RACING THROUGH THE CENTURY

THE STORY OF THOROUGHBRED RACING IN AMERICA

BY MARY SIMON

BOWTIE™

PRESS

IRVINE, CALIFORNIA

To my husband, Mark,
and my children Nora, and Rachel;
and to the memory of my late father, Paul Fleming,
which I hold dear to my heart.

—Mary Simon

Previously published in part as a series of articles in *Thoroughbred Times*.
Thoroughbred Times® is a registered trademark.

A Thoroughbred Times Book™

Ruth Strother, editor, project manager
Nick Clemente, special consultant
Michelle Martinez, editorial assistant
Rachel Rice, indexer
Cover and book design by Michele Lanci-Altomare

Special thanks go to Dr. Hyman Berman, professor of American History at
the University of Minnesota

Copyright © 2002 by BowTie ™ Press

Library of Congress Cataloging-in-Publication Data

Simon, Mary, 1954-
  Racing through the century : the story of thoroughbred racing in
America / Mary Simon.
    p. cm.
  ISBN 1-889540-92-7 (hardcover : alk. paper)
  1. Horse-racing–United States–History–20th century. 2.
Thoroughbred horse–United States–History–20th century. 3.
Horse-racing–United States–Pictorial works. 4. Thoroughbred
horse–United States–Pictorial works. I. Title.
  SF335.U5 S56 2002
  798.4'009730904–dc21
                                    2002001976

BowTie ™ Press
A Division of Fancy Publications
3 Burroughs
Irvine, California 92618

Printed and bound in Singapore
10 9 8 7 6 5 4 3 2 1

The photographs in this book are courtesy of: The Louisville Courier-Journal, cover, 3, 100; Tony Leonard, pp. 1, 200, 236, 249, 267; Photos by Z, pp. 2, 14, 235, 263, 270; Laurel Park photo by Francis DiGennaro, p. 4; Jerry Frutkoff, pp. 7, 214; Washington Park, p. 8; Painting by Jean Lacretelle, p. 10; Painting by Edward Troye from the Jockey Club collection, p. 11; Painting by George Stubbs, p. 12; Keeneland Library, pp. 13, 16, 40; Lithograph by N. Currier from a drawing by C. Severin, NYRA collection, p. 15; Keeneland-Cook, pp. 17, 20, 24, 28, 31, 32, 33, 38, 44, 45, 47, 50, 61, 62, 65, 73, 80, 82, 87, 92, 93, 96, 97, 103, 115, 116, 117, 288, 289; New York Racing Association, pp. 18, 68, 89, 132, 173, 185, 187, 188, 195, 198, 202, 209, 211, 213, 217, 222, 225, 226; Thoroughbred Times, pp. 21, 27, 29, 36, 43, 59, 66, 79, 86, 107, 110, 111, 118, 119, 133, 144, 148, 152, 156, 160, 161, 162, 163, 182, 197, 203, 206, 221; Bert & Richard Morgan Studios, pp. 19, 35, 53, 54, 69, 78, 84, 106, 114, 120, 121, 126, 129, 130, 131, 134, 136, 137, 138, 139, 147, 159, 167, 172, 174, 175; Vic Stein & Associates, p. 22; Arlington Park, pp. 23, 242, 251; Painting by E. Miner from the National Museum of Racing, pp. 37, 46; Grayson/Sutcliffe, pp. 42, 60, 72; Louis Goy, p. 56; *Cincinnati Enquirer*, p. 57; Painting by Foster Disinger from the National Museum of Racing, p. 70; National Museum of Racing, p. 71; W.W. Rouch & Co., pp. 76, 94, 95; C.C. Cook, p. 104; Skeets Meadors, pp. 124, 146, 170; Brownie Leach, p. 142; Knox Osbourne/Record, p. 143; Sirico Photos, p. 149; Hollywood Park, pp. 155, 192; Jim Raftery Turfotos, pp. 164, 189, 199, 220; Miller's Photo Service, p. 169; Bob Coglianese/NYRA, pp. 178, 191, 223, 227; Wide World Photos, p. 181; William Stravitz, p. 228; John Cornell Jr., p. 229; Rick Buckley, p. 232; Brant Gamma, p. 201, 234; Amy Zimmerman, p. 239; Dan Johnson, pp. 240, 250; Matt Goins, pp. 243, 262; Shigeki Kikkawa, p. 245; Rick Samuels, pp. 252, 253; Four Footed Fotos, p. 254; Chris Hoff, p. 255; Patricia McQueen, pp. 258, 269, 278, 279, 297; Mike Marten, p. 271; Suzie Picou-Oldham, p. 274; Benoit & Associates, pp. 276, 277.

Table of Contents

FOREWORD

The fabric that holds Thoroughbred racing together is history. You could say that history is at the heart of many sports, but without history, there would be no Thoroughbred racing. It is a sport where each and every one of its current athletes is a son or daughter of a past athlete, who in turn is a descendant of past athletes. And so it goes back to the beginning of the breed, with all horses tracing to three foundation sires. This thread that spans three hundred years of Thoroughbred racing requires all participants—bettors, breeders, owners, and trainers—to consider the history of each horse when making decisions. Appreciation and understanding of the sport and how it evolved are what this book is about. *Racing Through the Century* itself has a bit of history. It is a synthesis of a series of 11 articles published in the weekly newsmagazine *Thoroughbred Times* between December 1999 and November 2000.

Thoroughbred Times is something of an upstart in racing. I was hired as editor in chief to start *Thoroughbred Times* in 1985, which is exactly 90 years after The Jockey Club, the registrar of the Thoroughbred breed in North America, was founded, and 110 years after the first running of the Kentucky Derby. I previously had been executive editor of *The Thoroughbred Record*, which was a weekly magazine first published in 1875 that covered the Thoroughbred industry for more than 110 years. As fate would have it, *Thoroughbred Times* merged in 1988 with *The Thoroughbred Record*. This union gave us a bit more history at *Thoroughbred Times*, which provided a great resource for a project such as *Racing Through the Century*.

When we first conceived the idea for the series, we turned to Mary Simon. Some would suggest this was because we are married. Well, yes, we are married. I first met Mary in 1983, soon after she had written *A History of the Thoroughbred in California*, which was published while she was an editor for the *Thoroughbred of California*, a monthly magazine for members of the California Thoroughbred Breeders Association. Mary's love for me apparently was stronger than her love for Thoroughbreds in California, so she moved to Kentucky in 1986. Since that time, in addition to helping raise our two daughters, Nora and Rachel, she has been a contributing editor, staunch supporter, and a chief asset for the *Thoroughbred Times,* editing, among many other things, a weekly column that looks back in history through the pages of *The Thoroughbred Record*.

If the truth must be known, we turned to Mary to write the series for one simple reason: She is the best historian in Thoroughbred racing. This was confirmed when the 11-article series chronicling racing in the twentieth century received the prestigious Eclipse Award, an annual award that honors the best racehorses, people, and work by the media in Thoroughbred racing during the past year. The work has been greatly expanded in *Racing Through the Century* to help readers, new and old alike, better appreciate the rich fabric that makes up the sport of Thoroughbred racing. It is a journey made easier through facile writing by an author who has a thorough understanding and love of the subject.

—*Mark Simon, Editor in Chief,*
THOROUGHBRED TIMES

INTRODUCTION
Sport of Antiquity

The urge to compete has been an integral part of human nature almost since recorded time began. Whether born as a tool of survival or simply as a way to pass time enjoyably, the need to prove oneself stronger, faster, and better than others has been handed down faithfully through the ages. Sport was undoubtedly created to feed that consuming desire, and at some imprecise point in the mists of our past, the equine became a partner in this enterprise, utilized for pleasure, entertainment, and as a means of defining supremacy.

Horse racing officially appeared on history's horizon sometime before 1000 B.C. when Greeks figured out how to connect equines to two-wheeled carts called chariots and send them careening in front of madly whipping drivers, a dangerous but engaging game that would catch on with Romans and Egyptians as well. It was not, however, until the 33rd Olympiad of 644 B.C. that men appeared in formal competition astride those flying coursers instead of seated behind them—jockeys, they would be called in generations hence.

During their quest for world dominance, Romans brought the sport with them deep into Europe in the early years A.D., all the way to the isles of Britain where they established themselves for four hundred years. Though Roman rule eventually ended, horse racing lived on and flourished in its new home through the coming centuries.

Racing had by the late 1500s become a favorite pastime of English noblemen. Although Henry VIII seemed to prefer serial marriage and hunting, he kept a stable of racehorses as well. So did his daughter Elizabeth I and her cousin James I, under whose rule the famed Newmarket racecourse came into being early in the seventeenth century. Charles I was another in a long line of royal sporting enthusiasts, though after his 1649 beheading on charges of tyranny, horse racing was outlawed by Lord Protector Oliver Cromwell as "a danger to the peace and security of England."

Banishment of this much-loved entertainment lasted barely a decade. Following the Restoration of 1660 and the ascension of Charles II to the throne of England, horse racing returned on a higher plane than ever before. Charles was not only an avid spectator and two-fisted gambler, but on occasion he also rode competitively and even penned some early organizational rules. It was largely due to the "Merry Monarch's" passion for racing that it came to be described as the sport of kings.

In the time of Charles II, England's cold-blooded native horses were bred primarily for work and war, an increasingly unsatisfactory situation in a sporting sense. British horsemen attempted to resolve this by importing stallions of exceptional beauty from the deserts of the Middle East to cross with local mares. The result of this selective breeding program over time was a refined, fleet-footed equine possessed of strength, speed, stamina, and competitive fire—all the ingredients one could possibly want in a racehorse.

Three importations made following the reign of Charles II deserve particular mention. In 1688, Captain Robert Byerly captured an elegant black stallion from a Turkish officer at the Hungarian siege of Buda and brought him home as a spoil of war. Sixteen years later, British consul Thomas Darley smuggled a handsome Arabian colt out of the Syrian Desert and into the county of Yorkshire. And around 1729, a mysterious horse of romantically obscure Eastern lineage appeared at the Earl of Godolphin's stud near Cambridge. These, of course, were the Byerly Turk, the Darley

Arabian, and the Godolphin Barb, foundation sires of the modern Thoroughbred racehorse.

As racing continued to gain popularity in the eighteenth century British Isles, the structure of the sport gradually fell into place: permanent racecourses were built, rules of racing were written, classic races were inaugurated, records were kept, and pedigrees were compiled.

Thousands of miles away, colonial America struggled for its very existence, yet its sporting instincts were as true as those of its mother country. In 1665—a quarter of a century *before* Captain Byerly brought his famous Turkish charger to England—New York Governor Richard Nicolls had named America's first formal race-track Newmarket. Only a year after Lord Godolphin's Arabian stallion began covering British mares, the first "Thoroughbred" reached the colonies in the form of Bulle Rock, a long-in-the-tooth son of the Darley Arabian.

Disrupted by the chaos of a revolution and the extreme difficulty of communication in a vast and primitive empire, American horse racing of the 1700s was a wildly disorganized, anything goes, enterprise with little or no official record keeping. But progress nevertheless marched inexorably onward.

Although Bulle Rock made no lasting impact, others imported in that century helped create a uniquely American breed of running horse. Prior to the Revolutionary War, colonists were not far removed in attitude and outlook from their British cousins; and in the realm of horsemanship, the bond could not have been closer. The blood of the English Arabians flowed freely into the colonies during that time preceding the storm, adding quality and speed to native stock—just as they had done for Britain's own industry decades before. Prerevolution imports included the Godolphin Barb's grandson Fearnought and a filly simply known later as the

Cub Mare, both enormously influential progenitors in their adopted country. Janus, who stood barely 14 hands—pony-sized by today's standards—also arrived in that peaceful era and laid the framework for what would become the American quarter horse.

Most prominent of the postwar imported horses was Diomed, who turned up on these shores in 1798 as a 20-year-old castoff, 17 seasons removed from his historic victory in England's inaugural Derby Stakes. As fortune would have it, America seemed ideally suited to Diomed, and he to America. The old stallion lived on fruitfully for another decade, generously populating the countryside with his talented offspring and giving the nascent American Thoroughbred industry something powerful on which to build in the centuries ahead.

chapter 1

Prologue to a Century

> *The 1800s were a time of*
>
> *rapid change for horse racing*
>
> *and for America.*

American Derby day in 1893 at Washington Park, one of America's then premier racetracks.

THE YEAR WAS 1800. WASHINGTON, D.C., WAS THE NEW CENTER of American government, and Thomas Jefferson had just been elected third President of the United States following a mud-slinging campaign against John Adams. (Adams had blasted Jefferson as an atheist, while Jefferson had claimed Adams might set up a monarchy and enslave the common man.) Okay, so some things never change. But despite the familiar political ugliness, change— rapid and breathtaking—was the byword of the nineteenth century, dramatically altering American society at large and horse racing specifically.

America early in the last century was a strange and alien place by present standards. The nation comprised just 16 states in 1800. The earliest horseless carriages were 80 years away and the first locomotive was three decades in the future. Communication was laborious with no telegraph or telephones. Conveniences were few—even such basic conveniences as zippers, safety pins, aspirin, and canned goods had not yet been invented. Sport as we know it was almost nonexistent, with a single outstanding exception: horse racing.

Throughout that era, horses reigned supreme as Americans relied on them for both work and play. A racing enthusiast himself, Jefferson approved the senate's practice of adjourning early to attend local meets. Senators of the day might have marveled at the fabled 28-foot stride of Mr. Ball's great colt, Florizel, or they might have witnessed the unbeatable brilliance of First Consul during his 21-race winning streak. Perhaps they were present when a filly named Maria raced five heartbreaking 4-mile heats—20 miles—to victory.

American racing back then was as primitive as the larger world around it. There were no starting gates, only a few prepared dirt courses, no uniform rules of racing, and no organization to enforce those rules. Races were crudely timed, if they were timed at all. It was an era of often unrecorded and disputed genealogies—for example, some argued that five-time leading sire Sir Charles was foaled from a cart mare. Prior to the advent of train transport, which began in the 1830s, horses were led or ridden long miles to their engagements. (An 1838 newspaper article recorded a train accident involving a shipment of horses near Charleston, South Carolina: "The shock was tremendous as the rate of speed was over 10 miles an hour.")

OLD HICKORY AND DIOMED

The 1823 victory of American Eclipse over Henry in the great regional rivalry known as the North-South match at Long Island's Union Course proved a milestone in postcolonial racing. The $20,000-a-side event drew a significant portion of the New York populace and helped American Eclipse stake his claim as the first American earnings champion with $56,700. As purses escalated, that title would change hands eight times before the century was out.

A year later, avid racing man Andrew Jackson made his first bid for the presidency. The Nashville *Whig* had aggressively promoted his candidacy: "GREAT RACING!!! The prize to be run for is the Presidential Chair. . . . Already four states have sent their nags in. Why not Tennessee put in her stud? And if so, let it be Old Hickory!" Jackson lost that election but won the next and became possibly the only sitting president to campaign a racing stable.

*R. A. Alexander was an industry innovator
at the time of the Civil War.*

American Eclipse retired in 1823 as America's first acknowledged leading money winner with $56,700.

Imported from England for just £50,
Diomed recreated the early nineteenth century
American Thoroughbred in his own image.

An early finish photo depicting Salvator's 1890 victory over Tenney at Sheepshead Bay. Stud fees soared toward the end of the century, with services to Salvator being offered at $250.

At the same time, Leviathan was offered at stud for America's highest known fee—$75—but he was not the most notable stallion of the period. That honor went to Diomed, a British castoff after the Revolutionary War. The inaugural Epsom Derby winner had arrived on these shores in 1798 at the age of 20, acquired for a meager £50. He proceeded in over 11 seasons to reshape the American Thoroughbred in his own remarkable image, siring runners who were uniformly taller, heavier of bone, stronger, and faster than their contemporaries.

CHANGING TIMES

Early in the 1800s, American racing gradually began to split from the old country in a significant way. As England embraced shorter nonheat races, resulting in the development of its Derby and St. Leger, Americans remained steadfastly true to the old ways. Decades would pass before the heroic 4-mile-heat performers gave way to the speedier 1- and 2-mile "dash" specialists.

While the style of our racing evolved over time, change of another kind arrived like a thunderclap on March 17, 1850. That date marked the birth on a central Kentucky farm of Diomed's great-great-grandson Lexington—after which the American Thoroughbred would never be the same. Brilliant on the racecourse and even more accomplished at stud, Lexington would reign 16 times as the country's leading sire before his final chapter was written. One hundred and fifty years later, he maintains a regal presence in the far reaches of any pedigree containing the names of such influential twentieth century sires as Nasrullah or Mahmoud.

As the century progressed, races became ever shorter, purses were on the rise, and racing began to organize. Saratoga Race Course, Pimlico Race Course, Churchill Downs, and Fair Grounds opened for business; the Jockey Club was established to oversee the growing sport; the *American Stud Book* began tracking pedigrees; sporting publications launched in-depth weekly turf coverage; and starting gates were put to widespread use.

*By the late 1800s, prominent horse operations such as Spendthrift Farm
liberally advertised their stallions' services, offering
boarding rates of from $1 to $3 per week.*

A painting depicting Peytona defeating Fashion in an 1845 match
and illustrating how far horse racing has come.

Rapidly increasing purses led to earnings records that would have been unimaginable just a short time before. In 1889, the great Miss Woodford became not only America's leading money-winning mare, but also the first of either sex to top $100,000 in earnings. Juvenile earnings also soared with the growing popularity of two-year-old racing. Nothing showcased this trend more than the advent in 1888 of the Futurity Stakes, worth an astonishing $40,000 to the winner. Five years later, in 1893, a juvenile named Domino set a $170,790 single-season earnings record for a horse of any age, and one that would stand for decades.

Kingston—the last of the great iron horses of a dying era—retired in 1894 with 89 victories to his credit, a record untouched to this day. One hundred years later, America's top racehorses had evolved into fragile specimens who rarely made more than 30 starts during their careers.

As the new century progressed, the face of American breeding changed as well. Four-time leading sire Hanover died in the final year of the 1800s, but others stood ready to take his place, horses such as Commando, Star Shoot, and Hastings. Stallion fees had soared since the days of Leviathan. Services to leading 1899 sire Albert and champion Salvator were offered at $250 for the 1900 season, while a season to Spendthrift, future paternal great-grandsire of Man o' War, cost $150. Prominent farms advertised liberally in *The Thoroughbred Record* and included names familiar even today—Elmendorf, Dixiana, Hamburg Place, and Spendthrift Farm. They offered boarding rates ranging from $1 to $3 per week.

By late century, Kentucky represented the heart of America's Thoroughbred business, with more professional horsemen than any other region. The luxurious Phoenix Hotel, in Lexington, capitalized on this situation, becoming a mecca for well-heeled visitors to the Blue Grass. In the *Record*'s final issue of 1899, the Phoenix promoted itself as the ultimate in modernity, boasting "Steam Heat and Electric Lights in every room," plus an "Electric Elevator." America and its Thoroughbred industry were thus poised to enter a modern era of even greater change than the one that was coming to a close.

Isaac Murphy, the greatest of the nineteenth-century jockeys, compiled a 44 percent win record prior to his death in 1896 at age 35.

Legendary horseman John Madden, right, talks with jockey Walter Miller who in 1906
established a single-season record of 388 wins that stood for 46 years.

Like America, the Thoroughbred business in the twentieth century enjoyed good times and suffered through bad. Mirroring these times, Ruffian was unstoppable until her life ended tragically in 1975.

Golden moments were as prevalent in the twentieth century as they were in the eighteenth. In 1953, Native Dancer became television's first equine hero.

TAKING FLIGHT

A new world was born with the twentieth century; a fast-paced epoch of invention, revolution, and startling innovation that probably would have amazed even a forward thinker such as Thomas Jefferson. The rhythmic beat of hooves and sweet scent of harness leather gradually gave way to the roar of sputtering engines and the noxious fumes of gasoline. Traditional horse-drawn plows, the mainstays of farm culture for centuries, were replaced over time by loud, smoke-belching machines called tractors—the first one was officially patented in 1900—while gasoline-guzzling horseless carriages caused joyriding Americans to hit the roads in ever-increasing numbers. With the dawn of this automotive age, the future of all things equine seemed a question mark. If no longer required for work or transportation, what place remained for the horse in a rapidly modernizing society? The answer, of course, was in sport.

The days of the workhorse may have been numbered, but the future never looked brighter for the Thoroughbred. During the first nine decades of the 1800s, it is estimated that American breeders produced 3,950 Thoroughbreds. Then in the year 1900 alone, 3,476 foals were registered by a youthful organization known as the Jockey Club. By 1986, that annually reported number would peak at 51,296.

Purses were also on their way up, and in lockstep with that increased earning power, the value of Thoroughbred bloodstock skyrocketed. Earnings potential and auction prices would forever be tied together. In 1911, adverse conditions for racing had for the time being destroyed purse values and contributed to an anemic $230 yearling auction average. Once that situation was resolved, the market headed upward until the average North American auction yearling of 2000 was sold for $51,139.

In the twentieth century, like America itself, the business of Thoroughbreds enjoyed good times and suffered through bad. And like America, the Thoroughbred industry proved remarkably resilient. When a great antigambling wave slammed the country in 1908, the sport of kings was all but swept away in a bitter tide of legislation. When the bottom fell out of both the national and world economies in 1929, the Thoroughbred industry staggered through the Great Depression but came out stronger than ever. When America went to war in 1941, racing stood unified behind it, contributing millions to the relief effort and ultimately shutting down for a time to conserve precious resources. When the Cold War produced the terrifying specter of a nuclear World War III, Thoroughbred breeders expressed their concern in the names they gave their horses—Hail to Reason, Nothirdchance, Atomic Attack, Nuclear Weapon, On the Brink, Air Terror, to name a few.

A CENTURY OF PROGRESS

Racing's evolution was profound during this time. The pari-mutuel form of betting arrived from Paris to help save the sport from the corruption and questionable gambling practices that were killing it in the early years of the century. Belmont Park, Hialeah Park, Santa Anita Park, and Keeneland Race Course were among the major racetracks to open their gates.

The Breeders' Cup and the National Thoroughbred Racing Association; drug testing and blood-typing, lip tattoos, photo-finish cameras, electronic timers and totalizator boards, off-track betting, simulcasting, a dazzling array of exotic wagers, and racetrack video lottery terminals were innovations that landscaped racing's twentieth century. All were ideas whose time had come, like them or not. And 90 years after the first racehorse was trundled down a set of rudimentary railroad tracks toward a country engagement, equine air transport was becoming a reality—one that would eventually internationalize the sport in no uncertain terms.

Milestones whizzed by at a dizzying rate in almost every category. Money records toppled in the blink of an eye or at the drop of a hammer. A yearling sold for $13.1 million; a stallion was syndicated for $40 million; a single race was worth $5.1 million; and a racehorse earned nearly $10 million before the book closed on this remarkable century.

Leading trainer H. Guy Bedwell and owner J. K. L. Ross paired to win the first American Triple Crown in 1919 with Sir Barton.

Evangelist Billy Sunday with Man o' War, whose magnificence during the 1920s placed him among the sporting greats of all time.

Three of the best jockeys of the twentieth century. From left: Eddie Arcaro, John Longden, and Bill Shoemaker.
Together, they won 19,642 races between 1927 and 1990.

*Industry leaders of the 1940s included trainers
Ben Jones (left) and Jimmy Jones (right), flanking Calumet
Farms's owner Warren Wright (left center) and
Arlington Park owner Ben Lindheimer (right center).*

Racehorses are mortal creatures, and thus logic dictates that there must be an upper limit as to how fast they can run. Nevertheless, the evolution of speed records has been incredible. Elusive Quality's 1998 world record mile in 1:31.63 is approximately 50 lengths faster than *Voter's 1900 record of 1:38. What might the record be at the end of the twenty-first century?

GREAT HORSES, GREAT MOMENTS

Golden moments and racetrack heroics were as much in evidence during the twentieth century as in the one that preceded it. Among them: Unconquerable Colin, whose 15 for 15 record enthralled the prewar racing world of 1907 through 1909 and remains a yardstick of perfection in America; Man o' War, whose Roaring Twenties magnificence placed his name in the pantheon of sporting greats of all eras; the raw Triple Crown power of Citation, America's first equine millionaire; Native Dancer, TV's first equine hero back in 1953; Dr. Fager's 1968 world record mile of 1:32 ⅕ under a staggering 134 pounds and Secretariat's unforgettable 31-length Belmont Stakes triumph five years later; Exterminator, Kelso, and Forego—geldings who carried the sport on their backs in their respective eras; Ruffian, whose extraordinary career ended tragically and too soon in front of a 1975 national television audience; Seattle Slew's unbeaten excellence through the 1977 Triple Crown; Affirmed and Alydar's epic battles in the 1978 Kentucky Derby, Preakness, and Belmont Stakes; and the 16 consecutive wins and an all-time earnings record for Cigar in the mid-1990s.

The twentieth century was a complex, immensely interesting slice of American history that was filled with wars and revolutions, labor strikes and social reform movements, political concerns that spanned the globe and explorations of the far corners of that globe, depressions and recessions, epidemics and cures, and inventions from television to the atomic bomb. The industry of Thoroughbreds was a small part of this fascinating, tumultuous whole, colorfully interwoven as it has always been into the very fabric of our society. For better or for worse, racing has endured through it all.

chapter 2

A Decade of Turmoil

Racing appears to thrive through much of

this period before a "great moral wave"

strikes a corrupted sport.

IFE IS FILLED WITH SO MANY SMALL, ALMOST TRIFLING, EVENTS that we sometimes lose sight of the larger changes going on around us. We are caught up in building a business or making a living, and one day we turn around to find that our small children have grown and are heading out the door.

Thoroughbred racing is little different. As an industry, it is focused on what is happening here and now—how fast a horse runs or how well a yearling sells—and sometimes the larger trends developing within the industry are missed. For instance, did it take racing 20 or 30 years to realize that it was losing its on-track customer base? The dawn of a new century offers a suitable promontory for looking back over the trail we have followed and viewing the twists and turns our path has taken. We can see the major events along that trail and the opportunities that were seized as well as those that were missed.

The American decade 1901–1910 witnessed unparalleled optimism coexisting with bleak despair. Immigrants arrived by the millions, passing through

Belmont Park, which opened in 1905, proved to be a popular and often crowded attraction.

Ellis Island with hearts full of hope but encountering harsh realities in the teeming cities of a strange country. Industrialization was beginning to reshape American business and American life. The first major corporations came into being in this era, and the assembly line transformed the consumer economy. While affluent Americans increased their wealth, many workers lived in slums, ate contaminated food, labored long hours in conditions that were often dangerous, and watched their children die from a horrifying array of ailments.

At the beginning of the century, the average life span was a mere 47 years and there was no social safety net to catch anyone who stumbled along the way. Yet from a world perspective, America of 1901 must have seemed a thrilling land of promise. Flight was on the horizon, and motion pictures and the Model T were just around the corner. Hot dogs and hamburgers were delicacies first savored by the masses at the 1904 St. Louis World's Fair. The World Series was inaugurated. The country was at peace.

And so it was with horse racing—the good mixed with the bad. As the calendar flipped to 1901, the future of America's Thoroughbred industry appeared outwardly dazzling. With the force of uncorked champagne, money sprayed into bigger purses, higher stud fees, and soaring sales prices. More foals were produced annually to meet rising demand. It was hard not to make money in the business of Thoroughbreds. But as often happens when things could not look better, the bubble was fated to burst—explosively. Trouble brewed even as financier James R. Keene's great Commando blistered the track at the dawn of the century, and as Commando's unbeatable son Colin carried the Keene colors to victory after brilliant victory a few years later. Even as Keene's stable racked up unprecedented earnings, as record purses were dispensed, and as Belmont Park opened its glorious gates, a dark cloud was settling ominously on racing's horizon.

SIGNS OF THE TIMES

1901–1910 100 pounds of sugar costs $5.80

8,000 cars, with an average price of $1,550, are registered in the United States, compared to 130 million cars registered in the mid-1990s

Less than 150 miles of paved highways exist in the United States

Average salary is 22¢ per hour

1.7 million children are employed for as little as 25¢ per day

60 percent of the United States population is rural, compared to 25 percent in the late 1990s

A person's average life expectancy is 47.3 years

Leading causes of death are diphtheria, typhoid, tuberculosis, and whooping cough

Sears catalog sells wood-burning stoves for $17.48 and wooden iceboxes for $8.92

8.8 million immigrants arrive in America

Morris Park, its clubhouse shown above, was one of several racetracks that was closed during the era.

*Meddler was America's leading sire of 1904 and 1906.

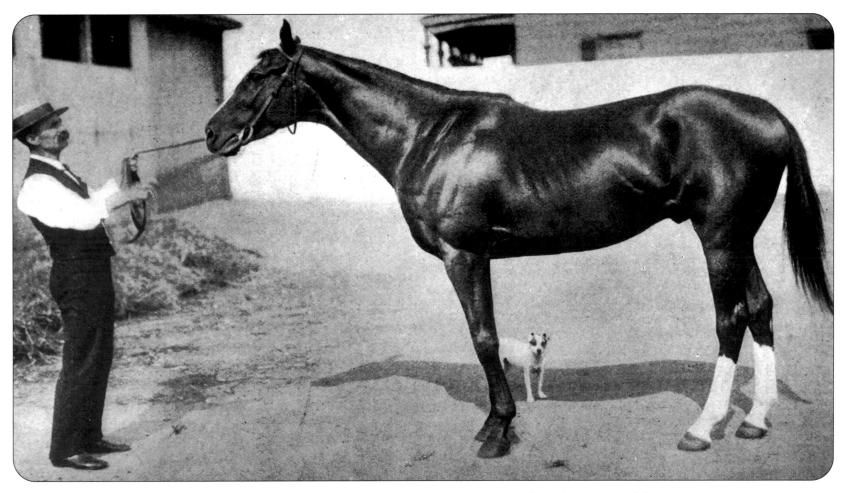

Hamburg was sold at auction for $70,000 in 1904 and became America's leading sire the following year.

You can never tell how far a frog will jump by looking at him.

—JOHN E. MADDEN

RAMPANT CORRUPTION

Racing may have been the sport of kings, but it was also part of a larger gambling industry. Increasingly, the taint of corruption was eroding public confidence in the sport as high-profile incidents were exposed. Keene's Sysonby—still viewed by turf historians as one of the all-time greats—suffered his only loss in the 1904 Futurity after being drugged by a groom. Delhi, the 1904 Belmont Stakes winner, later ran sluggishly and was found to have sponges inserted far up into his nostrils. Electrical prods, dopings, ringers, crooked jockeys, and diverse gambling scams were common journalistic fodder in those early days of investigative reporting.

Race fixing was becoming the ugly centerpiece of an elegant sport, one that deeply offended an increasingly powerful segment of the population, including New York Governor Charles Evans Hughes. Although too many of racing's elite failed to see how seriously the very soul of their sport was compromised by the malpractice of a few, Keene was not among the shortsighted. At one point he spoke darkly of a "great moral wave" that would bring racing to its knees. Pay attention, he cautioned, to what is happening in our sport. Act quickly to reform it—or suffer the consequences. But it was already too late.

By 1907, anti-racetrack wagering laws had been simmering for some time on legislative back burners across America. In June of 1908, the lid blew off the most potent of them all when New York's Agnew-Hart Bill was passed into law with the ardent blessing of Governor Hughes. A death knell was thus sounded. Without revenues from legalized gambling, racing soon found it impossible to support itself. In 1910, historic Saratoga was among the racetracks that ceased operation because "the sport could not be conducted properly under present conditions." A domino effect occurred thereafter as other states rushed to pass similar legislation. The national purse structure collapsed, declining by one-third in just two years, from a 1907 average of $949 per race to $643 in 1909. Leading owners, including Keene, shipped their horses overseas in a European invasion so successful that it would pave the way for the next great blow to the American Thoroughbred industry—England's 1913 passage of the Jersey Act.

HORSE SIGNS OF THE TIMES

1901–1910 Kentucky Derby is worth $4,850 to the winner

Trainer James Rowe Sr. is paid a $10,000 annual salary plus 10 percent purses by James R. Keene

Boarding rates in Kentucky range from $1 to $3 per week

1901 Jockey Club registers a record 3,784 foals

1902 Savable earns largest winner's purse of $44,500 in the Futurity Stakes

1904 Africander and Irish Lad become the first American runners of the twentieth century to top $100,000 in career earnings

Jockey Club reports 3,990 foals registered—a decade high

1906 Flying Fox's stud fee of $3,000 is the highest in the world

John Madden estimates that it costs $50 to raise a foal to its yearling year

HORSE SIGNS OF THE TIMES

1906 Walter Miller is the first jockey to ride 300 winners in a season

Roseben sets seven-furlong American record of 1:22 that stands for 41 years

1907 Commando sets single-season progeny earnings record of $270,345

Owner James R. Keene establishes single-season earnings record of $397,342

Average purse is $949 (just prior to Agnew-Hart bill)

1908 Center Shot sets American mile record of 1:37 ⅕ at Santa Anita Park

1909 At Tattersalls, in England, Flair sells for $80,000, a record price for a broodmare

Average purse is $643 (after Agnew-Hart bill)

1910 Jockey Club foal registrations drop to 1,950

Fair Play was a temperamental but talented runner, who later sired an even better one in Man o' War.

If only people would treat their Derby horses like their selling platers, they would get on much better. Nothing is so likely to spoil a horse than making a fuss over him.

—Trainer Matthew Dawson

Previously a victim of the corruption of the early 1900s,
Sysonby dusts Oiseau and Broomstick at Saratoga in 1905.

A well-dressed crowd enters the new Belmont Park in 1905.

GOLDEN MOMENTS

Despite the legislative attacks suffered by the sport, particularly in New York, several outstanding competitors appeared on racing's stage to illuminate the decade. Foremost among them was an undefeated bona fide superstar whose legendary conditioner, James Rowe Sr., later requested but a three-word epitaph: "He trained Colin."

James R. Keene's Colin was one of nine future Racing Hall of Fame members who campaigned during the decade. Man o' War's fiery sire, Fair Play, was another, along with Commando, Sysonby, Artful, Beldame, Roseben, Broomstick, and Peter Pan—several of whom have important races named in their honor today. This cast of great Thoroughbreds was well supported by the human element, including 11 jockeys and 12 trainers who would one day enter the Hall of Fame.

With such talent in the racing pool, golden moments were not lacking. In 1903, Africander became the first three-year-old Suburban Handicap winner, and homely Waterboy emerged as America's premier handicap performer after hanging for weeks in a sling with a fractured pelvis. Juvenile filly Artful packed 130 pounds in 1904 and sped to a 1:08 6-furlong American straightaway record that would stand for decades. Tanya conquered colts in the first Belmont Stakes run at Belmont Park in 1905, and Roseben lugged 147 pounds to an American record for 6 furlongs around a turn in the 1905 Manhattan Handicap. Sysonby sizzled 3 furlongs in :32 ⅗ to catch his field after being left at the post in the 1907 Great Republic Stakes. And Colin, on a painfully suspect tendon in the 1908 Belmont Stakes, used every ounce of his abundant courage to hold off the rush of Fair Play. The one event, however, that most profoundly touched the sport in those years took place not on a racetrack but in the halls of government.

He trained Colin.

—*HALL OF FAME TRAINER JAMES ROWE SR.'S DESIRED EPITAPH*

LEADING TRAINERS

Samuel Hildreth
Racing Hall of Fame. Leading money trainer 1909–1910. See also 1910s, 1920s.

John J. Hyland
Racing Hall of Fame. In this era, he trained champion Beldame and 1902 Belmont Stakes winner Masterman. (More prominent in 1890s.)

Andrew Jackson Joyner
Racing Hall of Fame. Leading trainer by wins in 1908. Trained Fair Play and champions Africander and Hamburg Belle during decade. Also trained successfully in England.

John W. Rogers
Racing Hall of Fame. Trainer for powerful Whitney Stable. Trained champions Artful, Tanya, Burgomaster, Nasturtium, Stamina, Blue Girl, Gunfire, and Perverse in this decade.

James Rowe Sr.
Racing Hall of Fame. Leading money trainer in 1908. Leader by wins in 1907. Trained champions Commando, Sysonby, Colin, Peter Pan, and Maskette in this decade. See also 1910s.

Tanya, *Meddler's daughter, represented a golden moment in the early 1900s when she captured the 1905 Belmont Stakes.

James R. Keene with Hall of Fame trainer James Rowe Sr. (right). Together, they raced Sysonby, Colin, and many other good ones.

One of the great weight carriers of all time,
Roseben set a 6-furlong American record in 1905 under 147 pounds.

TOUGH LESSON

On June 13, 1908, racing experienced its darkest hour when the New York Senate voted the Agnew-Hart Antiwagering Bill into law by a 26 to 25 margin. As a result of that single vote, prominent breeders dispersed their holdings, farms were sold, the market for Thoroughbreds shriveled to nothing, top stables and jockeys took their businesses abroad, and racetracks closed—among them E. J. "Lucky" Baldwin's elaborate haven of winter competition, the original Santa Anita Park. Painful as it was, Agnew-Hart needed to happen. Only the direst of circumstances seemed capable of awakening American racing men to the critical need for reform within their sport.

Ironically, while corrupt gambling practices nearly killed racing, another form of wagering helped resuscitate it. Pari-mutuels had long been considered Parisian oddities. Several of these curious machines had been brought to America years earlier and employed experimentally without success. In 1908, the year of Agnew-Hart, Churchill Downs's energetic general manager pulled some of the old machines out of storage, dusted them off, and put them back into use. Although it would not rid racing of its darker element, the pari-mutuel system itself proved efficient and fair, eliminating the need for potentially crooked middlemen and their cohorts. Once bettors grew accustomed to the new style of wagering, there would be no going back.

At the bottom of two-year-old racing, there can be nothing but greed.

—AUTHOR THOMAS MERRY

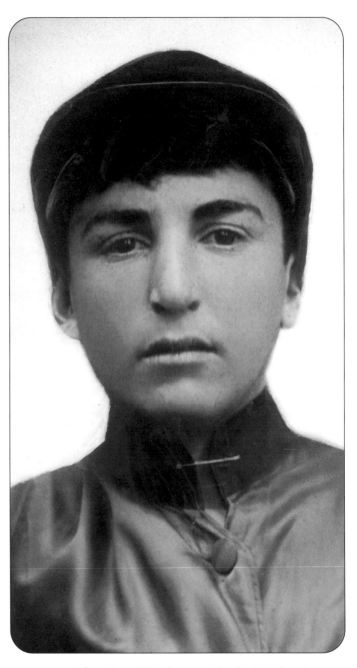

In 1906, Walter Miller became the first jockey to ride more than three hundred winners in a single season.

LEADING JOCKEYS

Tommy Burns
Racing Hall of Fame. Rode more than 1,300 winners in America and abroad, including champion Broomstick. Won 21 percent of his career races.

Eddie Dugan
Leading money rider in 1909. Won Belmont Stakes, Preakness Stakes (twice), Brooklyn Handicap (twice). Rode Fair Play and champions Stamina and Fitz Hebert.

Walter Miller
Racing Hall of Fame. Leading rider by wins in 1906–1907. First to ride more than 300 winners in a season (1906), setting a 46-year record. Rode more than 1,900 career winners, including champions Colin and Peter Pan.

Joe Notter
Racing Hall of Fame. Leading money rider in 1908. Rode champions Colin, Peter Pan, Maskette, Ballot, and Whisk Broom II.

Winnie O'Connor
Racing Hall of Fame. Leading rider of 1901 by wins. Rode more than 1,200 winners in America and Europe.

Frank O'Neill
Racing Hall of Fame. Rode primarily in Europe due to legislation unfavorable to American racing. Won important American races aboard champions Roseben and Beldame.

Vincent Powers
Racing Hall of Fame. Leading rider of 1909 by wins. Won 1909 Kentucky Derby on Wintergreen.

Carol Shilling
Racing Hall of Fame. Leading money rider in 1910. Rode 25 percent career winners. Won the 1912 Kentucky Derby on Worth. Other major victories include the Travers and Futurity Stakes.

Jimmy Winkfield
Won the 1901 and 1902 Kentucky Derbys aboard His Eminence and Alan-a-Dale. One of the last great African-American jockeys.

The man who reintroduced pari-mutuels to America was none other than Mr. Kentucky Derby himself, Churchill Downs's Col. Matt Winn. Like James R. Keene before him, Winn knew that racing must assume responsibility for its own mistakes and could never again turn a blind eye to corruption from within. "The big thing about racing is to keep it clean," Winn would explain years later. "Do that and it'll take care of itself. They talk a lot about the public putting racing out, but the public never put racing out of anywhere. Racing always puts itself out." This was a lesson bitterly learned in a long-ago decade of turmoil.

Mares are a necessary evil, only to serve as material to propagate the breed. They are only sisters to their brothers and daughters to their sires.

—BREEDING THEORISTS "ANTWERP & LAMPLIGHTER"

E. J. "Lucky" Baldwin, the breeder of four American Derby winners, passed away in 1909.

NECROLOGY

1901 Hindoo, 23. Racing Hall of Fame, Kentucky Derby winner, sire of Hanover

Pierre Lorillard, 68. International owner-breeder, raced Iroquois, first American-bred winner of the English Derby (1881)

1902 Firenze, 18. Racing Hall of Fame, second mare to earn $100,000

1903 Parole, 30. Racing Hall of Fame, 59 victories

1904 Luke Blackburn, 27. Racing Hall of Fame

*Ormonde, 21, in California. Undefeated European Horse of the Century

William Collins Whitney. Leading owner-breeder, bred 26 stakes winners in five years

1905 Frank Harper, 81. Owner of Racing Hall of Famers Ten Broeck and Longfellow

George "Pittsburgh Phil" Smith. Legendary gambler

Commando, 7. Racing Hall of Fame, leading sire of 1907

Robert W. Walden. Racing Hall of Fame trainer of seven Preakness winners and four Belmont Stakes winners

Wanda, 23. Champion, first to wear aluminum shoes

1906 Mike Dwyer, 59. Renowned gambler and owner-breeder; with brother, Phil, raced Racing Hall of Famers Hindoo, Hanover, Kingston, Miss Woodford, and Luke Blackburn

NECROLOGY

1906 Sysonby, 4. Racing Hall of Fame, once beaten in 15 starts

Major Barak Thomas, 80. Breeder of Domino, owner of Dixiana Farm

1907 Emperor of Norfolk, 22. Racing Hall of Fame

1908 John W. Rogers. Racing Hall of Fame trainer of Hall of Famer Artful and 1905 Belmont Stakes winner Tanya

1909 E. J. "Lucky" Baldwin, 81. Owner-breeder of four American Derby winners, built original Santa Anita racetrack

William Easton. Famed auctioneer, Fasig-Tipton Co.

Imp, 15. Racing Hall of Fame, 62 victories

Salvator, 23. Racing Hall of Fame, long-time world record holder for a mile

Sir Dixon, 16. Belmont Stakes, Travers, leading sire of 1901

*St. Blaise, 29. Auctioned in 1891 for world record $100,000

1910 *Albert, 28. Leading American sire of 1899

Salvidere, 6. Among leading two-year-olds of 1906

If a three-year-old is not able to go at least six furlongs, he ought to be put before the plough or between the shafts of a market wagon.

—E. J. "Lucky" Baldwin

I desire no other monument. This is the greatest thing I have ever done, and I am satisfied.

—E. J. "Lucky" Baldwin, then in his 80s, after completion of original Santa Anita racetrack, 1907

COLIN

BY OUTWARD APPEARANCES, COLIN WAS MERELY A HORSE—A FLESH and blood creature prone to physical flaws, injury, and exhaustion. He had a deformed hind leg and fragile fore tendons; and he was not immune to coughs and fevers. Yet, when he appeared on racing's stage early in the twentieth century, Colin transcended these frailties to achieve a perfection seldom attained in the mortal world. He became that rarest of athletes, one who requires no excuse or explanation and who proves emphatically that one can, indeed, win 'em all.

Colin was the equine equivalent of a rock star in that long-ago era when the world was a simpler place and racing reigned as one of America's most popular pastimes. When antiwagering legislation crippled the sport in New York during the summer of 1908, this horse could still draw thousands of fans, who were eager to see him in flawless action.

Foaled in the spring of 1905 at Wall Street financier James R. Keene's Castleton Farm, in Kentucky, Colin had the bloodlines to be a good one. His sire was American champion Commando, his dam was an English stakes winner—thus his pedigree represented a perfect blend of domestic speed and European stamina.

As a yearling, Colin was turned over to the great trainer James Rowe Sr., who was at first skeptical. Though a fine individual, the colt arrived in his barn with a hideously enlarged hock due to a pasture injury. Rowe's Hall of Fame patience prevailed after months of massage therapy and cold spray on the damaged joint, and on May 29, 1907, at Belmont Park, he revealed Colin to the public for the first time. The handsome bay was a sight to behold as he roared down the stretch ahead of 22 rivals to win easily. He never looked back thereafter, racing through a perfect 12 for 12 season, including victories in several of America's most important races, and establishing a twentieth century win streak for a two-year-old that would stand as a record for 65 years. To this day, it has been equaled but never surpassed.

By Futurity Stakes day on August 31, Colin was a genuine public idol. An estimated 50,000 fans swarmed Sheepshead Bay that afternoon, hoping to catch a glimpse of their four-legged hero, then screamed themselves hoarse as he made some of the finest young Thoroughbreds in the country look no better than ordinary.

Colin had successfully carried 129 pounds in 1907, an enormous burden for a two-year-old. When handicapper Walter Vosburgh offered to load 130 pounds on the colt's back, trainer Rowe politely declined and retired him for the season.

As a three-year-old in 1908, Colin emerged fresh to win the Withers Stakes over Fair Play, a talented though temperamental colt destined for greater fame a decade hence as the sire of Man o' War. It was a fitting prelude to another wondrous season.

During those years, it was not the Kentucky Derby that the Eastern racing elite most coveted, but New York's Belmont Stakes. Rowe began training his undefeated star with that race in mind. In the weeks leading up to the Belmont, however, unsettling rumors began circulating regarding Colin's physical condition: rumors that he had injured one front tendon, or perhaps both; that he had a sore, unsightly ankle; and he was sick, with a hacking cough. Only Rowe and Keene knew the truth and they weren't talking, but a problem there clearly was. Tempers flared around the Rowe stable and as race day approached, the trainer decided that Colin should not run. Keene, no true horseman himself, disagreed quite vehemently. The Belmont was a jewel he wanted to possess, and the wealthy financier was used to having his way. On May 30, Colin lined up with three others to contest the New York classic.

Rowe by now loved this colt almost as a son. He ordered jockey Joe Notter to go easy on Colin, not to push him beyond where his fragile legs could carry him. Then, in the midst of a violent thunderstorm, with the racetrack a roiling sea of mud, Rowe returned to his barn and stood alone, head down, heart in his throat. Though he could not see the race, the distant cheering of the crowd told him all he needed to know, rising as it did to a joyous crescendo above the downpour and thunder claps.

Despite Rowe's instructions, Notter rode one of the worst races of his Hall of Fame career that afternoon, pushing Colin early, then mistaking the finish and easing up too soon. Upon realizing his error, the horrified rider begged his mount to find a reserve of courage he had never called on before. As always, Colin responded. Utterly exhausted, weaving leg-weary and sore through the deepening mud, rain slashing his face, he somehow managed to thrust his nose in front of Fair Play's in the final stride to the finish. It was the race of his life, and one that would place him forever among the immortals of the sport.

In late spring of 1908, the New York Legislature decreed that racetrack wagering would no longer be allowed in the Empire State, thus Coney Island's Tidal Stakes on June 20 became a betless exhibition with Colin its featured attraction. It marked his 15th consecutive victory, and his last.

Racing's disintegration caused leading stables to ship abroad for competition, and in 1909 the Keene horses joined the exodus. Colin, unfortunately, was injured in training soon after his arrival in England and was retired without having started there. Keene initially kept him overseas for stud duty, but his career as a stallion there was not a happy one. He was poorly patronized by British breeders who scorned his American bloodlines, and what few mares he did receive often failed to get in foal. Colin returned home in 1913, where he sold for $30,000 at Keene's estate dispersal at Madison Square Garden. Five years later, as the sad fact of his sub-fertility was confirmed, he sold again at public auction, this time for only $5,100.

Colin eventually sired 81 foals, just four per annual crop. Though his numbers were small, his quality was high; he was represented by 14 percent stakes winners from foals, compared to the 3 percent average for all Thoroughbred stallions. More importantly, Colin defied the longest of odds in establishing a male line that would span the century—its most significant recent link being 1994 leading American sire Broad Brush, a grandson seven generations removed.

Colin, the unbeatable star of 1907–1908
won 15 consecutive races.

Colin's unconquerable heart beat for the final time during the 28th summer of his life. He was buried on the Virginia farm where he last resided. Rowe had preceded him in death by three years, a sorrowful occasion that had brought the flags at the Saratoga Race Course to half-mast. Though he had been responsible for the development of so many great runners, including Hall of Famers Sysonby, Miss Woodford, Commando, and Hindoo, Rowe always considered Colin to be the masterpiece of his career.

SYSONBY

WHEN JAMES R. KEENE FIRST SET EYES ON SYSONBY IN THE spring of 1902, he was immediately repulsed. Though this son of an English Derby winner possessed a royal equine pedigree, he was not built along the sleek, classic lines Keene had come to expect of his Castleton-breds. In fact, Sysonby was a squat, rather homely creature, Roman-nosed, lop-eared, and almost clownish in appearance, all of which morbidly offended Keene's finer sensibilities.

Curiously named for a lovely English hunting lodge, Sysonby would have been cast off early on had not Keene's son Foxhall intervened on his behalf. When Keene later ordered Sysonby shipped out of sight to race in Europe, trainer James Rowe Sr. argued that the colt was too sick to travel. It was an outright lie. Sysonby was brimming with good health and already showing Rowe something extraordinary in the huge, athletic stride that would soon carry him to fame and fortune. Thus, literally against his will, the Wall Street millionaire was "stuck" with one of the finest racehorses of the twentieth century.

Rowe brought this plain brown package to the races at Brighton Beach on July 14, 1904. He won by 10 lengths, then followed up with rapid-fire triumphs in the Brighton Junior, Flash Stakes, and Saratoga Special by a combined 24 lengths. Common he may have been in a physical sense, but there was nothing plain or ordinary about the competitive fire that burned white-hot within him. On the track, Sysonby was becoming a beast, a fearfully overpowering racing machine, whose breathtaking performances converted even Keene from harsh critic to ardent fan almost overnight.

In the lucrative Futurity Stakes on August 27, Sysonby lost for the only time in his career. It was a fluke. Clearly not himself, he finished a sluggish third behind the good filly Artful—a miraculous effort considering he had almost certainly been drugged. (Sysonby's groom later admitted to having "doped" the colt for a gambling payoff.) Keene went

to his grave believing that if Sysonby had not been tampered with that day, his record would have been as unblemished as that of future Castleton star Colin.

Sysonby's 1905 debut came in the Metropolitan Handicap on opening day at the brand-new Belmont Park, where he finished in a dead heat with the older Race King, while giving him a 10-pound weight advantage. After that, no mortal horse could touch him. Sysonby reeled off victories in the Tidal Stakes, Commonwealth Handicap, Lawrence Realization, Brighton Derby, Iroquois, Century, Annual Champion, and Great Republic Stakes, in the latter, running one of the most amazing races ever seen. At the drop of the starter's flag, Sysonby sprang away at a sharp angle, bolted to the outer rail, and lost at least 75 yards before recovering his usual ground-consuming stride. He then proceeded to scorch three furlongs in an unofficial world record of :32 ⅕ en route to yet another ridiculously easy triumph. It was an unearthly performance.

Keene and Rowe anticipated even greater things from Sysonby in 1906 when he attained a four-year-old's physical maturity, but fate intervened in the worst possible way. The champion returned from a gallop one morning in March sporting a small sore on one leg. It was treated and forgotten. Within days, however, Sysonby's body was covered with bleeding sores, and his tremendous strength slowly ebbed with each passing day. On June 17, 1906, Sysonby could fight the good battle no longer. The courageous colt lay down in his stall at Sheepshead Bay, and with a heartbroken Rowe at his side, Sysonby died at 1:05 P.M. Cause of death would subsequently be diagnosed as septic poisoning.

Sysonby was buried in front of the Keene stable, but he would not rest in peace. His skeleton was exhumed several months later and placed on exhibit at the American Museum of Natural History, in New York.

Sysonby may have been plain in a physical sense, but there was nothing ordinary about the competitive fire that burned within him.

He was a common, cheap-looking, lop-eared colt.

—Sysonby's groom, Ernest Shackleford

ROSEBEN

WEIGHT CARRIED IN COMPETITION WAS ONCE AN HONORED measure by which to assess the quality of an American racehorse. The better the horse, the more weight old-time handicappers would require him to carry; and the more he carried, the more he would concede to his rivals. Weight was the ultimate equalizer, designed to level the playing field between great and lesser performers, and to bring them together for exciting finishes.

If weight successfully carried defines racing quality, then Roseben was truly one of the greats of all time. It is quite possible that more cumulative pounds of lead were strapped onto the sturdy back of this 1901 gelding than onto that of any other horse, before or since. He was called the big train for obvious reasons: Roseben was huge, and he was strong. He crossed racing's stage in an era of iron-tough racehorses, but none was tougher than he.

Foaled in the early months of the last century, the Kentucky-bred son of *Ben Strome literally towered above his contemporaries from the outset. He was a gangly, long-legged monstrosity who was gelded early on and sent to the races in 1903 to serve as a gambling tool for his owners. Roseben matured slowly, and it was not until age four that this late bloomer showed the world what he was made of. He had distinct limitations. He was a sprinter, pure and simple—even a mile in top company was a stretch for him. But at shorter distances, the big gelding was racing's monarch between 1905 and 1907.

In seven years, Roseben started 111 times, winning 52 and finishing second or third on 37 occasions. In 59 of those starts, he carried 130 pounds or more; in 29, 14 of which he won, he packed at least 140 pounds. And incredibly, four times he triumphed with 147—under which weight in 1905 he set an American record for 6 furlongs that would last for more than 40 years.

It was a handicapper's rule of thumb that two pounds of additional weight carried was equal to one equine body length of distance at the finish of a race. By that standard, when Roseben conceded 50 to 60 pounds to his rivals and defeated them, he would theoretically have been 25 to 30 lengths their superior at equal weights, or the best by as much as $\frac{1}{16}$ of a mile.

The wear and tear of continuous racing under enormous weights eventually took its toll; as an eight-year-old, Roseben was still running hard but cashing fewer bets for his gambling owner, Davy Johnson. Injury finally halted a long, sad descent toward anonymity, when on July 1, 1909, at Sheepshead Bay, Roseben bowed a tendon in a lowly claiming race.

Johnson finally did right by his grand old campaigner. The aging gelding was given to a family friend in New York and put to light use as a lady's sidesaddle mount. Roseben is believed to have lived out his days in comfort on an Upstate farm, where he died around 1918.

Weight will stop a freight train.

—JAMES ROWE SR.

If weight successfully carried defines racing quality, then Roseben was truly one of the greats of all time.

horse and birth year	starts	wins	seconds	thirds	earnings
ARTFUL (filly) 1902	8	6	2	0	$81,125
BELDAME (filly) 1901	31	17	6	4	$102,135
BROOMSTICK (horse) 1901	39	14	11	5	$74,730
BURGOMASTER (horse) 1903	9	7	0	0	$66,580
COLIN (horse) 1905	15	15	0	0	$178,110
COMMANDO (horse) 1898	9	7	2	0	$58,196
DELHI (horse) 1901	23	8	2	1	$115,640
ENDURANCE BY RIGHT (filly) 1899	18	16	0	2	$26,405
FAIR PLAY (horse) 1905	32	10	11	3	$86,950
FITZ HEBERT (horse) 1906	44	31	7	3	$55,750
HAMBURG BELLE (filly) 1901	29	16	5	3	$84,640
HERMIS (horse) 1899	55	28	8	6	$82,815
MASKETTE (filly) 1906	17	12	2	0	$66,570
PETER PAN (horse) 1904	17	10	3	1	$115,450
ROSEBEN (gelding) 1901	111	52	25	12	$75,110
SIR MARTIN (horse) 1906	13	8	4	0	$78,560
SWEEP (horse) 1907	13	9	2	2	$63,984
SYSONBY (horse) 1902	15	14	0	1	$184,438
TANYA (filly) 1902	12	6	2	1	$71,372

important races won	special notes
Futurity S.	Racing Hall of Fame, only horse to defeat Sysonby
Suburban H.	Racing Hall of Fame, third mare to earn more than $100,000
Travers S.	Racing Hall of Fame, three-time leading American sire
U.S. Hotel S., Belmont S.	Champion
Belmont S.	Racing Hall of Fame, unbeaten in 15 starts
Belmont S.	Racing Hall of Fame, leading American sire of 1907, sire of Colin and Peter Pan
Hopeful S., Belmont S., Brooklyn H.	Classic winner
Champagne S., Holly H.	Champion, raced only at two, won Holly H. carrying 130 pounds and beating colts
Brooklyn Derby, Flash S., etc.	Racing Hall of Fame, three-time leading American sire and sire of Man o' War
Suburban H., Brooklyn H.	Champion
	Champion
Travers S., Suburban H.	Champion
Futurity, Spinaway, Alabama, Gazelle, Ladies; Matron, etc.	Racing Hall of Fame
Belmont S.	Racing Hall of Fame, among leading sires, sire of three champions and Pennant
Manhattan H., Tobaggan H.	Racing Hall of Fame, won 14 times with 140 pounds or more, set American 7-furlong record that stood for 41 years
Saratoga Special S., Coronation Cup (Eng)	Champion
Futurity, Belmont S.	Champion
Metropolitan H.	Racing Hall of Fame
Belmont S.	Champion

chapter 3

A Return to Big-Time Racing

America's industry rebounds from

adverse legislation and produces

some of racing's all-time greats.

T HE TROUBLED FIRST DECADE OF THE 1900s ENDED cataclysmically for America's Thoroughbred industry. Antiwagering laws from coast to coast caused the industry to implode, closing racetracks, dispersing studs, and sending thousands of the country's finest Thoroughbreds abroad to the only viable markets left to them. In the years that followed, American racing embarked on a thrill ride of epic proportions, one that carried it from the lowest of lows to unprecedented heights. From a period of near financial ruin, the industry segued into one that produced the first filly Kentucky Derby winner, the first $200,000 earner, and the first mile faster than 1:35. The period from 1911 to 1920 began in tatters and ended with Man o' War.

RACING LOST AND FOUND

The passage in 1908 of the Agnew-Hart Bill severely damaged New York racing, but an even more devastating blow arrived three years later via a nasty addendum to it. Legal loopholes allowed the sport to scrape by

H. P. Whitney's champion Whisk Broom II raced in Europe before capturing the 1913 New York Handicap Triple Crown.

through 1909 and 1910 with a discreet form of oral betting, although police continued to patrol the tracks, roughing up and occasionally arresting patrons on gambling charges. While this put a distinct chill on racing's pleasures, it did not satisfy the moral crusaders, who in 1911 crafted a pair of laws even more potent than Agnew-Hart. One restricted all forms of betting; the other mandated that racetrack directors face criminal charges if anyone was caught wagering on track grounds.

Industry leaders such as August Belmont, John Sanford, and Harry Payne Whitney willingly supported racing with their time, energy, and money, but they drew the line at imprisonment. Hence, in 1911 the gates of the great New York racetracks slammed shut. Similar legislation harmful to racing swept the country in those years, resulting in track closings as far away as California, leaving only Kentucky and Maryland with any kind of decent racing between 1911 and 1913.

SIGNS OF THE TIMES

1911 The first transcontinental flight takes 49 days and experiences 15 crashes

1916 Actor Charlie Chaplin's salary is $670,000

First U.S. self-service grocery store opens in Tennessee

1917 4.8 million cars and trucks are on U.S. roads, 720,000 are in the rest of the world, the average new car costs $720

U.S. military air service has 55 planes and 130 pilots

American Federation of Labor has 2 million members

1920 The gross national product is at $71.6 billion, more than double its $30.4 billion total of 1910

In decade U. S. Rubber introduces Keds tennis shoes

Go to France and bring

back the sepulcher of Napoleon,

then to England and buy the crown jewels,

then to India and buy the Taj Mahal—

then I'll put a price on Man o' War.

—OWNER SAMUEL RIDDLE

The Jockey Club chairman August Belmont (left) with renowned horseman Samuel Hildreth.

Sir Barton, America's first Triple Crown winner,
won the Kentucky Derby as a maiden in 1919.

HORSE SIGNS OF THE TIMES

1911   Jockey Club registers 2,040 foals

390 sales yearlings average $230

Average purse is at a twentieth century low of $371

1912   James R. Keene's Castleton Stud, in Kentucky, sells for $225 per acre

Star Charter is the year's leading earner with $14,655

1916   Jockey Club registers a decade high 2,128 foals

1918 $863 average purse surpasses the 1907 pre-Agnew-Hart bill record of $860

1919   Jockey Club registers 1,665 foals, a twentieth century low

1920   400 sales yearlings average $1,727

Kentucky Derby winner's purse is a record $30,375

When turf writer O'Neill Sevier predicted a quarter-century recovery period, he overlooked two important parts of the equation: the historic resilience of a popular pastime (racing), and American outrage at being denied a cherished personal freedom (wagering). (Reformers then were also targeting theater, Sunday sporting events, and alcohol consumption.) As indignation swelled, a group of wealthy horsemen began stockpiling a fund with which to hold future race meets. The future came quickly. Although the Agnew-Hart Bill moldered on the books until 1934, the liability law was apparently softened or even dropped by May 30, 1913, for that afternoon, the Belmont Park band struck up "Auld Lang Syne" as Thoroughbreds were led to post in New York for the first time since 1910.

JERSEY ACT

The impact of that brief period was far-reaching. With earning capabilities at an all-time low and bloodstock virtually worthless, American breeders sent more than 1,500 horses overseas between 1908 and 1913. Among those horses were at least 24 past, present, or future United States champions, including Artful, Tanya, Colin, Henry of Navarre, Sir Martin, Maskette, Hermis, Novelty, Peter Pan, Irish Lad, and Ballot. Some eventually came back, but many did not. Leading sires *Rock Sand and *Meddler, also part of the exodus, were lost forever to American breeding.

He was the only horse I ever saw that could come into the homestretch on top by 15 lengths and get beat by 80!

—COL. PHIL CHINN ON FUTURE LEADING SIRE HIGH TIME

An inevitable backlash occurred as foreign countries saw their bloodstock markets threatened. The British, who were especially appalled by the equine flood reaching their shores, suddenly concluded that American pedigrees were not what they ought to be and began aggressively campaigning against the American imports. This process culminated in 1913 with the Jersey Act, a piece of work every bit as shameful as Agnew-Hart. Instead of the previous requirement of eight crosses of genetic purity, admission to England's *General Stud Book*, which lists all recognized English Thoroughbreds and their pedigrees, now demanded that a horse trace back in all lines to foundation stock recorded in its earliest volumes. The Jersey Act effectively excluded horses of old American lineage since many early records had been lost in the chaos of a bloody revolution and bitter civil war. Never mind that the breed had recovered to produce runners capable of beating any horse, on any racetrack, anywhere in the world. As of 1913, the American Thoroughbred was formally mongrelized in the eyes of the international breeding community.

A WORLD AT WAR

The pendulum soon swung the other way. The opening gunshots of World War I in 1914 closely followed racing's return in New York, producing a situation of ironic symmetry. American racing was on the mend but lacked enough native stock to support it. England's sport was sharply curtailed by war, but there were plenty of Thoroughbreds around. The American bloodstock industry, formerly a desperate exporter, overnight became an energetic importer, much to its everlasting advantage. Ironically, the Jersey Act only hurt the British. Long after the war's end in 1918, American horsemen continued to replenish their studs with the best English blood that money could buy. British breeders could not reciprocate because until 1949, American horses were considered to be unworthy of the British stud book.

American owner H. B. Duryea won the 1914 English Derby with Durbar II.

This cartoon from the Cincinnati Enquirer
lampooning the Jersey Act was reprinted in
The Thoroughbred Record *on October 30, 1920.*

On the racetrack, quality proved a two-way street. American-bred horses had won some of Europe's big races a half-decade earlier, but between 1916 and 1920, numerous English and French Thoroughbreds, including champions *Short Grass, *Sun Briar, *Hourless, *Omar Khayyam, *Johren, *Sunbonnet, *Enfilade, and *Constancy, plus classic winner *War Cloud and future influential sire *Chicle, were performing at the apex of U.S. racing.

Although World War I enabled American breeders to acquire much-needed bloodstock at reasonable prices, purses remained small by pre-Agnew-Hart standards. In 1916, Friar Rock banked just $11,150 for winning the Belmont Stakes and Brooklyn and Suburban Handicaps, which in 1908 had been worth $62,265 to the winners. Of the 70 leading American earners through 1920, only 3 had run primarily between 1911 and 1920; 29 had campaigned in the previous decade and 38 in the 1800s. While it did not improve American purses, the war affected the nation's racing in other tangible ways, both good and bad: Churchill Downs grew potatoes in its infield for allied troops; racetrack-sponsored Liberty Bond sales netted millions; and "gift" horses were auctioned to benefit the Red Cross.

In April 1917—the very month that the United States entered the war—Belmont Park suffered two devastating fires, one of which killed 26 horses. The fires were blamed on German sympathizers who erroneously believed the track would be used for troop mobilization. Later that fall, a ship carrying a consignment of English bloodstock to America was torpedoed off the Irish coast. Among the horses lost in the icy Atlantic was a valuable son of Polymelus for whom A. B. Hancock Sr. had high hopes as a stallion.

LEADING TRAINERS

H. Guy Bedwell
Racing Hall of Fame. Leading money trainer in 1918–1919. Leader by wins six times in the decade. Best horse: 1919 Triple Crown winner Sir Barton.

Louis Feustel
Racing Hall of Fame. Leading money trainer in 1920. Trained Man o' War.

Samuel Hildreth
Racing Hall of Fame. Won 1916–1917 Belmont Stakes with Friar Rock and *Hourless. See also 1900s, 1920s.

Henry McDaniel
Racing Hall of Fame. Best runners in this era: champions Exterminator and *Sun Briar. See also 1920s.

James Rowe Sr.
Racing Hall of Fame. Leading money trainer in 1913 and 1915. Trained Regret, first filly Kentucky Derby winner (1915). See also 1900s.

J. F. Schorr
Leading money trainer in 1912. Trained 1914 Belmont Stakes winner Luke McLuke.

Kay Spence
Leading trainer by wins three times in 1918, 1919, and 1920. Later trained 1920s champion Princess Doreen.

Frank D. Weir
During decade, he trained champion Old Rosebud. Previously, he trained champion Roseben.

That horse isn't fast enough to run past me.

—Owner Willis Sharpe Kilmer on Exterminator at three

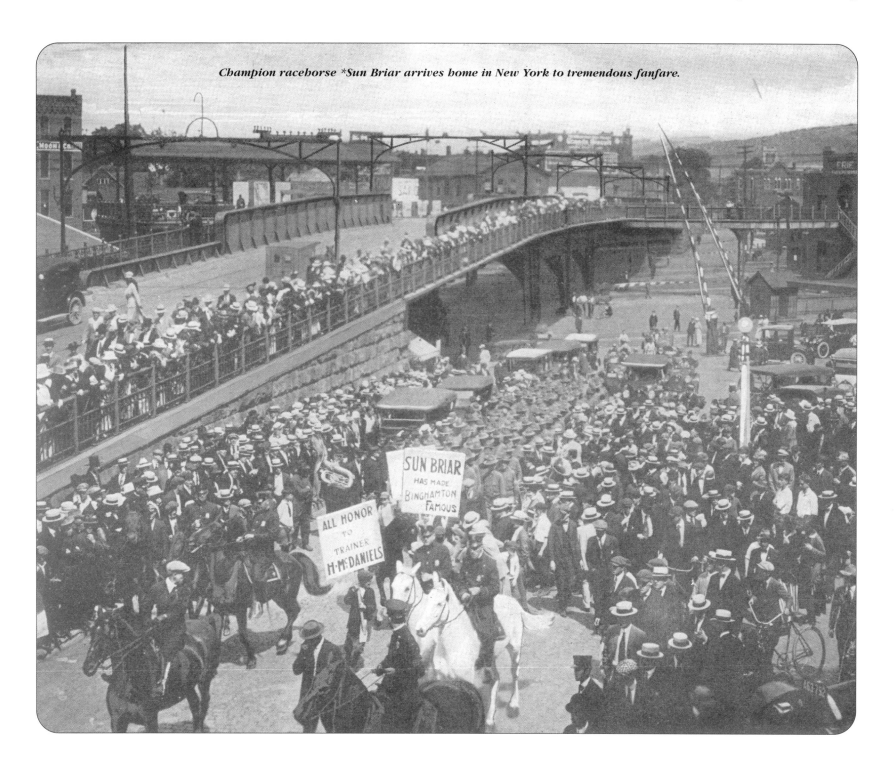

*Champion racehorse *Sun Briar arrives home in New York to tremendous fanfare.*

Star Shoot was a five-time leading sire in North America.

Roamer, who made it into the Racing Hall of Fame, was born and died in this era.

GREAT GELDINGS, FANTASTIC FILLIES

Even in the shadow of war, the decade was memorable for its outstanding runners, including future Racing Hall of Fame geldings Roamer, Old Rosebud, and Exterminator. In 1918, Roamer became the first ever to crack the mythical 1:35 mile, while Old Rosebud's 2:03 ⅖ Kentucky Derby record of 1914 endured for 17 seasons. Exterminator proved victorious 19 times under weights of 130 to 138 pounds. Together they won 129 races and set or equaled 29 records from 5 to 18 furlongs at 14 different racetracks.

Arguably, the most spectacular individual performance of the era did not belong to any of the above but to a now forgotten gelding named Iron Mask. It happened on March 8, 1914, at Mexico's Juarez racetrack, across the border from El Paso, Texas. The grandson of Domino carried 150 pounds that day and sped 5½ furlongs in 1:03 ⅖, setting an American record that lasted for 30 years.

Mack Garner was a leading rider of the decade.

Roamer is a freak.

His legs are like iron, and his heart must be as

big as my head. I never expect to see another like him.

—*TRAINER JACK GOLDSBOROUGH*

LEADING JOCKEYS

James Butwell
Racing Hall of Fame. Leading money rider in 1912. Leader by wins in 1920. Rode more than 1,400 winners in 21-season career, including champions Roamer, Sweep, and *Omar Khayyam.

Mack Garner
Racing Hall of Fame. Leading money rider in 1915 in only his second year of competition. Eventually won 1,346 races, including 1934 Kentucky Derby aboard Cavalcade.

William Knapp
Racing Hall of Fame. Won 1918 Kentucky Derby on Exterminator. Rode champion *Sun Briar and was on Upset when he handed Man o' War his only defeat in the 1919 Sanford Stakes.

Clarence Kummer
Racing Hall of Fame. Leading money rider in 1920. Rode Man o' War in nine of his victories. Also rode champions Exterminator, Sir Barton, and Sarazen.

John Loftus
Racing Hall of Fame. Leading money rider in 1919. Captured 1919 Triple Crown on Sir Barton, won eight races aboard Man o' War, and 1916 Kentucky Derby with George Smith.

Frank Robinson
Leading money rider in 1917. Leader by number of winners in 1916 and 1918. Won 1918 Belmont Stakes and the Suburban Handicap on *Johren.

Iron Mask's female counterpart was Pan Zareta, also a magnificent weight carrier who took a back seat to no male in the realm of blazing speed. Between 1912 and 1918, the "gangly mare with the chestnut hair" inspired poetry and passion as she won more races (76) under more weight (up to 146 pounds) than any mare who had ever lived. Ironically, neither Iron Mask nor Pan Zareta survived the decade. The gelding died in 1916, and the mare succumbed two years later to pneumonia in a damp stall at the fair grounds in New Orleans. She was buried in the track infield, where her gravesite draws tourists to this day.

Pan Zareta appeared on the scene just as angry women of all ages began engaging in Emma Pankhurst's "argument of the broken pane," which promoted violent methods of achieving equality. In the increasingly volatile international quest for suffrage, windows were smashed, fires set, and bombs planted. One militant suffragette named Emily Davison carried the battle to Epsom Downs on Derby Day, 1913, when she rushed onto the course and brought down the King's horse—losing her life in the process.

I would sooner train a good horse than be President of the United States.

—*John E. Madden*

Between 1915 and 1917, H. P. Whitney's Regret did her part for the female cause, albeit peacefully. The daughter of Broomstick routinely whipped the boys and in 1915 became the first filly to win the Kentucky Derby, thus helping a very good race evolve into a classic one. In the ceremony that followed, Whitney exclaimed: "This is the greatest race in America. I don't care if she ever runs again." But she did, all the way into the Racing Hall of Fame.

THE GREATEST OF THEM ALL

As it happened, this decade of revival saved the best for last. On June 6, 1919, in the sixth race at Belmont Park, a chestnut son of Fair Play won his public debut "in a canter, under stout restraint." This was Man o' War, a genetic specimen unacceptable for admission in the *General Stud Book*, but who could gallop faster than most champions raced, required no whip to smash record after record at all major distances, carried monstrous weights, and drew mammoth crowds back to American racetracks.

In 16 months of competition, Man o' War redefined equine greatness. He lost a race at two that he should have won, proving only that he was mortal. Otherwise, he was perfection itself. In 1920, Big Red established five American and two track records in 11 starts and won his races by a combined 164 lengths. Man o' War capped his extraordinary career on October 12, 1920, simply galloping away from another future Racing Hall of Famer, 1919 Triple Crown winner Sir Barton. The $80,000 winner-take-all purse sent Man o' War to stud the richest American Thoroughbred in history with $249,465. But the tale the stopwatch told was perhaps more indicative of what manner of beast he really was. In victory that autumn afternoon, the flame-coated chestnut carved 6⅖ seconds off Kenilworth Park's well-established record for 1¼ miles. An era thus ended, and a legend was born.

NECROLOGY

1911 Flying Fox, 15. English Triple Crown winner, leading sire in France

Isinglass, 21. English Triple Crown winner, one-time world's leading money winner with $285,063

1912 Kingston, 28. Holds all-time win record with 89 wins, leading sire in 1900

Daniel Swigert. Founder of Elmendorf Farm, great-grandfather of Leslie Combs II

Worth, 3. Champion at two, 1912 Kentucky Derby winner

1913 James R. Keene, 73. Financier; leading owner-breeder; owner of Castleton Stud, raced Domino; bred and raced Hall of Famers Commando, Colin, Peter Pan, and Sysonby

Foxhall Daingerfield. Manager of Castleton Stud, member of Kentucky Racing Commission

Tommy Burns, 34. Racing Hall of Fame jockey, rode 1,333 winners

Stephen Sanford, 87. Prominent owner-breeder

1914 *Rock Sand, 14. English Triple Crown winner, broodmare sire of Man o' War. (Died in France.)

James Ben Ali Haggin, 93. Financier; owned Elmendorf Farm; raced numerous champions, including Africander and Hamburg Belle

1915 Hamburg, 20. Champion and leading sire in 1905

1916 *Meddler, 26. Leading sire in 1904 and 1906. (Died in France.)

NECROLOGY

1916 Danny Maher, 35. Racing Hall of Fame jockey, leading rider in England

Herman B. Duryea, 54. Raced Epsom Derby winner Durbar II

Iron Mask, 8. Great sprinter and weight carrier

1917 Hastings, 24. Leading sire in 1902 and 1908, sire of Fair Play

Phil Dwyer, 74. Head of Brooklyn and Queens County Jockey Clubs; with brother Mike, raced champions Hindoo, Miss Woodford, Hanover, Luke Blackburn, Kingston.

1918 Roseben, 17. Racing Hall of Fame, carried 140 pounds or more 29 times

Ben Brush, 25. Racing Hall of Fame, leading sire in 1909

Pan Zareta, 8. Racing Hall of Fame, great sprinter and weight carrier

Jacob Pincus. Racing Hall of Fame trainer

1919 Celt, 14. Leading sire in 1921

*Star Shoot, 21. Leading sire five times

Frank Robinson. Leading jockey by wins in 1916 and 1918

1920 Andrew Miller, 63. Owned Roamer and *Life* magazine

Roamer, 9. Racing Hall of Fame, world record miler

Green B. Morris, 83. Leading owner

H. P. Whitney (right), the most successful American owner-breeder of the decade, with owners J. S. Cosden (left), and Ral Parr (center).

If he were led into a sales ring and none realized who he was, he would sell for $200.

—WRITER MOSE GOLDBLATT ON ROAMER

MAN O' WAR

MAJOR AUGUST BELMONT II MADE A FATEFUL DECISION IN THE spring of 1918. World War I was then at full boil, with more than a million American troops risking their lives on the battlefields of Europe. Under the circumstances, it seemed unthinkable to Belmont that he remain at home in the pastoral safety of his farm, Nursery Stud, planning matings and watching young Thoroughbreds grow up. He chose instead to support his country in war, and thus announced the sale of his entire yearling crop without reserve at the upcoming August Saratoga sales.

Belmont's patriotic sacrifice cost him far more than he could possibly have anticipated, for among the 21 Nursery yearlings auctioned off on August 17, 1918, was a colt like no other the American turf had ever seen—or would ever see. This powerfully built flame-coated son of Fair Play and Mahuba had already been named by Mrs. Belmont when sale day arrived. To honor her husband, she had called him Man o' War. At $5,000, he was the priciest of the Nursery yearlings, though several from other consignments brought more. A relative newcomer to racing named Samuel Riddle became on that afternoon arguably the luckiest man who ever raised a finger to bid. "This is the cheapest horse ever sold," he said to his wife immediately after the sale. Truer words were never spoken.

Over the next two years, trainer Louis Feustel developed Man o' War into the yardstick by which we will eternally measure all great Thoroughbreds. This, however, was no easy task for the future Hall of Fame conditioner. Man o' War had inherited a measure of his sire's difficult temperament. He was a strong-willed and opinionated handful, a gluttonous eater, habitual biter, and notorious runaway in early workouts. It required a masterful piece of horsemanship to bring out his best.

At two in 1919, this son of Fair Play ripped through a 10-race season, winning 9, losing only when purposely trapped by rival jockeys along the rail in the Sanford Memorial. Six times that summer Man 'o War carried 130

pounds, an astonishing assignment for a juvenile, even in those days of burdensome weights.

If he had been awesome at two, Man o' War simply defied description at three. Never has America witnessed such a spectacular streak of unbroken brilliance as this strapping red colt revealed in 1920. He started 11 times and 11 times he won, each race a virtuoso performance. In 8 of those races, he set track, American, or world records from 1 to 1⅝ miles while carrying up to 138 pounds.

Man o' War was not entered for the 1920 Kentucky Derby because Riddle felt it too much to ask of a three-year-old so early in the year. He did, however, win the Preakness and Belmont Stakes, taking the latter by 20 lengths in an American record for 1⅜ miles. He then captured the Withers Mile under a stout pull in American record time of 1:35 ⅕; gave 32 pounds and an eight-length beating to his only rival in the Stuyvesant Handicap; and was challenged head-to-head in the Dwyer Stakes by the talented John P. Grier, to whom he conceded 18 pounds and defeated in the fastest 1⅛ miles ever run to that day.

Man o' War subsequently won the Miller Stakes under 131 pounds; equaled Saratoga's 1¼-mile record in the Travers Stakes; and clipped 4⅕ seconds off the American standard for 1⅝ miles in the Lawrence Realization, defeating his lone rival by an estimated 100 lengths—more than the entire length of the homestretch. In the Jockey Club Gold Cup, he set yet another American record, this time for 1½ miles; and in the Potomac Handicap under a career-high 138 pounds, he clocked the fastest 1¹⁄₁₆ miles ever recorded at Maryland's Havre de Grace racetrack. On the rare occasion when Man o' War did not break a speed record, concerns arose that something was amiss.

In what would be his final start, Man o' War found a seemingly worthy rival in 1919 American Triple Crown champion Sir Barton. But in that historic

> *Man o' War will never be*
>
> *permitted to leave this country. . . .*
>
> *I am merely his custodian, holding him in*
>
> *trust for the American Thoroughbred of the future.*

—OWNER SAMUEL RIDDLE

match at Kenilworth Park, Man o' War treated the future Racing Hall of Famer as though he were a lowly claiming horse, galloping off by 7 lengths to win exactly as he pleased. Man o' War smashed the track record for 1¼ miles by 6⅖ seconds—running the distance approximately 38 lengths faster than it had ever been run before at the Canadian track. The $80,000 he earned that day brought Man o' War's career earnings to $249,465 and established him as the top money-winning American Thoroughbred to that time.

Riddle and Feustel toyed with the idea of racing Man o' War at four, but abandoned it when famed handicapper Walter Vosburgh promised to "put the heaviest weight on him that any horse has carried in my lifetime" if he won his first race of 1921. There were few mortal rivals left to conquer, anyway—no trainer in his right mind wanted to break the heart of a good horse in futile competition against Man o' War, and the clock itself had proved an inadequate foe. Thus, he was forced into retirement in Kentucky, standing briefly at Hinata Farm before moving to Faraway Farm, where he would remain until his death years later.

There is no telling how great a sire Man o' War might have become had he been in the hands of a top breeder. As it was, he was utilized by the Riddles as a private stallion limited to 25 mares annually through 22 seasons. His broodmares were, for the most part, not of the quality that Man o' War deserved. The magnificent stallion's genetic potency was such that he overcame even this. Seven of his eight champions emerged from his first four crops, and in 1926 with only three crops racing, he led the American sire list and established a progeny earnings record of $408,137.

Man o' War eventually sired 64 stakes winners from 379 named foals—17 percent compared to the breed average of 3 percent. Although he never duplicated his own freakish greatness, he got several true standouts, including future Racing Hall of Fame members War Admiral and Crusader, and champions American Flag, Edith Cavell, Scapa Flow, Maid at Arms, Florence Nightingale, and Bateau. As with Colin, Man 'o War's male line survived over time.

During his lifetime, Man o' War struck his proud, high-headed stance before thousands of awed visitors as cameras clicked and groom Will Harbut eloquently sang his praises as the "mostest hoss." In May of 1947, an era ended when after a quarter of a century the gates to Faraway Farm were closed to the public. Man o' War's 30-year-old heart was beginning to fail, and he had endured several agonizing bouts of colic, each weakening him more.

MAN O' WAR continued

When the time came that the once powerful stallion could no longer rise to his feet, Mr. Riddle asked noted veterinarian Dr. William McGee to intervene in the name of mercy. Around noon on Saturday, November 1, Man o' War's struggles ceased. His body was placed in a large oak casket lined with the gold and black colors of Riddle's famous silks. It was said that a thousand people or more came to pay their respects at the funeral on November 4, along with newsreel crews and radio broadcasters. The incomparable champion was buried in a plot adjacent to his long-time paddock at Faraway Farm, and sometime afterward a larger-than-life bronze by sculptor Herbert Haseltine was placed on the site.

Man o' War's grave was relocated in the late 1970s to the newly built Kentucky Horse Park, where, at the end of a long tree-lined driveway, the 20-hand-high Haseltine bronze silently greets thousands of visitors to the Blue Grass each year. Even in death, Man o' War remains racing's number one goodwill ambassador.

Eight decades have come and gone since he left the great Sir Barton in a cloud of dust at Kenilworth Park. Countless champions have dominated the sport in their respective eras, but none like Man o' War. He remains without equal.

Champion of champions Man o' War defeats John P. Grier
in the race of his life—the 1920 Dwyer Stakes.

If he wins his first race at four, I'll put the heaviest weight on him that any horse has carried in my lifetime.

—HANDICAPPER WALTER VOSBURGH ON MAN O' WAR

EXTERMINATOR

HE WAS NOT GREAT IN THE SENSE THAT MAN O' WAR WAS—HE was no flaming meteor streaking with blinding brilliance across racing's horizon, here now and gone in a year or two. Exterminator was a different sort of hero, a homespun fellow who the common man could embrace as his own. His pedigree was not upper crust, nor was he a perfect physical specimen. But he was all heart.

The American public loved him for qualities that had nothing to do with sheer greatness. They cherished his splendid longevity and stood in awe of the versatility that allowed him to win from 5½-furlong sprints to 2¼-mile marathons in deep mud and over rock-hard surfaces from Canada to Mexico. Most of all, they admired his Bunyanesque strength. He was thin and angular, lovingly nicknamed Old Bones, yet he could shoulder the heaviest weights over the longest distances against the best competition, and he did it over and over again as the calendar years flipped by.

Between 1918 and 1924, Exterminator fueled America's love for a good fairytale. Foaled at Almahurst Farm, in Kentucky, on May 30, 1915, and sold for $1,500 as a yearling to J. Cal Milam, he was a lightly raced, unremarkable two-year-old. After flashing some ability early the next spring, he was sold privately to Willis Sharpe Kilmer to serve as a pre–Kentucky Derby work companion for the champion *Sun Briar.

Kilmer, who had made a fortune promoting his family's popular line of patented medicines (including Swamp Root, a "remedy" for kidney and liver ailments), practically worshiped the expensive French-bred *Sun Briar, but it was Exterminator who would bring him lasting fame. When *Sun Briar began sulking in his morning trials, his honest and hard-trying stablemate took his place in the 1918 Kentucky Derby—and won at odds of 30 to 1.

As a four-year-old in 1919, Exterminator developed into a handicap star, and with his improved performances came added weight. Thirty-five times he was asked to carry 130 pounds or more, and he won with as much as

138. While Roseben packed higher weights over short distances, Exterminator hauled his massive loads many furlongs farther, a more demanding task in the final analysis.

Exterminator actually hit his prime at age seven, long after most top horses have left the track. His crowning moment came in the 1922 Brooklyn Handicap in which he carried a steadying 135 pounds, conceding 9 to future Hall of Famer Grey Lag. When the pair hooked up in a ferocious battle to the finish, neither would give in; Exterminator ultimately employed his last ounce of strength to defeat his tenacious rival by inches.

Depleted both mentally and physically by that titanic effort, Exterminator was never the same thereafter. Age and weight caught up with him quickly, though Kilmer kept him running hard. In 1924, the now nine-year-old gelding was at last allowed to throw in the towel, heading home to Sun Briar Court, in New York, with 50 wins, 17 seconds, and 17 thirds in 100 starts, and earnings of $252,996. He had passed the great Man o' War and was ranked second only to Zev among all-time American money-winning Thoroughbreds.

A gregarious sort, Exterminator was given a pony named Peanuts as a retirement buddy. Like Man o' War in Kentucky, Exterminator welcomed thousands of visitors over the years. Unlike Man o' War, Exterminator was gentle and calm, a favorite with schoolchildren who showed up to help celebrate his birthday each May 30. In 1943, 28-year-old Exterminator made a final and very popular public appearance at Belmont Park to promote the sale of war bonds.

Kilmer had died of pneumonia in 1940. His farm had been sold, but his will provided that Exterminator be lovingly cared for in his familiar surroundings for the remainder of his days. Old Bones passed away at age 30 on September 25, 1945, and was buried next to *Sun Briar, the workmate he had eclipsed more than a quarter of a century before, on a hill overlooking the Susquehanna River.

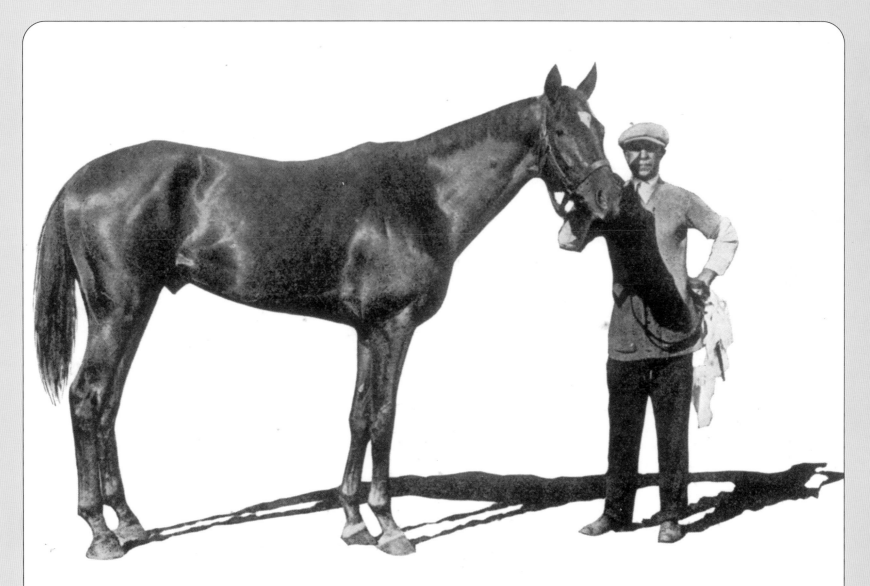

EXTERMINATOR

WINNER OF THE TWO 1918 KENTUCKY CLASSICS

THE KENTUCKY DERBY (1¼ MILES) AND LATONIA CUP (2¼ MILES)

REGRET

AT ABOUT 1:30 P.M. ON MAY 7, 1915, A GERMAN U-BOAT'S torpedo ripped an explosive hole in the hull of the luxury liner *Lusitania* as it sailed along the coast of Ireland. Within 18 minutes, 1,198 passengers had disappeared forever into the frigid Atlantic waters, among them, Alfred Gwynn Vanderbilt, brother-in-law of noted American racehorse owner and breeder Harry Payne Whitney. The deep mourning in which the Whitney family suddenly found itself juxtaposed eerily with the festive activity preceding the 41st renewal of the Kentucky Derby to be run the next day—and for which Whitney's undefeated Regret was favored. While some family members felt she should be withdrawn from the race, the sporting Whitney decreed that the Derby would go on with his great filly facing the starter.

It was a historic decision. Approximately 27 hours after the sinking of the *Lusitania,* Regret took the lead from the start and drew away to become the first of her sex to have the traditional wreath of roses draped across her shoulders. It would not happen again for another 65 years.

The 1915 Run for the Roses was significant not only because of Regret's status as the first filly winner, but because of the enormously favorable publicity generated in the aftermath of her popular victory. Derby promoter Matt Winn subsequently credited Regret with putting the Kentucky classic on the road to becoming an American institution.

Regret was 1 of 192 stakes winners bred by Whitney. Foaled in 1912 at his Brookdale Farm, in New Jersey, she was a lovely chestnut daughter of champion Broomstick and the Hamburg mare, Jersey Lightning. From the start, Regret looked and acted the part of a good one, and her distinctively blazed white face was rarely seen anywhere but in front

once the starter's flag fell. Trained by the great James Rowe Sr., she was never defeated by another filly and was only twice beaten by males. This member of the so-called weaker sex won all three of her races as a two-year-old, defeating top male rivals in the Hopeful, Sanford Stakes, and Saratoga Special. The Kentucky Derby signified her 1915 debut, a training strategy that would never even be considered in modern times.

Regret tasted defeat for the first time at age four, and once again at five, although the latter marked one of her finest efforts on the racecourse.

Among the entrants for the 1917 Brooklyn Handicap were three Kentucky Derby winners (Regret, Old Rosebud, and *Omar Khayyam), future Hall of Fame inductee Roamer, future leading sire *Chicle, and handicap stars Borrow, Stromboli, and Boots. It was arguably the most amazing group of Thoroughbreds seen on an American racetrack at one time. Regret finished second that day, a desperate nose behind stablemate Borrow in a new American record time for 1⅛ miles.

Regret was retired after 1917 with 9 victories in 11 starts; only once was she beaten by more than a few inches. Expectations were high for Regret in her new career as a broodmare, but in this she proved a disappointment to Whitney. Only 1 of her 10 foals managed to win a minor stakes, though several of her daughters became quality producers.

Regret's legacy would not be a genetic one. For 65 years she stood alone in the history books as the only filly winner of the Kentucky Derby. In 1980, Genuine Risk joined her, followed eight years later by Winning Colors. Regret died on April 14, 1934, and was buried at the Whitney Farm, near Lexington, Kentucky.

In 1915, Regret (left) became the first filly Kentucky Derby winner.

horse and birth year	starts	wins	seconds	thirds	earnings
BILLY KELLY (gelding) 1916	69	39	15	7	$99,782
BOOTS (gelding) 1911	29	11	4	3	
BORROW (gelding) 1908	91	24	20	12	$87,396
CLEOPATRA (filly) 1917	26	8	10	4	$55,939
CUDGEL (horse) 1914	59	28	13	7	$68,954
EXTERMINATOR (gelding) 1915	100	50	17	17	$252,996
FRIAR ROCK (horse) 1913	21	9	1	3	$20,365
*HOURLESS (horse) 1914	15	9	1	2	$45,475
IRON MASK (gelding) 1908	32	12	12	4	
JOHN P. GRIER (horse) 1917	17	10	4	2	$37,003
*JOHREN (horse) 1915	22	9	5	3	$49,156
MAN O' WAR (horse) 1917	21	20	1	0	$249,465
OLD ROSEBUD (gelding) 1911	80	40	13	8	$74,729
*OMAR KHAYYAM (horse) 1914	32	13	6	5	$58,436
PAN ZARETA (filly) 1910	151	76	31	21	$39,082
PENNANT (horse) 1911	12	9	1	2	$25,315
PURCHASE (horse) 1916	23	14	2	2	$39,706
REGRET (filly) 1912	11	9	1	0	$35,093
ROAMER (gelding) 1911	98	39	26	9	$98,828
SIR BARTON (horse) 1916	31	13	6	5	$116,857
*SUN BRIAR (horse) 1915	22	8	4	5	$74,355
WHISK BROOM II (horse) 1907	26	10	8	1	

important races won	special notes
Sanford S., Eastern Shore S., etc.	Champion
Suburban H.	Stakes winner in England; in U.S. set or equaled four American, Canadian, or track records; defeated Roamer four times in six meetings
Brooklyn H., etc.	Defeated three Kentucky Derby winners and Roamer in 1917 Brooklyn H., setting new world record for 1⅛ miles
Champagne S., CCA Oaks, Alabama S., Pimlico Oaks, etc.	Champion
Brooklyn H., etc.	Great weight carrier, twice handicap champion, won eight times with 130 pounds or more
Kentucky Derby, Saratoga Cup, etc.	Racing Hall of Fame, retired as leading American money winner
Belmont S., Suburban H., Brooklyn H.	
Belmont S., etc.	Champion, defeated *Omar Khayyam in match race
	Great sprinter and weight carrier, set new American record under 150 pounds
Aqueduct H., etc.	Gave Man o' War the race of his life in 1920 Dwyer S.
Belmont S., etc.	Champion
Preakness S., Belmont S., etc.	Racing Hall of Fame, widely regarded as America's greatest champion, retired as leading American money winner
Kentucky Derby, etc.	Racing Hall of Fame, won 1914 Kentucky Derby in track-record 2:03 ⅖, 14 additional stakes
Kentucky Derby, Travers S., Saratoga Cup, Brooklyn Derby	Champion, first foreign-bred winner of Kentucky Derby
	Racing Hall of Fame; carried 146 pounds to victory at Juarez racetrack, giving as many as 54 pounds to rivals for $300 purse
Futurity S.	
Jockey Club (Gold Cup), Dwyer S., etc.	
Kentucky Derby, Hopeful, Sanford, Saratoga Special S., Saranac H.	Racing Hall of Fame, first filly to win Kentucky Derby
Saratoga H. (three times), Travers S., etc.	Racing Hall of Fame, set new world record for mile in 1:34 ⅕
Kentucky Derby, Preakness S., Belmont S.	Racing Hall of Fame, first American Triple Crown winner
Travers S., etc.	Champion
Suburban H., Brooklyn H., etc.	First winner of Handicap Triple Crown in only three U.S. starts

Roaring Through the Twenties

Racing's unbridled optimism and fiscal

extravagance mirrored the American

experience before the Depression.

ROARING TWENTIES. NO OTHER DECADE IN AMERICA'S twentieth century possessed a designation so enduring or so vividly descriptive of the time. The 1920s did indeed blast onto the scene with a roar of exuberance, marking the end of a somber era of war. On the surface, at least, it was a time of outrageous fun—flappers and the fox trot are indelible images of this, the jazz age. As Americans worked fewer hours for increased pay, they had more money to spend and more time to spend it. Automobiles transported them everywhere: to movies, to ballparks, and, yes, to the racetrack. Technological wonders such as the washing machine and indoor plumbing made life easier, while radio changed forever the way people perceived their world.

Horse racing rode the crest of this postwar celebration of life. Although puritanical attitudes still existed—witness Prohibition—racing seemed inoculated against them. When antiwagering proposals appeared on local dockets, they were routinely smacked down by legislators fed up with smothering moralism.

PARI-MUTUEL EXCESSES

The shrine at which racing worshipped during these golden years was the pari-mutuel. Fueled by the enormous revenue-generating success of this form of wagering, the Thoroughbred industry grew beyond belief. Elaborate new racetracks were the overt symbol of this prosperity—at least 15 of note were constructed in the United States during the 1920s, including Arlington and Washington Parks, in Chicago, and Hialeah Park, in Florida. Purses went through the roof, again thanks to those marvelous French betting machines. The 1926 American Derby at Arlington was the country's inaugural $100,000 stakes event; by 1929, the Kentucky Derby, Preakness, and Belmont Stakes were all worth at least $50,000.

If earnings power had been sluggish in the previous decade, the opposite was now true as purse distribution climbed from $8.4 million to $13.7 million. In 1923, Zev became the first American racehorse to bank $200,000 in a season; by 1930, Gallant Fox had raised that bar to $300,000. Jockey Earle Sande, trainer James Fitzsimmons, breeder H. P. Whitney, and owner Harry Sinclair each established earnings records that would stand for years.

Bloodstock prices also went into orbit. Starting in 1925, Saratoga's elite yearling sale annually hammered down American records. A Man o' War filly that summer became America's first $50,000 yearling. A colt fetched $70,000 in 1927; and in 1928, New Broom—described by one incredulous observer as "the most ordinary-looking yearling I ever saw"—commanded $75,000. (That record price stood for 26 years.)

America seemed conflicted in this postwar era, yearning for friendly foreign relations yet severely limiting immigration from eastern and southern Europe with passage of the 1924 National Origins Quota Act, a law that grew out of ethnic prejudice. Such sentiments did not extend to Thoroughbreds, as racing in the United States became strikingly global in view. Although American-bred horses had previously competed in Europe and vice versa, the public's desire for international contests reached a boiling point in the early 1920s.

Earl Sande, legendary rider, set a
1923 earnings record that stood for 20 years.

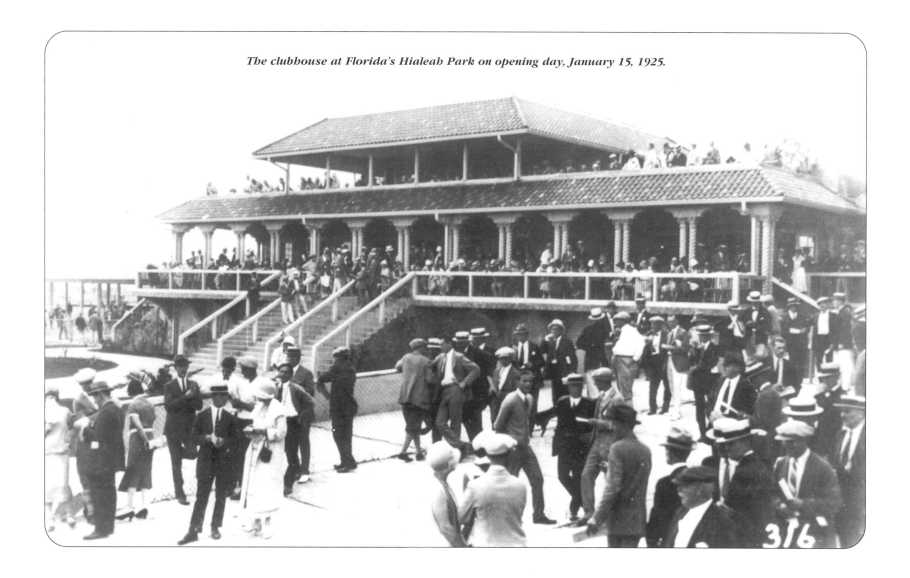

The clubhouse at Florida's Hialeah Park on opening day, January 15, 1925.

He was the best I ever trained—

probably the best the Turf had ever seen.

—*RACING HALL OF FAME TRAINER JAMES FITZSIMMONS ON ILL-FATED, UNDEFEATED DICE*

By the mid-1920s, Zev had earned more money than any other American Thoroughbred.

SIGNS OF THE TIMES

1921–1930 Airlines carry fewer than 10,000 commercial passengers a year

Movies cost $50,000 or less to make

Average American salary is $2,000 per year

Greta Garbo makes $5,000 per week

Model T. sells for around $300

Average automobile horsepower is 20

Number of cars and trucks in America increases from 9.2 million to 26.5 million

First commercial television sets sell for $75

Average life expectancy is 59 years

1922 Henry Ford earns $264,000 a day and is declared a billionaire by the Associated Press

1925 Female textile workers are paid 16¢ an hour and work 56-hour weeks

1930 Six million Americans are unemployed shortly after the start of the Great Depression

Transcontinental air service takes 36 hours

The first such event was staged at Belmont Park on October 20, 1923, matching oilman Harry Sinclair's Kentucky Derby winner Zev against Epsom Derby winner *Papyrus for a total purse of $100,000. The British were unenthused, believing the odds insurmountable against their candidate—as, indeed, they proved to be. *Papyrus sailed through two storms in seven days, had no time to acclimate, and faced his first race on dirt—rather than the grass surface he was accustomed to in England. To make matters worse, race day brought ankle-deep mud, and *Papyrus struggled mightily on smooth-plated shoes inappropriate for a slippery, wet surface. Zev won by five lengths before 60,000 screaming nationalists, putting him squarely on the road to a money-winning record. This match also marked the first-ever radio broadcast of a racing event. It was the year's high point for Sinclair, who was later indicted on federal bribery charges in the Teapot Dome oil reserve scandal. Though acquitted, the master of Rancocas Stable spent three humiliating months in jail for "contempt of Senate."

Why, I expect he is one of the dumbest horses I ever saw. He don't know the difference between 115 and 135 pounds.

—TRAINER HENRY MCDANIEL ON EXTERMINATOR

Noted racing men August Belmont II (left), racing official J. S. Wallace (center),
and oilman and master of Rancocas Stable Harry F. Sinclair.

HORSE SIGNS OF THE TIMES

1921 2,035 foals are registered

395 yearlings sell for an average of $2,273

1922 Man o' War's fee is $2,500 with ten outside subscriptions available

1923 Earl Sande rides winners of $569,394, a record that stands for 20 years

1924 North American purse money exceeds $10 million for first time

1925 Man o' War yearling filly brings American record of $50,500

Yearling sales average peaks at $3,207 and remains the record for 20 years

1926 Man o' War sets progeny earnings record of $408,137

1929 Futurity winner Whichone earns a record $105,730 purse

1930 Gallant Fox becomes first $300,000 single-season earner

5,137 foals are registered

Yearling average cost plummets to $1,966

The match left British horsemen tasting lemons. "That this (race) will live in turf history is beyond question," the 1923 *Bloodstock Breeders' Review* sourly conceded. "That it is a forerunner of similar enterprises is open to doubt." But it was a forerunner. A year later, Pierre Wertheimer sent French champion *Epinard over for a series of International Specials. The handsome chestnut finished second each time to Wise Counsellor, Ladkin, and Sarazen, but his failure to win only confirmed the English suspicion that such contests were folly. If Americans wanted international competition, they grumbled, let them come to Ascot and contest the Gold Cup—an invitation that would not be accepted by a viable contender for several decades. Thus, the great experiment ended.

When Arlington Park opened a few years later and tried to generate interest in an annual international race, none could be found. A quarter-century passed before the idea gained a lasting foothold in Laurel Park's Washington, D.C., International Stakes—on turf. As for *Epinard, his popularity was such that he divided his early stud years between Kentucky and France, becoming the first "shuttle" stallion.

When a man can breed a Quarter Horse to a plow mare and get a horse that can beat everything in America, it's time for me to sell out.

—JOHN E. MADDEN ON SARAZEN

ROYAL AND PLEBEIAN BLOOD

Even as international racing went on extended hiatus, U.S. breeders continued to demand foreign bloodstock. Because England's Jersey Act still banned most American pedigrees from the *General Stud Book*, imports maintained a distinctly westward flow. Future leading sires *St. Germans, *Sickle, and *Challenger II were among the imports as was the great matron *La Troienne. And then there was *Sir Gallahad III.

December 15, 1925, was a day of such colossal importance to America's Thoroughbred industry that it requires special mention. On that day, the great French racehorse *Sir Gallahad III arrived on American shores. An animal of exceptional beauty, lineage, and class, his syndication by A. B. Hancock Sr. was considered even then a towering home run. "Bred as he is and endowed with great racing abilities, he appears an ideal stallion for American breeders," wrote one English bloodstock authority. "It will be surprising if, under the able management of Mr. Hancock, he does not take high rank as a sire." Indeed, *Sir Gallahad III would reign 4 times as America's premier sire and 12 times as its leading broodmare sire.

Blue blood was all right, but Americans raised on Horatio Alger's rags-to-riches tales hankered for a good Cinderella story. Racing obliged by serving them up in abundance throughout the 1920s. Champion Sally's Alley was sired by a $375 Army remount stallion; Sarazen was described by John Madden as being "by a Quarter Horse, out of a plow mare;" Exterminator's sire, *McGee, was the only foal of a horse who was subsequently gelded; Wise Counsellor sold in utero for $100; and Black Gold was from an Oklahoma claiming mare.

Colonel E. R. Bradley won two of his four Kentucky Derbys in the 1920s.

LEADING TRAINERS

William Duke
Racing Hall of Fame. Trained 1925 Kentucky Derby winner Flying Ebony, 1925 Preakness Stakes winner Coventry, and 1924 French Derby winner Pot au Feu.

James Fitzsimmons
Racing Hall of Fame. Leading money trainer 1930. Best runner of era: 1930 Triple Crown winner Gallant Fox. See also 1930s, 1940s, 1950s, 1960s.

Thomas J. Healey
Racing Hall of Fame. During 1920s, he trained four winners of Preakness Stakes: Pillory (1922), Vigil (1923), Display (1926), Victorian (1928). See also 1930s.

Samuel Hildreth
Racing Hall of Fame. Leading money trainer four times. Leader by wins in 1921 and 1927. Trained champions Grey Lag, Zev, and Mad Play. See also 1900s, 1910s.

Max Hirsch
Racing Hall of Fame. In this decade, he trained champion Grey Lag as two-year-old and 1924–1925 Horse of the Year Sarazen. See also 1930s, 1940s.

Henry McDaniel
Racing Hall of Fame. Leading trainer by wins in 1922. Trained 1928 Kentucky Derby winner Reigh Count and former leading money earner Sun Beau. See also 1910s.

Herbert J. Thompson
Racing Hall of Fame. Won four Kentucky Derbys in this decade with Behave Yourself, Bubbling Over, Burgoo King, and Brokers Tip.

THE DECADE'S BEST

No single racehorse towered above all others in the 1920s as Man o' War and Colin had before and as Citation and Secretariat would later. Still, 15 Racing Hall of Fame members competed during these years. Foremost among them was Exterminator, the wonderful gelding whose career spanned eight seasons and nine trainers. He was a faded chestnut, angular and almost skinny in appearance—thus the affectionate nickname Old Bones. But his Herculean strength was evident with every pound of lead the handicappers loaded onto his back. "Weight will stop a freight train," trainer James Rowe had warned; Exterminator reached that threshold at 140 pounds. Other than that, he had no apparent limitations, scoring a twentieth century record of 34 stakes victories and retiring as America's richest Thoroughbred.

Best of the rest in this decade was Rancocas Stable's Grey Lag, who at top form flirted with greatness. So too did subsequent champions Sarazen, Blue Larkspur, Reigh Count, and 1930 Triple Crown winner Gallant Fox. Despite an 11 for 11 juvenile season, superstar status eluded Morvich, who never won again after taking the 1922 Kentucky Derby. Zev, Crusader, and Sun Beau were big money winners but lost too many races to rank among the immortals. Equipoise and Twenty Grand were true turf giants, but as two-year-olds of 1930 they belong more to the 1930s.

Best of the era's fillies was Princess Doreen. As tough and almost as popular as Old Bones, the iron mare won 34 races and broke Miss Woodford's 40-year female earnings record of $174,745. Other notable distaff runners included 1921 Preakness winner Nellie Morse; multiple champions Black Maria and Bateau; and Rose of Sharon, considered best of either sex at the age of three in 1929 before succumbing to pneumonia.

Known as the iron mare, Princess Doreen retired in 1927 as the leading distaff money winner.

In 1924, Nellie Morse became the fourth and last filly to win the Preakness Stakes.

HEARTBREAK

An alarming epidemic of infertility swept the ranks of top horses in this era. Grey Lag sired just 17 foals. Zev averaged 6 per crop. Mad Play, Kentucky Derby winners Whiskery, Black Gold, and Twenty Grand, and Man o' War's champion daughter Bateau were all completely infertile. Drugs may have been a culprit. In that era before postrace testing, even top stables engaged in doping. Rumor had it that Sam Hildreth—trainer of Grey Lag, Mad Play, and Zev—was a pharmacological master, though this was never proven, and he was eventually inducted with honor into the Racing Hall of Fame.

Heartbreak is a part of any era, but the 1920s had more than its share. Black Gold died on the racetrack, as did Scapa Flow, one of Man o' War's fleetest sons. Preakness winner Broomspun was kicked fatally in the shoulder. Undefeated 1927 juvenile Dice hemorrhaged. Handicap star Captain Hal was accidentally overdosed with a strychnine-laced medication, while Sunny Man was victim of a more sinister poisoning before the 1925 Kentucky Derby, for which he would have been a favorite.

Fire was an especially horrible byproduct of the times. With sprinkler systems and some noncombustible building materials still in the future, barn fires took a deadly toll. Sinclair's unbeaten $150,000 acquisition, Inchcape, perished in a fire at Rancocas Farm along with 1920 Brooklyn Handicap winner Cirrus. *Prince Palatine, male-line ancestor of Round Table, also died by fire, as did Coffroth Handicap hero Sir Harry, and multiple stakes winner and producer Bonnie Mary. Late in 1928, Mrs. John D. Hertz's Horse of the Year Reigh Count narrowly escaped that same awful fate when dragged blindfolded from a burning barn at his owner's Illinois farm.

LEADING JOCKEYS

Frank Coltiletti
Racing Hall of Fame. Rode champions Crusader, Sun Beau, Black Maria, and Edith Cavell. Won many important races, including Travers, Metropolitan Handicap, and Futurity Stakes.

Laverne Fator
Racing Hall of Fame. Leading money rider in 1925–1926. Rode more than 1,000 winners, including champion Grey Lag, Black Maria, Pompey. Won Travers (twice) and Futurity Stakes (twice).

Albert Johnson
Racing Hall of Fame. Leading money rider in 1922. Won Kentucky Derby with Morvich (1922) and Bubbling Over (1926). Also won 1925–1926 Belmont Stakes on American Flag and Crusader. Rode champion Exterminator.

Linus "Pony" McAtee
Racing Hall of Fame. Leading money rider in 1928. Won 1927 and 1929 Kentucky Derbys aboard Whiskery and Clyde Van Dusen. Rode champions Twenty Grand and Exterminator.

Ivan Parke
Racing Hall of Fame. Leading money rider in 1924. Leading rider by wins in 1923 and 1924. Rode only three seasons (1923–1925) and won 23 percent of his races.

Earle Sande
Racing Hall of Fame. Leading money rider in 1921, 1923, and 1927. In 1923, he set earnings record of $569,394 that stood for 20 years. Rode 3,700 winners, including Gallant Fox to 1930 Triple Crown sweep. Won Kentucky Derbys with Zev (1923) and Flying Ebony (1925).

Raymond "Sonny" Workman
Racing Hall of Fame. Leading money rider in 1930 and 1932. Rode 1,169 winners, including champions Equipoise and Top Flight.

Jim Dandy beats Gallant Fox in the 1930 Travers Stakes at 100-1 odds.

THE CRASH

America had problems aplenty as the decade progressed. The country's carefree face concealed an interior simmering with intolerance and paranoia, including a fear of communism; antialien sentiments; the rebirth of the Ku Klux Klan with its night raids and lynchings; and the rise of gangsterism.

Through it all, Presidents Warren G. Harding and Calvin Coolidge presided over a period of unprecedented economic growth, outrageously conspicuous consumption, and increasingly irresponsible speculation even on the part of average Americans. By September 3, 1929, the Dow Jones Industrial Average had soared to 381.17. President Herbert Hoover professed to have "no fears for the future of our country. It is bright with hope."

Seven weeks later, on October 24, Hoover's "bright hope" was extinguished in a nightmarish flood of ticker tape. On Black Thursday, $4 billion was lost in the New York Stock Exchange; by year's end, stock values had plummeted by $15 billion. Life savings were gone, banks and factories were closed, and soup lines were formed. America had entered the Great Depression.

THE TORCH IS PASSED

The 1920s witnessed a changing of the guard in American racing. When August Belmont II died in 1924, William Woodward filled the breach of leadership. Legendary conditioners James Rowe Sr., Sam Hildreth, and John Madden died in 1929, the year in which Ben A. Jones and James Fitzsimmons started to develop their first champions. Harry Payne Whitney breathed his last in 1930 but left behind a son who would carry the family torch with pride. Fair Play, too, was gone—just as his son Man o' War stood on the threshold of immortality as a sire.

America's Thoroughbred industry again found itself in trouble, but this time things would be different. Even as the depression years took their terrible toll, the foundation of the sport remained solid; its future resided in good hands. Racing would survive.

NECROLOGY

1921 Hal Pettit Headley, 65. Noted breeder, owner of Beaumont Farm in Kentucky

Ultimus, 15. Sire of successful sires High Time, Stimulus, and Supremus; leading juvenile sire of 1924

1922 Richard Croker, 81. American and Irish owner-breeder, one-time Tammany Hall political boss, raced Epsom Derby winner Orby, brought Americus to England

1923 Beldame, 23. Racing Hall of Fame champion

Lord Jersey, 53. English owner, Jockey Club official, author of the Jersey Act

1924 August Belmont II, 72. Renowned owner, breeder, and industry leader; chairman of the Jockey Club; president of Westchester Racing Association; breeder of Man o' War

Edward Corrigan. Owner, racetrack proprietor; built Hawthorne Race Course in Chicago

Adolph Spreckels, 67. Bred champion and Kentucky Derby winner Morvich, president of Pacific Coast Jockey Club

1925 Alan-a-Dale, 26. Kentucky Derby winner

The Finn, 13. Champion and classic winner, leading sire of 1923, sire of Racing Hall of Fame champion Zev and Kentucky Derby winner Flying Ebony

Fred Taral, 58. Racing Hall of Fame jockey

1926 William P. Burch, 80. Racing Hall of Fame trainer

William Duke, 68. Racing Hall of Fame trainer, trained Flying Ebony and Coventry (Preakness Stakes winner)

1927 James Cox Brady, 45. Owner of Dixiana Farm, paid auction record $50,500 for Man o' War filly in 1925

NECROLOGY

1927 Fred Burlew. Racing Hall of Fame trainer

Disguise, 30. Among the leading sires, last surviving offspring of Domino

James McLaughlin. Racing Hall of Fame jockey

Willie Simms, 47. Racing Hall of Fame jockey

Payne Whitney, 52. Owner of Greentree Stable, brother of Harry Payne Whitney, and father of John Hay Whitney

1928 Black Gold, 7. Racing Hall of Fame, won 1924 Kentucky Derby

*Whisk Broom II, 21. Racing Hall of Fame champion, successful sire

1929 Mars Cassidy, 67. Legendary starter

Fair Play, 24. Racing Hall of Fame champion, three-time leading sire in 1920, 1924, and 1927

Sam Hildreth, 63. Racing Hall of Fame trainer, three-time leading owner, nine-time leading trainer

John E. Madden, 74. Racing Hall of Fame trainer; renowned owner-breeder, industry leader; founded Hamburg Place; bred five Kentucky Derby winners

James Rowe Sr. Racing Hall of Fame trainer of champions Hindoo, Miss Woodford, Luke Blackburn, Colin, Commando, Sysonby, and Delhi

1930 E. H. "Snapper" Garrison, 62. Racing Hall of Fame jockey

Clarence Kummer, 31. Racing Hall of Fame jockey, Man o' War's regular rider in 1920

Prudery, 12. Champion at two and three, dam of two classic winners

Harry Payne Whitney, 58. Six-time leading owner, eight-time leading breeder; bred a record 192 stakes winners

A lot of people think a bet on a horse race is a sin and never stop to think that practically everything in life is a gamble. One takes a chance on the price of stocks or bonds rising and no one thinks anything of it. If that speculative element of life were removed, there would be little left to live for.

—*Clarence Darrow*

GREY LAG

THE STORY OF GREY LAG IS A CLASSIC ONE IN REVERSE. He descended from the noblest of riches to the most tattered of rags before finding some semblance of peace in the twilight of his life.

Grey Lag was bred in 1918 by famed horseman John E. Madden, who curiously named him for a species of goose. Despite the *grey* reference, this son of *Star Shoot was a brightly marked, blazed-faced chestnut with three flashy white ankles—although he did have an unusual patch of gray on his back.

In 1919, Madden packaged the gaudy colt with a now-forgotten filly and sold the pair for $10,000 to an up-and-coming young conditioner named Max Hirsch, who, in turn, began developing him into a prospect of great promise. By the time rival trainer Sam Hildreth showed up the following summer to inspect Grey Lag for client and well-known oilman Harry F. Sinclair, Hirsch had hung a rather audacious $40,000 price tag on him. Hildreth was not fazed. What did bother him, though, was that patch on the colt's back. Upon viewing this peculiarity, Hildreth—who had an irrational aversion to gray horses—turned an expensive thumb's down.

Of course, those gray hairs did not slow Grey Lag down one bit. He won the subsequent Champagne Stakes impressively, after which his asking price shot up to $60,000. At this point, Sinclair overruled his superstitious trainer and bought himself a great one. Hildreth found himself in charge of a colt he did not like or want, but who he would come to regard as one of the best he had ever known in half a century of racing.

Hildreth shoved his distaste aside and guided Sinclair's expensive acquisition to a championship season as a three-year-old. A bruised foot kept Grey Lag out of the 1921 Kentucky Derby, but he returned to win eight in a row—a streak that included the classic Belmont Stakes; the Dwyer Stakes in 9-furlong American record time; the Knickerbocker Handicap under 135

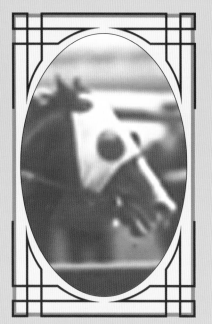

pounds; and the Brooklyn Handicap over a star-studded field that included the great Exterminator, 1920 Kentucky Derby winner Paul Jones, champions Mad Hatter and Eternal, and John P. Grier, who in 1920 had given Man o' War the race of his life.

Grey Lag won 9 of 11 starts at ages four and five, and never finished worse than second. In one losing effort, he dropped a nose decision to Exterminator after engaging that immortal in an epic battle of heart and courage. While that effort effectively ended Exterminator's career at the apex of racing, Grey Lag went on to bigger and better things, including a victory in the 1923 Suburban Handicap under 135 pounds. It was after that race that Madden proclaimed him the best he had ever bred— and he had bred more than 180 stakes winners.

In 1924, Grey Lag was retired to the life of a stallion at Sinclair's Rancocas Farm, in New Jersey, where he proved all but infertile. He received some of America's finest mares during three breeding seasons, but sired just 19 foals, among them a useless gelding named Repenter out of Kentucky Derby winner Regret.

By all rights, after his stud career had failed, Grey Lag should have remained an honored pensioner at Rancocas. Hildreth and Sinclair instead returned him to the races at the age of 9—a disgraceful, mercenary gesture considering all he had meant to them in his days of glory. Still, the old warrior remained competitive, winning several races, and at age 10 finishing third in the important Excelsior Handicap.

Grey Lag was again retired in 1928 and given away as a riding horse. Sinclair lost track of him. As the aging champion went from owner to owner at the dawn of the Great Depression, Sinclair was recovering from his own spate of bad fortune. The founder of Sinclair Consolidated Oil Corporation (later Atlantic Richfield), he had earlier been accused of bribing government officials to gain rights to the Teapot Dome U. S. Navy Oil Reserve. Though

At ages four and five, Grey Lag won 9 of 11 starts and never finished worse than second.

acquitted of those charges, he had spent nine months in prison for contempt of court and Congress.

Sinclair was horrified to learn in 1931 that at the age of 13, Grey Lag was in training yet *again,* this time competing in the cheapest of races at obscure Canadian tracks. On July 1, 1931, he had finished 9th of 10 in a $1,000 claiming event at Dorval Park, beaten by 18 humiliating lengths.

Sinclair sent an agent north to acquire Grey Lag and return him home to Rancocas. On the trip back, the future Racing Hall of Fame inductee made a brief stopover in the Rancocas training barn at Empire City Race Course. "The old-timer looked around as he was led under the shed," trainer Frank Taylor later recalled. "He whinnied when he saw the familiar green and white buckets and boxes, and made it evident in every way that he realized his return to the good old times and better days. He was finally put into a box, as happy and contented a horse as the world ever saw."

And he did, indeed, live happily ever after.

GALLANT FOX

GALLANT FOX CAME ALONG AT THE WRONG MOMENT IN TIME for what he was. His pedigree was too royal, his looks too perfect, his owner too wealthy. He had it all, and the American people simply could not relate to him during the panicky early days of the Great Depression.

One month before Black Tuesday, October 29, 1929, launched the stock market's relentless downward spiral, Gallant Fox had shown his heels to a field of good two-year-olds in Aqueduct's Junior Champion Stakes. By the time he became the first Kentucky Derby winner to break from a starting gate and then sweep triumphantly through the 1930 Triple Crown, banks and factories were starting to fail. He earned $308,275 over a six-month period in 1930, while millions of Americans survived on an average per capita income of $750. As his wealthy owner William Woodward Sr. uncorked expensive champagne and hosted fashionable parties at his 28,600-square-foot mansion on New York's East 86th Street, a growing number of homeless and unemployed people stood in soup lines. Gallant Fox may not have been the stuff of which legends were made during this era of heartbreak in America, but he was a good one nonetheless.

He was called the Fox of Belair after Woodward's historic Belair Stud, in Maryland, though he first saw light of day at Claiborne Farm, in Kentucky, on March 23, 1927. A year and a half later, the son of *Sir Gallahad III arrived in the barn of Hall of Fame trainer James Fitzsimmons, where he matured into a well-balanced, 1,200-pound, blaze-faced beauty, standing nearly 17 hands in height and possessed of a singular white-rimmed eye that made him appear wild. When his greatness became evident, some said that he scared his rivals by rolling that wicked eye at them in the heat of battle, though his standard equipment of hood and blinkers made that feat improbable if not impossible.

Gallant Fox proved difficult, even for a gifted horseman such as Fitzsimmons. While Gallant Fox was abundantly talented, his natural herd instincts held sway over the competitive blood coursing through his veins. He loved to gallop alongside rivals and lost interest quickly unless another horse was breathing down his neck. In the mornings, multiple companions were sometimes employed to work in relay with him, just to keep him focused.

Gallant Fox's juvenile season netted but two victories from seven starts, though Fitzsimmons suspected better days ahead when he approached retired jockey Earl Sande with an interesting proposition: Return to the saddle in 1930 to handle Gallant Fox, and receive 10 percent of the colt's seasonal earnings. The future Hall of Fame rider had been financially ruined by the stock market crash, so yes was his response. It was the right one. Over the next few months, Sande deposited more than $30,000 into his personal account, a kingly sum during a time of national deprivation.

Sande and the colt with movie star good looks captured 9 of 10 races that year, including a spectacular romp through the Triple Crown and marathon victories in the Saratoga Cup, Lawrence Realization, and 2-mile Jockey Club Gold Cup. After 70 years of training, Fitz would recall the son of *Sir Gallahad III as the best natural distance horse he had ever been around.

Gallant Fox's single losing effort of 1930 brought him at least as much fame as had his wonderful victories. It came during the dog days of summer in Saratoga's Travers Stakes, when after a wearying speed duel in the mud between Gallant Fox and Whichone, a 100 to 1 long shot named Jim Dandy blew past them both to win easily. Seven decades later, Saratoga continues to commemorate this most stunning of upsets with an annual Travers prep race called the Jim Dandy Stakes.

Gallant Fox retired that autumn as America's top-earning Thoroughbred to that time, with a career bankroll of $328,165. His money record was an irony, however, coming as it did when so many Americans were living at or below subsistence level.

In the stud, he became what author Kent Hollingsworth would refer to as "an extraordinary two-crop sire." His first crop featured 1935 American

Gallant Fox was called the Fox of Belair after owner Woodward's historic Belair Stud, in Maryland.

Triple Crown hero Omaha, making Gallant Fox the only American Triple Crown winner to sire another. From his second crop came 1936 Horse of the Year Granville and European star Flares. Gallant Fox sired 20 stakes winners in all over a 21-year period, but virtually all of his best were clustered in those first two crops.

Gallant Fox died on the afternoon of November 13, 1954, just 2½ hours before the 16th running of the Gallant Fox Handicap was contested at Jamaica Race Course, in New York. At 1⅝ miles, the Gallant Fox remains today America's longest graded stakes race run on the dirt, a fitting tribute to a long ago champion.

MORVICH

IN THE FALL OF 1919, ADOLPH SPRECKELS SPECULATIVELY EYED two of the colts foaled that year at his Napa Stock Farm, in Northern California. Though sons of the same stallion, Runnymede, they were physical opposites—Runstar, a flawless golden beauty and Morvich, a common bay blemished by a pair of crooked forelegs. The heir to the Spreckels sugar fortune was understandably smitten by one, while utterly dismissing the other.

It was Man o' War's juvenile season and as that great one streaked across the racing world like a blazing meteor, it is possible that flame-coated Runstar conjured up similar thrilling images in Spreckels's mind. Not so the stocky brown colt who had been dubbed Morvich, some said for a pathetic literary character in a book his owner had read or, perhaps, simply for a Scottish locale. Whatever the name's source, Spreckels apparently had little use for the flesh and blood colt who embodied it.

While Runstar raced the wind in his early trials at Napa, Morvich appeared whimsically distractible and slow of foot. Spreckels and trainer Bob Carroll had no means of measuring the lion's heart that beat deep within his plain brown chest. Morvich was first entered in a claiming stake in New York, a $3,000 selling tag attached to him. At 50 to 1 odds he woke up with a vengeance. Eyewitness accounts had him winning by 20 lengths, but those crooked legs and homely looks discouraged potential buyers. Future Hall of Fame conditioner Max Hirsch eventually took a chance and removed Morvich from the Spreckels's barn for $5,000 and quickly resold him for a $2,000 profit to trainer Fred Burlew, who, curiously, continued to race Morvich in selling company—with no takers.

Between 1919 and 1920, Man o' War had generated many new friends for racing, among them, Wall Street broker Benjamin Block, who, in the summer of 1921, made a decisive move from fan to participant. In doing so, he purchased from Burlew a half-interest in Morvich, and soon after bought the

remaining interest to race the crooked-legged colt in his own orange- and jade-blocked silks.

Morvich looked nothing whatsoever like Man o' War but shared something far more profound with that superstar, as America would soon learn. Though laid back and sweet natured around the barn, Morvich transformed into a fiery competitor on the racetrack. This free-running spirit raced in front from start to finish with weights of up to 130 pounds, winning for Block a series of prestigious two-year-old races, including the Hopeful and United States Hotel Stakes, Saratoga Special, Eastern Shore Handicap, and Pimlico Futurity. He won each of his 11 races in 1921 and earned $115,234.

The Kentucky Derby was to be his 1922 debut, and he trained for the 1¼-mile race with a controversial series of short, fast drills. Critics had a field day. Not only was Morvich bred to be a sprinter, they said, but he was being trained as one. No way would he have the stamina required to travel the classic Derby distance.

On May 13, 1922, Morvich defied those critics to etch his name in the history books alongside that of Regret as one of only two runners to race undefeated through the Kentucky Derby. (Majestic Prince and Seattle Slew would join them in 1969 and 1977, respectively.) Morvich led from the drop of the starter's flag and easily turned back all challengers to score his 12th victory in as many starts. The instant he flashed across the finish line at Churchill Downs that afternoon, Morvich became an American icon. "Today…courage was the quality which won the Derby," Kentucky Governor Edwin P. Morrow enthused afterward in the flowery celebratory language of the time. "Over a grueling distance, setting his own pace, out in front from start to finish, there like a beacon of light a gallant steed shone bright and true. He tried in bone, muscle, and sinew, and tried above all else in heart and spirit. He never faltered, never failed, and would not be denied."

Morvich's heroic status unfortunately faded fast. After the Derby, he seemed to lose his zest for battle, and in four subsequent starts ran with no evidence of the heart and spirit that Governor Morrow had so lauded. Those inexplicable losses stripped away from Morvich the mantle of immortality just as it was descending upon his bay shoulders, and undoubtedly denied him future admission into the Racing Hall of Fame.

The former champion was retired to stud in Kentucky, where breeders distrusted his regional origins and sent few quality mares his way. The cold Blue Grass winters eventually wore him down, and at the age of 20 he was vanned without fanfare back to his birth state of California.

The old stallion thrived in the mild climate of the West, and another seven seasons passed before death claimed him. Morvich ultimately sired 12 stakes winners, including several fine sprinters, but for the most part was regarded as a failure. He was an anomaly, a freakish four-legged marvel who briefly revealed himself with wondrous perfection on racing's stage, but who could not in any way be genetically duplicated.

And what of Spreckels's beloved Runstar? His career amounted to naught until 1924, when he defeated an ancient Exterminator in Tijuana's $50,000 Coffroth Handicap. Spreckels went to his grave soon after, believing in his heart, however stubbornly and irrationally, that Runstar was the superior of Morvich. Runstar began a subsequent decline into mediocrity and beyond, and in 1926 could be found competing for $800 Mexican claiming purses. Mercifully, Spreckels was not around to witness the humbling of his would-be champion.

Morvich went 12 for 12 through the 1922 Kentucky Derby but never won again.

. . . He never faltered, never failed, and would not be denied.

—Kentucky Governor Edwin P. Morrow

TOP RUNNERS

horse and birth year	starts	wins	seconds	thirds	earnings
ANITA PEABODY (filly) 1925	8	7	0	1	$113,105
BATEAU (filly) 1925	35	11	5	9	$120,760
BLACK GOLD (horse) 1921	35	18	5	4	$111,553
BLACK MARIA (filly) 1923	52	18	14	6	$110,350
BLUE LARKSPUR (horse) 1926	16	10	3	1	$272,070
CHANCE PLAY (horse) 1923	39	16	9	2	$137,946
CRUSADER (horse) 1923	42	18	8	4	$203,261
DICE (horse) 1925	5	5	0	0	$42,625
EQUIPOISE (horse) 1928	51	29	10	4	$338,610
EXTERMINATOR (gelding) 1915	100	50	17	17	$252,996
GALLANT FOX (horse) 1927	17	11	3	2	$328,165
GREY LAG (horse) 1918	47	25	9	6	$136,715
JAMESTOWN (horse) 1928	19	12	3	2	$189,685
JOLLY ROGER (gelding) 1922	49	18	9	9	$143,240
MAD HATTER (horse) 1916	98	32	22	15	$194,525
MORVICH (horse) 1919	16	12	2	1	$172,909
NELLIE MORSE (filly) 1921	34	7	9	3	$73,565
NIMBA (filly) 1924	13	7	1	1	$74,045
PRINCESS DOREEN (filly) 1921	94	34	15	17	$174,745
REIGH COUNT (horse) 1925	26	12	4	0	$180,795
ROSE OF SHARON (filly) 1926	14	10	2	1	$64,069
SARAZEN (gelding) 1921	55	27	2	6	$225,000
SUN BEAU (horse) 1925	74	33	12	10	$376,744
VANDER POOL (horse) 1928	32	19	3	6	$52,095
WHICHONE (horse) 1927	14	10	2	1	$192,705
WISE COUNSELLOR (horse) 1921	27	11	3	4	$115,570
ZEV (horse) 1920	43	23	8	5	$313,639

important races won	special notes
Futurity S.	Champion
CCA Oaks, Suburban H., Whitney S., Selima S., Gazelle S., etc.	Champion at three and four
Kentucky Derby, Louisiana Derby, Chicago Derby, Ohio Derby, etc.	Racing Hall of Fame
Metropolitan H., Whitney S., Ladies H. (twice), Kentucky Oaks, etc.	Champion at three, four, and five
Belmont S., Withers S., Classic S., etc.	Racing Hall of Fame, Horse of the Year
Jockey Club Gold Cup, Saratoga Cup, etc.	Horse of the Year in 1927
Belmont S., Suburban H. (twice), Jockey Club Gold Cup, etc.	Racing Hall of Fame, 1926 Horse of the Year
Great American S.	Undefeated champion at two
Pimlico Futurity	Racing Hall of Fame, two-time Horse of the Year
Saratoga Cup, etc.	Racing Hall of Fame
Kentucky Derby, Preakness S., Belmont S.	Racing Hall of Fame, Horse of the Year in 1930, Triple Crown winner, leading money winner
Belmont S., Suburban H., Metropolitan H., etc.	Racing Hall of Fame; Horse of the Year in 1921; champion at three, four, and five
Futurity S., etc.	Cochampion at two
Grand National Steeplechase (U.S.)	Racing Hall of Fame steeplechaser, two-time winner of American Grand National, legendary weight carrier
Jockey Club Gold Cup, Metropolitan H., etc.	Champion
Kentucky Derby, etc.	Undefeated (11 for 11) champion at two
Preakness S., etc.	Champion
Metropolitan H., Alabama S., CCA Oaks, Lawrence Realization, etc.	Champion
Bowie H., Independence H. (twice), etc.	Racing Hall of Fame; champion at three, four, and five
Kentucky Derby, Coronation Cup (England), etc.	Racing Hall of Fame, 1928 Horse of the Year
Kentucky Oaks, Ashland Oaks, Latonia Oaks, etc.	Champion
Metropolitan H., Champagne S., etc.	Racing Hall of Fame, Horse of the Year 1924–25
Hawthorne Gold Cup (twice), etc.	Racing Hall of Fame, three-time champion handicap horse, leading money earner
Youthful S., etc.	Unbeaten through first 15 races at two and three
Futurity S., Champagne S., Saratoga Special, Whitney S., Withers, etc.	Champion
International Special, etc.	Champion
Belmont S., Kentucky Derby, International Match Race, etc.	Racing Hall of Fame, 1923 Horse of the Year

Hard Times, Good Times

The infamous 1933 Kentucky Derby finish
between winner Broker's Tip (right),
ridden by Don Meade, and Head Play (left),
ridden by Herb Fisher.

THE PERIOD FROM 1931 THROUGH 1940 WAS PERHAPS THE most difficult and perilous in the country's history. America was battered by national calamity and international tragedy, falling into economic depression after the stock market collapse in 1929 and inexorably marching toward war as Nazism snuffed out freedom in western Europe and a threat from Japan became more ominous. It was a time of economic devastation and despair. In 1931 alone, 20,000 American suicides were reported and unemployment hit 25 percent; robbing banks became a dark American pastime; a drought of biblical proportions turned America's heartland to dust; while Nazism, Fascism, and totalitarianism found their way onto the world's stage.

In contrast to the high-flying 1920s, a blanket of sadness shrouded much of the 1930s, and horse racing was not exempt from its suffocating embrace. The sport had previously survived an antiwagering movement, but the pervasive economic disaster of the early to middle part of this era was something else entirely. Formerly successful businessmen who might have once spent money on racehorses now sold apples on street corners. The average price paid for a yearling at public auction in the United States plummeted to a $570 average in 1932, with the best averaging just $903 at Saratoga, down 75 percent from the precrash sale of 1929. Gross purse distribution declined 40 percent from its all-time high as even the Kentucky Derby was slashed in value. Stud fees were also cut: *Sir Gallahad III dropped from $3,000 to $1,500.

Adding to the era's grim mood was a continuous assault on racing by William Randolph Hearst's newspapers, which viewed racetracks as morally reprehensible gathering points for "thieves, gamblers, louts, dope gangsters, and violators of women." While horse racing has always attracted a wicked element along with the good, it was hardly the den of iniquity portrayed by Hearst, himself no paragon of virtue. Still, such publicity spoon-fed to the masses on a daily basis could only hurt the sport of kings.

HOPE IS REBORN

At his 1933 inauguration, President Franklin Delano Roosevelt assured panicked Americans that the only thing they had to fear was fear itself. He then launched his controversial New Deal—a broad legislative program that cost the federal government billions of dollars but created employment, provided retirement benefits, established a minimum wage, insured bank deposits, halted home foreclosures, and supported crop prices. Hope was reborn, and a decimated economy slowly recovered. At the end of the decade, revived defense spending in response to threats to world peace ended the economic depression of the thirties.

The Thoroughbred industry became healthy as well. Purses soared by decade's end to unprecedented heights, and yearling sales gained strength, though it would be many years before the extravagant spending of the 1920s would be seen again. Racing's leaders included Joseph E. Widener and William Woodward Sr.—wealthy, influential men who loved the sport and were willing and able to fight its battles.

SIGNS OF THE TIMES

1931 20,000 suicides are reported

1933 25 percent unemployment in United States

1939 Passengers pay $375 for first transatlantic flight from New York to Marseilles

In decade Average doctor's salary is $3,382

A dental filling costs $1

Bread sells for 5¢ per loaf, potatoes sell for 2¢ a pound

Gasoline costs 18¢ per gallon

New Studebaker is advertised for $840

The human desire to gamble cannot be stamped out by legislation. . . . Let us regulate that which we know exists and will continue to do so.

—ASSEMBLYMAN TOM MALONEY ON 1933 BILL
TO LEGALIZE PARI-MUTUEL WAGERING IN CALIFORNIA

*Ethel Mars was a leading buyer of yearlings for her successful
Milky Way Stable during the 1930s.*

Vice chairman of the New York Jockey Club Joseph E. Widener fought to bring New York horse racing back to its former glory.

Open racetrack gambling will lure the unsuspecting and bring in its wake train embezzlement, defalcation, imprisonment, wrecked homes, and demoralized communities.

—ASSEMBLYWOMAN ELEANOR MILLER,
ARGUING AGAINST CALIFORNIA'S PARI-MUTUEL BILL

HORSE SIGNS OF THE TIMES

1931 A record 5,266 foals are registered

1932 Saratoga yearlings average $903, down 75 percent from 1929

1933 Purse distribution plunges to $8.5 million from $13.1 million in 1931

Mary Hirsch is denied trainer's license by Jockey Club

1934 *Sir Gallahad III's stud fee drops to $1,500 from $3,000 in 1932

Kentucky Derby purse reduced to $30,000 from $50,000

1935 Mary Hirsch becomes first licensed female trainer

1939 Foal crop tops 6,000 for first time, reaching 6,316

1940 Gross purse distribution reaches a record $16 million

Widener, vice chairman of the New York Jockey Club, crusaded tirelessly to return the sport in the Empire State to its former glory. He argued that 1908 wagering restrictions had crippled the industry, that it was dying a slow, agonizing death, and that only pro–pari-mutuel laws could save it. Widener took this argument to anyone in power who would listen, from then New York Governor Roosevelt on down the political ladder. It was a battle he ultimately won, to the benefit of all. In 1940, mechanical wagering generated $13 million in revenue for the state of New York.

Jockey Club Chairman Woodward campaigned 1935 Triple Crown winner Omaha, but more importantly, that year he fired some of the angriest, most articulate words in opposition to England's discriminatory Jersey Act. He argued that the British should immediately accept the *American Stud Book* in its entirety or face the consequences. "If we do not get together, we will grow apart," Woodward warned. "I want *one* great breed of Thoroughbred the world over, mutually recognized. If this does not result, we will have two breeds, and they will gradually be as far apart as the sun and the moon."

EXPANSION

Despite its wobbly economic situation, racing showcased remarkable innovation and growth in the 1930s. Increasingly sophisticated starting gates were developed, photo-finish cameras were installed at the finish lines, and saliva testing for drugs gained widespread use. By 1936, 22 state racing commissions had been appointed to oversee the sport; the first national poll was conducted to designate divisional champions; and modern grass courses became the rage as did electronic totalizators—machines that publicly posted the odds on horses in each race. Also, the Grayson Foundation was established to provide philanthropic support for equine research, including research in the area of racetrack breakdowns; Keeneland Race Course, Del Mar Thoroughbred Club, and Santa Anita, Hollywood, and Gulfstream Parks opened for business; a $100,000 handicap was inaugurated; and pari-mutuels were legalized in numerous states, including Florida, New York, California, and, for a time, Texas.

Trainer James Fitzsimmons (left) and owner William Woodward (right) paired up to win the 1930 and 1935 American Triple Crowns.

LEADING TRAINERS

James Fitzsimmons
Racing Hall of Fame. Leading money trainer in 1932, 1936, and 1939. Trained 1935 Triple Crown winner Omaha; 1939 Kentucky Derby winner Johnstown; and 1936 Horse of the Year Granville. See also 1920s, 1940s, 1950s, 1960s.

Thomas J. Healey
Racing Hall of Fame. In this era, he trained champions Top Flight and Equipoise. See also 1920s.

Max Hirsch
Racing Hall of Fame. Won 1936 Kentucky Derby with Bold Venture. See also 1920s, 1940s.

Robert A. Smith
Racing Hall of Fame. Leading money trainer in 1933 and 1934. Trained 1934 Kentucky Derby winner Cavalcade and Preakness winner High Quest.

Tom Smith
Racing Hall of Fame. Leading money trainer in 1940. Trained 1938 Horse of the Year Seabiscuit and champion *Kayak II. See also 1940s.

I suspect my being a member of the Jockey Club is due to my ownership of Man o' War. That august body could hardly be expected to elect a horse a member, so they made me one instead.

—SAMUEL RIDDLE

Industry leader Hal Price Headley (right) with leading jockey Charles Kurtsinger (left).

The sport was expanding so rapidly during these years that some industry insiders believed it might soon reach a dangerous saturation point. In other words, could there be too much of a good thing? The Jockey Club chairman seemed to think so. "I sincerely hope we have come to the fullness in amount of racing and that no more states join the procession, for we cannot stand it," Woodward worried aloud. Such concerns turned out to be unfounded, at least at that point in time. Horse racing seemed to thrive on expansion. As the Great Depression faded into history, Americans again began to look for fun and once more found it at the racetrack. Breeders happily responded by producing foals in record numbers—more than 6,000 in 1939—and the cycle of growth continued.

Although the 1930s featured many standout racehorses, including 17 future Racing Hall of Fame members and 2 Triple Crown winners, 3 in particular captured the hearts of America—C. V. Whitney's Equipoise, Australasian wonder *Phar Lap, and claimer-turned-champion Seabiscuit.

Equipoise came first, campaigning at the height of the Great Depression from 1930 to 1935. Although bred in the purple and owned by one of America's wealthiest blue bloods, there was nothing pretentious about this son of Pennant. He was universally embraced as the "people's horse," and affectionately nicknamed the Chocolate Soldier for his dark chestnut coat and gallant heart.

Champion at two, three-time handicap champion, Horse of the Year in 1932–1933, and a world record miler, Equipoise was at times compared favorably to Man o' War. Because fans adored him, Whitney raced his "soldier" beyond his best years, until he bowed a tendon at age seven in the inaugural Santa Anita Handicap. With total earnings of $338,610, Equipoise ranked second only to Sun Beau, whose career had preceded the worst of the Depression. In better economic times, Equipoise would certainly have been first to cross the $400,000 earnings threshold, but that was left to a later hero.

The only American-bred of the era to rival Equipoise in popularity was Seabiscuit, an undersized Wheatley Stable reject after an uninspiring 5 for 35 juvenile season in 1935. Sold privately to California car salesman C. S. Howard and in the care of trainer "Silent" Tom Smith, Seabiscuit developed into a

LEADING JOCKEYS

John Adams
Racing Hall of Fame. Leading rider by winners in 1937. Won 1939 Santa Anita Handicap with *Kayak II. Rode a career 3,270 winners.

Eddie Arcaro
Racing Hall of Fame. Rode first of 4,779 career winners in 1932. Won 1938 Kentucky Derby on Lawrin. Leading money rider of 1940, which was the first of many national titles.

Charles Kurtsinger
Racing Hall of Fame. Guided War Admiral to victory in the 1937 Triple Crown. Also won the 1931 Kentucky Derby and Belmont Stakes with champion Twenty Grand.

John Longden
Racing Hall of Fame. In 1938, rode to first of five national riding titles. Eventually, he became the first to ride 6,000 career winners.

Alfred Robertson
Racing Hall of Fame. Among leading riders of this era, he rode 1,856 career winners. Rode champions Top Flight and Whirlaway.

megastar, reigning as 1938 Horse of the Year and twice earning America's handicap championship. Of his 89 starts, 2 became a part of racing lore—the two-horse 1938 Pimlico Special and the 1940 Santa Anita Handicap. In the former, Seabiscuit conquered Triple Crown winner War Admiral in record time, an event that represented a high-water mark in American match racing. Rarely in the twentieth century would there be a match so important and so wholly satisfactory without a dark cloud hanging over it. In the Big 'Cap, Seabiscuit returned from injury and stud duty to win in his third attempt, crowning a fairy-tale career and retiring as the world's first $400,000 earner.

Arguably, the best racing story of the decade was a brief one, and it was a heartbreaker. *Phar Lap illuminated the Depression's darkest hour when he arrived in America for the 1932 Agua Caliente Handicap. The huge New Zealander had been a hero at home, where he had won major races under unbelievable imposts. When handicappers in his home region seemed willing to kill him with weight—he carried as much as 150 pounds—*Phar Lap was exiled north to friendlier environs.

. . . 'damn the brass,' it was the horse we wanted to see. I feel certain the American public would have paid a million dollars, hard times and all, to have saved the red gelding's life.

—*TURF WRITER NEIL NEWMAN ON *PHAR LAP*

The popular Seabiscuit began his career as a claimer but ended it
as the world's leading money winner.

I want one great breed of Thoroughbred the world over, mutually recognized. If this does not result, we will have two breeds, and they will gradually be as far apart as the sun and the moon.

—WILLIAM WOODWARD, ARGUING AGAINST ENGLAND'S JERSEY ACT IN 1935

AGUA CALIENTE
HANDICAP WINNER
MARCH 20, 1932

The Australasian wonder horse *Phar Lap won the 1932 Agua Caliente Handicap,
then died mysteriously 17 days later.

He arrived in the U.S. amid snapping flashbulbs and swarming reporters, a homely gelding with a Cinderella pedigree and unorthodox training regimen. Paul Bunyanesque stories soon abounded: *Phar Lap possessed a 35-foot stride and mile-a-minute speed, and he had shattered Australasian records while galloping through knee-high grass. This was nonsense, of course, but the hysteria made for good press, and Americans fell in love. Their new champion rewarded them by dismissing a good field and setting a track record in the process.

The best lay ahead, or so it was thought, with a tentative schedule that might have put *Phar Lap up against Equipoise and Twenty Grand. Instead, he died—just 17 days after his victory, far from the racetrack crowds, on a quiet northern California farm where he had been sent to rest. While official reports attributed his death to accidental poisoning from grazing on treated pasture, trainer Tommy Woodcock believed otherwise. "His life was ever in danger from the moment he landed in America, and his interrupted preparation (due to a cracked hoof) was the only reason he was allowed to live and run in that race," Woodcock later said. "Gangsters with a knowledge of racing thought it impossible for a horse to win the Mexican classic without a solid preparation. They laid heavily against him. . . . I knew in my heart that 'Bobby' was poisoned. But gangsters are not placed behind bars on evidence as flimsy as what I had, so I kept my suspicions to myself. To have voiced them would have resulted in my following in the footsteps of the horse I loved."

Other bittersweet moments defined the era. Chase Me, a former field hunter and child's pony, won his first seven starts before being fatally injured in the 1934 Metropolitan Handicap. Dark Secret, widely regarded as America's best long-distance runner since Exterminator, suffered a fatal leg injury 200 yards from the finish of the 1934 Jockey Club Gold Cup but battled on courageously to win by a nod. The biggest loss of the decade came on August 4, 1938, when 10-year-old Equipoise died of a massive infection at the C. V. Whitney Farm. Four years later he would reign posthumously as America's premier sire.

NECROLOGY

1931 Broomstick, 30. Three-time leading sire

"Father" Bill Daly, 92. Famous trainer of jockeys

*McGee, 31. Leading sire of 1922, sire of Exterminator

James Rowe Jr. Leading trainer of 1929, son of Racing Hall of Fame trainer James Rowe Sr.

Sweep, 24. Leading sire of 1918 and 1925

1932 Colin, 27. Racing Hall of Fame, undefeated champion

*Phar Lap, 6. Australasian champion, winner of Agua Caliente H.

1933 Peter Pan, 29. Racing Hall of Fame champion, among the leading sires

Tod Sloan, 59. Racing Hall of Fame jockey

1934 Regret, 22. Racing Hall of Fame, first filly to win Kentucky Derby

1936 Laverne Fator, 36. Racing Hall of Fame jockey

Andrew "Mack" Garner, 36. Racing Hall of Fame jockey

*Teddy, 23. Among the leading sires, sire of *Sir Gallahad III and *Bull Dog

1937 High Time, 21. Leading sire of 1928, sire of Sarazen and others

NECROLOGY

1937 Ogden Mills, 53. Co-owner of Wheatley Stable

Sir Barton, 21. Racing Hall of Fame champion, first American Triple Crown winner

H. J. "Dick" Thompson, 56. Racing Hall of Fame trainer, trained all four of Col. E. R. Bradley's Kentucky Derby winners

Nash Turner, 56. Racing Hall of Fame jockey

1938 Black Toney, 27. Sire of two Kentucky Derby winners

Bubbling Over, 15. Kentucky Derby winner, sire of Kentucky Derby winner Burgoo King

Equipoise, 10. Racing Hall of Fame, leading sire of 1942

Walter Vosburgh, 83. Turf authority, legendary racing secretary and handicapper

1939 *Chicle, 26. Leading sire of 1929

John Sanford, 88. Vice chairman of Jockey Club from 1913 to 1921

1940 Crusader, 17. Racing Hall of Fame

Willis Sharpe Kilmer, 71. Noted owner-breeder, owned Exterminator

Sarazen, 19. Racing Hall of Fame

FEMALE LEADERS

The 1930s launched a feminine revolution of sorts, both human and equine. Notable among the latter was C. V. Whitney's ornately marked Top Flight, whose victory over males in the 1931 Futurity made her the first $200,000 juvenile earner and richest American female of the time. That same year, Mrs. Payne Whitney joined the short list of female Kentucky Derby–winning owners when her Twenty Grand captured the roses for Greentree Stable. Isabel Dodge Sloane of Brookmeade Stable in 1934 became America's first female leading owner, while Ethel Mars annually was a leading yearling buyer for her Milky Way Stable. In 1935, Mary Hirsch, 22-year-old daughter of Max Hirsch, became the first woman awarded a trainer's license by the Jockey Club after previously having been denied one to avoid setting a precedent.

BUILDING BLOCKS

The 1930s continued the trend of quality bloodstock importations, and A. B. Hancock Sr. remained the man behind the movement. In 1936, Hancock organized a $250,000 syndicate to purchase promising young sire *Blenheim II; four years later, Whitney acquired that stallion's classic-winning son, *Mahmoud. Both became influential sires.

By 1938, the industry had a new marquee name—Metro-Goldwyn-Mayer chief Louis B. Mayer. His attempt to buy Man o' War was snubbed, as was his million-dollar wartime offer for England's Hyperion. In 1939, he settled for *Alibhai, a Hyperion yearling colt of astonishing speed who later bowed in both forelegs without having started. Mayer subsequently paid $100,000 for *Beau Pere, an Australian-based stallion little known in America. *Alibhai and *Beau Pere would rank among the leading progenitors of the 1940s. As Mayer built his empire, the United States enjoyed a rare interlude of economic revival and peace. But it would not last. A tumultuous international situation was heating up to where American neutrality was no longer possible. War lay on the horizon.

In 1934, Isabel Dodge Sloane, the mistress of Brookmeade Stable (shown here with Henry Carnegie Phipps), became the first woman to top the American owners list.

If wealthy, idle, and tired businessmen will take up the breeding of Thoroughbreds as a pastime, they will at least enjoy life, even though they die poor.

—JOHN MADDEN

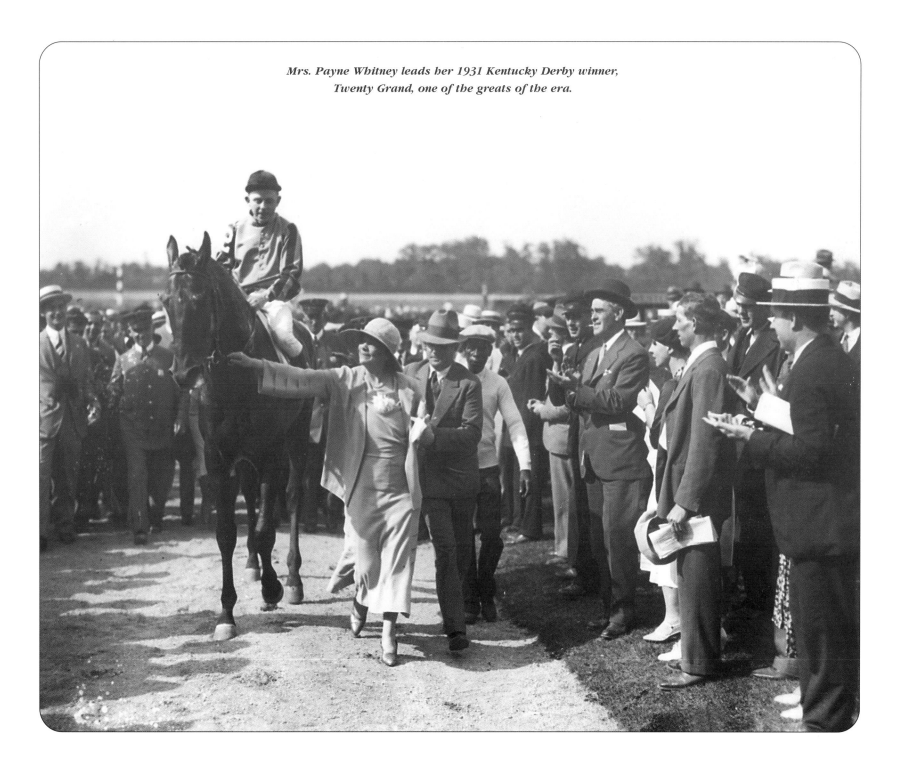

*Mrs. Payne Whitney leads her 1931 Kentucky Derby winner,
Twenty Grand, one of the greats of the era.*

EQUIPOISE

LIFE IS NOT ALWAYS FAIR OR DEATH TIMELY. HARRY PAYNE WHITNEY might have contemplated such bitter facts as he lay on his deathbed in the waning hours of October 26, 1930. He was aware that in his stable at Aqueduct racetrack was a two-year-old of rare quality, possibly the best he had ever bred. He also knew he would not live to see this colt realize whatever his potential might be. The 58-year-old sportsman passed away that evening, leaving his son Cornelius to carry on the family's distinguished racing tradition, launched in the 1890s by H. P.'s father, W. C. Whitney.

H. P. had hoped to run the fleet son of Pennant in the Pimlico Futurity on November 5, 1930, and so it came to be that 10 days after the famous breeder's passing, Equipoise became the first Thoroughbred to race in the name of Cornelius Vanderbilt Whitney. On that gloomy afternoon in Maryland, Equipoise stormed through mud so deep and sticky it literally ripped the front shoes right off of his hooves. He thundered past future Hall of Fame champion Twenty Grand, and galloped to the very edge of greatness in what newspapers hailed as the race of the decade.

Equipoise was a Depression Era racehorse, as was Gallant Fox, with a wealthy owner and elite pedigree. So why was William Woodward's 1930 Triple Crown winner so tepidly received by the masses, while Whitney's champion came to be universally admired, indeed loved? It had to do with what people could sense rather than what they could see. While Gallant Fox had amazing ability but questionable courage, Equipoise possessed a single-minded determination to win at any cost. And whereas the former often eased up once the lead was attained, the latter would ram his way around, through, and over rivals so aggressively that he was disqualified from victory three times for interference.

This average-sized colt with an anything but average heart was a handsome dark chestnut of unusual brownish tone, which when viewed in tandem with his combative racing attitude earned him the nickname Chocolate

Soldier. The fire that burned within Equipoise was an invisible essence, but one that endeared him to a public in search of inspiration. C. V. Whitney remarked years later in a vastly different world of advanced technology that Equipoise had possessed "that ineffable something which no computer will ever be able to discern: competitive spirit."

Courage, class, and ability Equipoise had aplenty, along with one rather serious physical flaw—thin-walled hooves that rendered him periodically lame. In 1930, he had won 8 of 16 starts and the juvenile championship, but a cracked foot kept him out of Twenty Grand's Kentucky Derby of 1931 and limited his sophomore campaign to just three races.

Equipoise blossomed as an older runner and for several years accomplished things that modern day racehorses are rarely asked or expected to do. He carried 128 pounds to a world record 1:34 ⅖ mile that would stand for nearly two decades and hauled up to 135 pounds to victory over America's classic distance of 1¼ miles. On chronically sore feet, Equipoise managed to win 29 of 51 starts, including 24 important stakes, and he finished in the top three on 43 occasions.

In 1935, racing in California was coming back after 25 years of darkness following 1909 antiwagering legislation. The magnificent new Santa Anita Park, in Arcadia, hoped to start things off with a bang by offering a $100,000 purse for its inaugural Santa Anita Handicap. At age seven, Equipoise was unsound and past his prime, but the enticing possibility of an earnings record kept him in training when he should have been retired. He worked erratically that winter with the hundred-grander as his goal, and on race day itself he shouldered high weight of 130 pounds against the best older runners in the country. But even the most generous of hearts could not compensate for failing bone and sinew. A seventh-place finish on a bowed tendon marked the end of the racing trail for America's beloved Chocolate Soldier.

Chocolate Soldier— the people's horse.

C. V. Whitney's champion Equipoise was beloved by Depression Era racing fans.

Equipoise retired with a bankroll of $338,610, just $36,134 short of Sun Beau's record. Upon arrival that spring at the Whitney Farm, in Kentucky, he was greeted by five hundred appreciative horsemen and fans who were assembled for the occasion by the Lexington Board of Commerce. For the next three years, Equipoise became the second most popular equine attraction in America, behind only Man o' War.

On August 3, 1938, noted veterinarian Dr. Charles Hagyard was unexpectedly called to Equipoise's stall. The normally robust eater had a slightly elevated temperature and was ignoring his feed. Though there at first seemed little cause for concern, his condition deteriorated rapidly in the coming hours; on the evening of August 4, Equipoise died from a raging internal infection.

He was 10 years old. The loss of this promising young stallion was heartbreaking, even more so when the quality of his first foals to race became apparent.

In 1942, Equipoise would reign posthumously as America's most successful sire. He left behind just 74 foals, 20 of stakes class, including champion Level Best and Kentucky Derby winner Shut Out. His sons ultimately accomplished little; Shut Out sired some good fillies, and Swing and Sway became the paternal grandsire of Racing Hall of Fame champion Carry Back. Daughters of Equipoise accounted for a fair number of stakes winners, among them 1946 Triple Crown winner Assault. Though a leading sire, it was Equipoise's remarkable racing achievements of the 1930s that placed the Chocolate Soldier forever among the immortals of the turf.

*Phar Lap

AMERICAN RACING ASSOCIATIONS DURING THE GREAT DEPRESSION were forced to slash purses or face financial ruin—even the Kentucky Derby felt the cold blade of the knife. A surreal oasis in this landscape of economic horror could be found at Agua Caliente racetrack, in Tijuana, Mexico, where a stupendous prize of $50,000 was somehow scraped together for its 1932 Gold Cup. Caliente management realized that in addition to big money, a special equine attraction was needed, and it ultimately found what it was looking for an ocean away, in a most unlikely place.

Australia and New Zealand of the early 1930s may as well have been Jupiter and Saturn as far as American racing was concerned. Top Thoroughbreds simply did not emerge from that mysterious corner of the globe. Or did they? A rangy red gelding nicknamed Bobby soon put that thesis to the test.

*Phar Lap (Sengalese for *lightning*) embodied just the Cinderella story Americans most appreciated. He was neither handsome nor well bred, but he transcended his lowly origins to win 37 races over vast distances in record-shattering times under backbreaking imposts. Australasia's fascination with *Phar Lap had in 1930 crossed over to a dark-tinged hysteria. Along with adulation came threats upon his life, ostensibly from criminal gambling elements, culminating in a botched sniper assault on the morning of his Melbourne Cup victory.

By 1931, *Phar Lap had run out of homeland competition, handicappers there appeared eager to break him down with imposts of 150 pounds and more, and his life seemed ever in jeopardy. Owner D. J. Davis was considering his options when Caliente representatives appeared with an offer of big money, physical safety, and a comparatively feathery Gold Cup handicap of 129 pounds. It was too good to refuse.

Once *Phar Lap arrived in Mexico, trainer Tommy Woodcock sent him to the track each day for short, leisurely gallops with scarcely any emphasis on speed—a highly unorthodox conditioning regimen by American stan-

dards. These workouts, combined with rumors of unsoundness, high weight, and the fact that he was acclimating to a new hemisphere, should have discouraged the betting public—but they did not.

*Phar Lap went off the 3 to 2 favorite over a Gold Cup field that included 1929 Preakness winner Dr. Freeland and 1930 American Derby victor Reveille Boy. Woodcock instructed jockey William Elliott to simply "canter down the front side and when you get to the back side, gallop on home." And so he did. Slow to start, *Phar Lap accelerated with each passing furlong, then explosively blew past his remaining rivals in the fastest 1¼ miles ever recorded at Caliente. The hefty purse brought his earnings to $332,250, placing him second in the world only to Sun Beau.

Track managers across America suddenly viewed Bobby as potentially the greatest equine drawing card since Man o' War, and images of match races with Twenty Grand and Equipoise danced like promotional sugarplums in their collective mind. While the big gelding's future was being mapped out, he was sent to a farm near Menlo Park, California, where two weeks later, the best laid plans went tragically awry.

On the morning of April 4, 1932, the Gold Cup winner awakened with abdominal distress. April 5th brought a stunning announcement: *Phar Lap was dead. Symptoms seemed to indicate colic until an autopsy revealed arsenic in his system. Some postulated that he had accidentally ingested chemicals from a nearby pasture that had been sprayed. Others—including Woodcock—believed something more sinister was at play, with the trainer later suggesting that *Phar Lap had been murdered by American gangsters. Foul play was never proven.

*Phar Lap did not have the dignity of a proper burial. His heart was excised and shipped to the Australian Institute of Anatomy, where it was revealed to be of extraordinary size and weight. His skin went to a taxidermist, who draped it over a frame to create a life-sized replica of the

Phar Lap embodied just the Cinderella story Americans most appreciated.

champion. The pathetic remains of Bobby went on tour that summer, a freak show some called it, including a Futurity Day appearance at Belmont Park, before heading back to Australia and Melbourne's National Museum.

*Phar Lap's true measure was not taken on these shores. He never met the best that American racing had to offer, though few who saw him at Caliente that day could doubt that he would have been up to the task. The cold statistics of this sport do not relate his story well—*Phar Lap was so much more than weight carried, times recorded, money earned. He was an inspiration to millions in a time of need, and the world truly mourned his loss. "The son of Night Raider bade fair to draw more money through the racing turnstiles from the Pacific to the Atlantic than any horse had ever drawn," writer Neil Newman lamented. "But 'damn the brass,' it was the horse we wanted to see! I feel certain the American public would have paid a million dollars, hard times and all, to have saved the red gelding's life."

TOP FLIGHT

ACCORDING TO NINETEENTH CENTURY TRAINER J. B. PRYOR, "When a filly can beat colts, depend on it—she's a good one." Such a filly was C. V. Whitney's Top Flight. She was not big or powerful. In repose, she exuded no aura of confidence. Her slower gaits were unimpressive, almost clumsy, and when the mood struck, she could be a stubborn handful. Her most distinctive physical feature was a broadly blazed face that looked like the work of a manic artist. Yet she exemplified the favorite axiom of James Fitzsimmons, the legendary horseman who believed that it was what you *couldn't* see that mattered most.

Like Equipoise, Top Flight was a deathbed gift to C.V. Whitney from his father Harry Payne. Though the elder Whitney had recognized the innate talent of the former, he could never have guessed what fate had in store for this garishly marked but well-named filly.

Top Flight was not bred like the usual Whitney horse, though she combined the family's revered lines of Peter Pan, Broomstick, and Hamburg. Her sire, *Dis Donc, was a huge, mean, unsound stallion who had lost his only start. He was by a leading French sire and was half-brother to an even meaner but more talented runner named *Chicle, himself a future leading sire. Only a royal pedigree kept this scary giant of a stallion in the Whitney stud, where he was lightly used before being exiled on lease to Canada in 1930.

Among the mares sent his way in 1928 was a high-strung head-case named Flyatit, a daughter of Peter Pan from a great female family. Why two such difficult horses were brought together remains a mystery, but the result of this mating arrived at the Whitney farm on April 15, 1929—fortunately without most of the temperamental baggage of her progenitors. Whitney trainer Tom Healey was underwhelmed upon first viewing Top Flight, but he soon learned the wisdom of not judging a book by its cover. "She possesses speed in abundance," he enthused to a reporter in 1931, "and no fault can be found with her action when she falls into full

stride. . . . She's not big, but she's a classy little trick." Certainly he liked her well enough to debut her in Aqueduct's Clover Stakes, which she won in near-record time. Top Flight undoubtedly grew in stature and beauty as she reeled off successive victories in Arlington's Lassie, the Saratoga Special (against colts), and the Spinaway and Matron Stakes.

The Futurity Stakes, worth $94,780 to the winner, was the most lucrative race run in the United States that season. Top Flight won it under 127 pounds over male rivals, including Burgoo King and Faireno who together would sweep the American Triple Crown of 1932. Top colts were again her victims in the Pimlico Futurity, after which she retired to winter quarters unbeaten in seven starts. Her impressive $219,000 bank account not only eclipsed Domino's 38-year-old juvenile record, but also sent her soaring past England's Sceptre as the leading distaff money winner of the world.

Top Flight's three-year-old season was anticlimactic. Though again a champion, she was no longer unbeatable. She dominated other fillies in the Acorn and Alabama Stakes, Arlington and Coaching Club American Oaks, and Ladies Handicap, losing to her sex only in the Delaware Handicap. Against males she tried and failed three times.

Soundness issues sent the Whitney champion into permanent retirement late in 1932 with a record of 12 wins in 16 starts and earnings of $275,900. Fourteen years would pass before her dethronement as the world's money queen.

As a broodmare, Top Flight went to some of America's finest stallions, including Man o' War, but in this arena she disappointed. Her seven foals were unsound, unlucky, or untalented. Only one was a stakes winner. Top Flight's true legacy was born in that long ago Depression year of 1931, when she towered above her contemporaries like an equine Amazon, utterly unconquerable and simply the best.

In 1931, C. V. Whitney's champion filly Top Flight became the first juvenile to top $200,000 in earnings.

. . . She's not big, but she's a classy little trick.

—WHITNEY TRAINER TOM HEALEY ON TOP FLIGHT

TOP RUNNERS

horse and birth year	starts	wins	seconds	thirds	earnings
BATTLESHIP (horse) 1927	33	18	3	3	$29,275
BIMELECH (horse) 1937	15	11	2	1	$248,745
BLACK HELEN (filly) 1932	22	15	0	2	$61,800
BOLD VENTURE (horse) 1933	11	6	2	0	$68,300
CAVALCADE (horse) 1931	22	8	5	3	$127,165
CHALLEDON (horse) 1936	44	20	7	6	$334,660
DARK SECRET (horse) 1929	57	23	12	6	$89,375
DISCOVERY (horse) 1931	63	27	10	10	$195,287
EIGHT THIRTY (horse) 1936	27	16	3	5	$155,475
EQUIPOISE (horse) 1928	51	29	10	4	$338,610
ESPOSA (filly) 1932	96	19	23	13	$132,055
GRANVILLE (horse) 1933	18	8	4	3	$111,820
HIGH FLEET (filly) 1933	30	15	9	5	$49,345
JOHNSTOWN (horse) 1936	21	14	0	3	$169,315
*KAYAK II (horse) 1935	26	14	8	1	$213,205
MATA HARI (filly) 1931	16	7	0	2	$66,699
MATE (horse) 1928	63	19	12	17	$297,860
MYRTLEWOOD (filly) 1932	22	15	4	2	$40,620
OMAHA (horse) 1932	34	7	9	3	$73,565
*PHAR LAP (gelding) 1926	51	37	3	3	$332,250
SEABISCUIT (horse) 1933	89	33	15	13	$437,730
STAGEHAND (horse) 1935	25	9	3	6	$200,110
SUN BEAU (horse) 1925	74	33	12	10	$376,744
TOP FLIGHT (filly) 1929	16	12	0	0	$275,900
TOP ROW (horse) 1931	39	14	8	9	$213,820
TWENTY GRAND (horse) 1928	23	14	4	3	$261,790
WAR ADMIRAL (horse) 1934	26	21	3	1	$273,240

important races won	special notes
Winner of England's Grand National Steeplechase	Racing Hall of Fame steeplechaser
Belmont S., Preakness S., etc.	Racing Hall of Fame
CCA Oaks, Florida Derby, etc.	Racing Hall of Fame
Kentucky Derby, etc.	
Kentucky Derby, etc.	Racing Hall of Fame
Preakness S., etc.	Racing Hall of Fame
Jockey Club Gold Cup (twice), etc.	
Brooklyn H., Whitney S. (twice), etc.	Racing Hall of Fame
Travers S., etc.	Racing Hall of Fame
Metropolitan H., etc.	Racing Hall of Fame, won 24 stakes
Empire City H., etc.	Twice handicap champion mare
Belmont S., Travers S., etc.	Racing Hall of Fame
CCA Oaks, etc.	Champion filly at three
Kentucky Derby, etc.	Racing Hall of Fame
Santa Anita H., etc.	Champion at four
Breeders' Futurity, etc.	Champion filly at two and three
Preakness S., etc.	
Ashland S., etc.	Racing Hall of Fame
Kentucky Derby, Preakness S., Belmont S.	Racing Hall of Fame, third American Triple Crown winner
Agua Caliente H.	Australasian legend
Santa Anita H., Pimlico Special, etc.	Racing Hall of Fame, won 26 stakes, leading money winner
Santa Anita H.	Champion at three
Hawthorne Gold Cup, etc.	Racing Hall of Fame, leading money winner
Futurity S., etc.	Racing Hall of Fame, leading money-winning mare
Santa Anita H., etc.	
Kentucky Derby, Belmont S., etc.	Racing Hall of Fame
Kentucky Derby, Preakness S., Belmont S.	Racing Hall of Fame, fourth American Triple Crown winner

War and Peace

Racing prospered through another

major war and into the nuclear age.

As HORSE RACING ENTERED THE 1940s, ITS FUTURE seemed bright. America's most popular spectator sport had recovered from the Great Depression, and fans were going racing in record numbers decked out in their new wrinkle-free polyester outfits. Like the jet-propelled planes then in development, daily handle spiraled into the stratosphere—$1-million betting days at major tracks were no longer unusual. Flourishing pari-mutuels translated into tremendous earnings power for horses. Money-winning records toppled again and again—five horses held the world title between 1941 and 1950. The once unimaginable $500,000 milestone was eclipsed early in the decade; then came $600,000, $700,000, and $800,000 before Stymie closed the era with $918,485.

Despite what had gone before—war, economic depression, gangsterism—the 1940s began as an age of simplicity and innocence, a time when America could still fall in love with a racehorse. Some 50,000 visitors signed newly retired Seabiscuit's California guest book in 1941, while Man o' War continued to draw adoring crowds in Kentucky. On the racetrack, Calumet Stable's charismatic Whirlaway generated a firestorm of enthusiasm.

Unfortunately for racing, those golden days did not last. They came to a sobering end on the morning of December 7, 1941, when the Japanese bombed Pearl Harbor. On that day of infamy, a war that had seemed so distant to most Americans came into sharp and terrifying focus. World War II impacted America's Thoroughbred industry more negatively than the previous global conflict. Whereas World War I had at least allowed American breeders broad access to coveted European bloodstock, the Second World War brought racing in the United States to a grinding halt.

RACING GOES TO WAR

Within months of the United States declaring war, gas rationing and curtailment of public transportation adversely affected racetrack attendance and handle, causing purses to be slashed. A crushing decline in yearling auction prices followed—a 48 percent nosedive on the average, from $1,215 in 1941 to $638 in 1942. "It was," wrote noted turf journalist Joe Estes, "the most cruel devaluation of Thoroughbreds in many years." By 1943, however, the Thoroughbred market was on its way up again as the wartime economy gathered steam.

Throughout the war, racing supported its country with patriotic passion. The Thoroughbred Racing Associations (TRA) was formed in 1942 largely to help organize war-related fundraising. Mrs. Payne Whitney contributed half of Shut Out's $44,520 winner's purse from the Belmont Stakes that year to the fundraising effort, while William Woodward pledged most of champion Vagrancy's earnings. By 1945, the industry had raised $25 million toward war relief.

Despite its enthusiastic support, American racing was all but torpedoed by the war. Gas rationing and a 1943 ban on pleasure driving caused cancellation of numerous race meetings, while others were conducted in more populous areas (for example, Keeneland Race Course based near the

Lt. Col. C. V. Whitney (left) and Lt. Alfred G. Vanderbilt (right) enjoy an afternoon at Belmont Park in May of 1943.

then small town of Lexington, Kentucky, conducted its meetings 80 miles away at Churchill Downs—in much larger Louisville). California racing was called off altogether by presidential order, with Hollywood Park transformed into an army storage unit and Santa Anita into a "relocation center" for U.S. citizens of Japanese ancestry—America's own shameful version of a concentration camp. Travel restrictions made the Saratoga yearling sale impossible for Kentucky breeders, who soon thereafter formed the Breeders' Sales Co. and began to conduct what is now known as the Keeneland July sale.

All of this was a prelude to the industry's climactic war-related moment of late 1944, when War Mobilization Director James Byrne became the grinch who stole racing, with issuance of the following order:

> The operation of racetracks not only requires employment of manpower needed for more essential operations, but also manpower, railway transportation, tires and gasoline in movement of passengers to and from the track, and in movement of horses and their attendants. The existing war situation demands the utmost effort that the people of the United States can give to the support of its armed forces in production of needed war materials. The operation of racetracks is not conducive to this all-out effort.

> Therefore, with the approval of the President, I urge that management of these tracks take immediate measures to bring present race meetings to a close by January 3, 1945, and to refrain from resuming at all tracks until war conditions permit.

The lights promptly went out at racetracks across America.

Has Citation bowed? If he's bowed in both front tendons, I'll go. One is not enough.

—*TRAINER ED CHRISTMAS ON SENDING ESCADRU TO THE PREAKNESS*

GOOD STORIES ABOUND

Fortunately, the hiatus was relatively brief. Germany surrendered on May 8 and racing resumed on May 12 at Narragansett Park, near Providence, Rhode Island. When Japan surrendered in September, World War II was over. But it was an uneasy peace that descended on a world scarred by war and brutal politics, and, though victorious, America's national psyche had been subtly altered: Roosevelt's sudden death in April had imparted a broad sense of vulnerability; Rosie the Riveter returned from factory to kitchen, not altogether pleased at the prospect; soldiers came home, nearly 300,000 fewer than had gone off to war; and the rising red scare bred paranoia—when fluoride was added to community water supplies, some denounced it as a Communist plot to poison the masses. Though Americans were ready to let the good times roll once more, their former exuberance had been tempered by recent events.

Still, the 1940s provided some of racing's great stories, including four Triple Crown sweeps. Whirlaway, Calumet's Mr. Longtail, opened the decade with a triumphant breeze through the Kentucky Derby, Preakness, and Belmont Stakes. Erratic, temperamental, almost impossible to handle, the son of *Blenheim II had terrorized riders with his penchant for bolting to the outer rail. A unique eye cup devised by trainer Ben Jones and jockey Eddie Arcaro's heroic strength transformed the colt from outlaw to superstar. Whirlaway's wonderful stretch runs, tail flowing out behind him like a red banner, remain a cherished part of racing lore.

Then there was Alsab, the era's penultimate rags-to-riches tale—a $700 yearling of peasant lineage who outgamed Whirlaway by a nose in a famous 1942 match race at Narragansett Park. That courage eventually carried him into the Racing Hall of Fame. And against all odds, Alsab established a male line that is surviving into the twenty-first century.

I've heard him called "slab-sided" and a "freak with no breeding," all of which might be true. But he was a racehorse— and that was all that mattered.

—TURF WRITER/HORSEMAN JOHN H. CLARK ON ALSAB

HORSE SIGNS OF THE TIMES

1941 A record 6,805 foals are registered

1941–1948 Annual purse distribution rises from $18 million to $54.5 million

1942 Yearling average falls to $638 after U.S. enters World War II

1946 Yearling average soars to $5,909 after war

Kentucky Derby offers $100,000 purse for the first time

1947 Purse distribution tops $50 million

Automatic hot-walking machine is introduced

Bull Lea becomes the first to sire $1 million earners in a single season

1950 Foal crop tops 9,000 for first time

Future Racing Hall of Fame trainer Ben Jones poses with Whirlaway, the first of Calumet's two Triple Crown winners.

Mrs. John D. Hertz's 1943 Triple Crown winner, Count Fleet, habitually crushed his opponents by huge margins, including a spectacular 25-length victory in the Belmont Stakes, during which he suffered what would be a career-ending injury. John Longden guided the great colt home that afternoon, past an infield billboard that eerily instructed In Case of Air Raid, Keep Calm. A half-century later, the Hall of Fame jockey remained steadfast in his belief that Count Fleet was simply the best he'd ever known or seen.

High-headed, flame-coated Stymie was *not* the best, but he was nevertheless beloved by racing fans. Nobody told Stymie that he had the blood of a peasant—that his sire was a flop and neither his dam nor his siblings could run a lick. He stepped onto racing's stage in 1943 with few pretensions and was claimed by trainer Hirsch Jacobs in his third start for $1,500 from King Ranch, where he was bred. Six years later, Stymie became the first Thoroughbred to surpass $900,000 in career earnings.

One who did not get away from the Texas-based King Ranch was Assault, although, like Stymie, he displayed little early promise. As a foal, Assault had stepped on a sharp object and permanently deformed his right forefoot. (The nickname-loving press later dubbed him the Club-Footed Comet.) Trainer Max Hirsch shook his head when he first saw Assault. "When he walks or trots, you'd think he's going to fall down," Hirsch marveled. But in full stride, Assault was Mr. Smooth, with speed aplenty to wrap up the 1946 Triple Crown.

Breed 'em all to Bull Lea.

—*Trainer Ben Jones's 1940s breeding theory*

Hirsch Jacobs, one of the winningest trainers of the 1940s, claimed Stymie for $1,500.

*Robert Kleberg, the master of King Ranch, admires his 1946 Triple Crown winner,
Assault, fondly referred to in the press as the Club-Footed Comet.*

Gallorette, shown here with jockey J. D. Jessop, earned more money ($445,535)
than any other mare through the first half of the twentieth century.

Cosmetics queen Elizabeth Arden Graham's successful Maine Chance Stable led all American owners by money won in 1945.

DISTAFF DISTINCTION

While the 1930s failed to produce many top fillies, the 1940s seemed to crank them out by the barnful. Six, in particular, stood out: Twilight Tear, Busher, Gallorette, Bewitch, Two Lea, and Bed o' Roses—each destined for the Racing Hall of Fame. The first two were honored in 1944 and 1945 as Horse of the Year, a title awarded to only seven distaffers in one hundred years.

The good fillies of the 1940s were no delicate hothouse flowers. They were a rugged troop of tomboys who carried weight, ran heart-breaking distances, and, because of limited earning opportunities for their sex, routinely challenged—and beat—the best of their male counterparts. Among these outstanding race mares was Twilight Tear, who prior to 1947 had been regarded by the legendary horseman Ben Jones as the best he had ever trained—and he had already trained Triple Crown winner Whirlaway. Gallorette defeated males seven times, endured five bruising campaigns, and was the first mare to earn more than $400,000, while Argentine-bred *Miss Grillo had no superior of either sex when long distance races returned briefly to favor in the 1940s.

CALUMET

If there was an industry story in the 1940s to rival the war, it was that of Warren Wright's magnificent Calumet Stable. As legendary sportswriter Red Smith put it, "Calumet laid it over the competition like ice cream over spinach." Calumet reigned as America's top owner seven times during the decade, edged only by a trio of prominent women—Mrs. Payne Whitney, Elizabeth Graham, and Isabel Dodge Sloane (in 1942, 1945, and 1950 respectively). In 1947, Wright's stable was first to bank $1 million in a season, then replicated that feat for three years running. As breeder, Calumet led six times in the 1940s; its $1.8 million in 1947 almost doubled its own previous American record. Runners who carried the feared devil-red and blue silks of Calumet Stable during the 1940s read like a who's who of the sport, among them Racing Hall of Famers Whirlaway, Twilight Tear, Armed, Citation, Bewitch, Coaltown, and Two Lea; and father-and-son Kentucky Derby winners Pensive and Ponder.

*Jimmy Jones brings in Citation (with Eddie Arcaro up) after his
1948 Belmont Stakes victory and Triple Crown sweep.*

LEADING TRAINERS

James Fitzsimmons
Racing Hall of Fame. Trained champion Vagrancy in this decade. See also 1920s, 1930s, 1950s, 1960s.

John M. Gaver
Racing Hall of Fame. Leading money trainer in 1942. Won 1942 Kentucky Derby with Shut Out; also trained 1949 Horse of the Year Capot and champion Devil Diver in this decade. See also 1950s.

Max Hirsch
Racing Hall of Fame. Won 1946 Triple Crown with Assault and 1950 Kentucky Derby with Middleground. See also 1920s, 1930s.

Bert Mulholland
Racing Hall of Fame. Trained 1940s champions Platter, Stefanita, Battlefield, and major winners Lucky Draw and Eight Thirty.

Hirsch Jacobs
Racing Hall of Fame. Leading money trainer in 1946. Leader by wins four times (1941–1944). Trained champion, leading money earner Stymie. See also 1950s, 1960s.

Ben Jones
Racing Hall of Fame. Leading money trainer in 1941, 1943, and 1944. Trained Triple Crown winners Whirlaway (1941), Citation (1948), and Kentucky Derby winners Pensive and Ponder in this decade. See also 1950s.

H. A. "Jimmy" Jones
Racing Hall of Fame. Leading money trainer in 1947, 1948, and 1949, in former year becoming first to top $1 million in a season. Trained era champions Citation, Bewitch, Armed, Coaltown, and Two Lea. See also 1950s.

Tom Smith
Racing Hall of Fame. Leading money trainer in 1945. Trained champions Star Pilot and Beaugay, and 1947 Kentucky Derby winner Jet Pilot. See also 1930s.

Calumet had been established by Wright in the 1930s. Luck and a willingness to spend money brought the stable quickly into the national spotlight. Much of its success was attributable to a $14,000 Saratoga yearling purchase of 1936, when Wright signed the ticket for Bull Lea. Although a moderate racehorse, when Bull Lea's sons and daughters were placed in the hands of Calumet trainers Ben and Jimmy Jones, magic happened. The five-time leading sire got six Racing Hall of Famers, including one of the best of the century in Citation. No wonder Ben Jones advised Wright to "breed 'em all to Bull Lea."

If Calumet had only Citation to its credit, that would have ensured the stable an honored place in racing history. Champion at two and three, Triple Crown hero, and winner of 16 consecutive races, Citation did all that was asked of him and more. The inevitable parallels to Man o' War were drawn and, indeed, deserved. Citation's acceleration was dizzying—in the Belmont Stakes he nearly ran out from under Arcaro who later admitted "he went so fast he scared me."

A late-season injury threw Citation out of training for more than a year. Warren Wright died in 1950 but dictated in his will that Citation be given a chance at millionaire status. Although he became the first Thoroughbred to achieve that goal at age six in 1951, Citation was never again the horse he had been in his first two seasons of glory.

I'll tell you something, but if you tell anybody else, I'll say it's a lie. I worked that horse a half and he shaded :44. I can't believe my watch!

—*Trainer Jimmy Jones on Coaltown*

Calumet's winning team in 1948 includes Ben Jones (second from left), General Jonathan Wainwright presenting Gold Cup (center left), Warren Wright (center right), Jimmy Jones (second from right), and Eddie Arcaro (right).

Armed draws away from Assault in the $100,000 match race at Belmont Park on September 27, 1947. He won by eight lengths.

Bill Shoemaker (on scale) began his career in 1949,
while Eddie Arcaro was at the height of his fame in the 1940s.

LEADING JOCKEYS

Eddie Arcaro
Racing Hall of Fame. Leading money rider in 1942, 1948, and 1950. Won the Triple Crown twice in this decade with Whirlaway (1941) and Citation (1948).

Ted Atkinson
Racing Hall of Fame. Leading money rider in 1944 and 1946, becoming the first to top $1 million in single-season earnings in 1946. Rode champions Devil Diver and Gallorette.

Doug Dodson
Leading money rider in 1947, setting a record of $1,429,949. Rode Faultless to victory in the 1947 Preakness. Also rode champions Bewitch and Armed.

John Longden
Racing Hall of Fame. Leading money rider in 1943 and 1945. Leader by wins in 1947 and 1948. In 1943, he guided Count Fleet to Triple Crown victory.

Conn McCreary
Racing Hall of Fame. Rode 1,200 winners, including champions Stymie, Twilight Tear, and Armed. Won the 1944 Kentucky Derby and Preakness on Pensive.

Stymie came around the turn with his copper mane flying in the wind, making good horses look as if they just remembered a pressing engagement with the quarter pole.

—JOE PALMER

Ted Atkinson, champion jockey and future Hall of Famer, was at the top of his game in the 1940s.

GOOD, BAD, AND UGLY

The era also showcased a darker side of racing. "Ringing," illegally substituting one horse for another in a race, made scandalous headlines throughout the 1940s. Other forms of malicious tampering gained public notice as well through highly aggressive media campaigns. Particularly insidious was the practice of "sponging," a method of altering the outcome of a race by inserting small sponges far up a horse's nasal passages, thereby prohibiting his ability to breathe sufficiently under exertion. A number of high-profile doping scandals were exposed with the development of new, more sophisticated drug-testing methods. Among the most notable of these scams was a Hollywood Park case where it was discovered that nine horses had been stimulated with caffeine. The culprit behind this one was never caught.

By mid-decade, "racing was in jeopardy of losing its patronage," according to Thoroughbred Racing Associations's President Harry Parr III. In late 1945, the sport took a major step forward in dealing with the criminally negative issues that threatened its very existence. That year, the TRA hired a 35-year-old former FBI agent named Spencer Drayton to head up its new Thoroughbred Racing Protective Bureau. Drayton, who had been recommended for the post by none other than J. Edgar Hoover himself, was given broad latitude in which to combat evil forces within the industry. Parr announced that Drayton would have "absolute and complete power to engage the necessary personnel and direct their operations to deal with any dishonest practices affecting racing, and to prosecute all offenders." Drayton responded by hiring a group of highly trained FBI men, including Edmund Coffey, who had earlier helped the FBI develop its renowned fingerprinting system of identification. The well-staffed new TRPB was off and running.

One of the Bureau's most important contributions to American racing came in 1947 with the introduction of lip tattooing as a means of identifying horses. With this method, the underside of a horse's upper lip was

NECROLOGY

1941 Foxhall Keene, 74. Owner-breeder-sportsman

Upset, 23. Only horse to defeat Man o' War

1942 American Flag, 20. Champion, classic winner

Robert A. Smith, 73. Racing Hall of Fame trainer

1943 A. J. Joyner, 83. Racing Hall of Fame trainer

*Sickle, 19. Leading American sire of 1936 and 1938

Joseph E. Widener, 71. Industry leader, racetrack executive

Zev, 23. Racing Hall of Fame

1944 Thomas Healey, 78. Racing Hall of Fame trainer

Sun Beau, 19. Racing Hall of Fame

The Porter, 29. Leading sire of 1937

Mrs. Payne Whitney, 68. Owner of Greentree Stable

1945 Exterminator, 30. Racing Hall of Fame

Mrs. Ethel Mars, 61. Owner of Milky Way Stable

1946 E. R. Bradley, 86. Owner-breeder of four Kentucky Derby winners

Charles Kurtsinger, 39. Racing Hall of Fame jockey

Morvich, 27. Unbeaten through the 1922 Kentucky Derby

George Woolf, 36. Racing Hall of Fame jockey

1947 Perry Belmont, 96. Among the founders of the Jockey Club

Blue Larkspur, 21. Racing Hall of Fame

NECROLOGY

1947 Lavelle Ensor, 47. Racing Hall of Fame jockey

Will Harbut. World's most famous groom, groomed Man o' War

John Hervey [Salvator, pseud.], 77. Noted turf writer and historian

Man o' War, 30. Racing Hall of Fame, leading sire

Winnie O'Connor, 63. Racing Hall of Fame jockey

Seabiscuit, 14. Racing Hall of Fame

*St. Germans, 26. Leading sire of 1931

1948 *Challenger II, 21. Leading sire of 1939

Henry McDaniel, 80. Racing Hall of Fame trainer

Reigh Count, 23. Racing Hall of Fame

Twenty Grand, 20. Racing Hall of Fame

P. A. B. Widener, 52. Owner of Elmendorf Farm

1949 *Sir Gallahad III, 29. Leading sire and broodmare sire

Top Flight, 20. Racing Hall of Fame

Colonel Matt Winn, 88. Dean of American race-track operators

1950 Chance Play, 27. Leading American sire of 1935 and 1944

C. S. Howard, 69. Owner of Seabiscuit, *Noor, and others

Myrtlewood, 18. Racing Hall of Fame

Caroll Schilling, 68. Racing Hall of Fame jockey

Warren Wright, 75. Master of Calumet Farm

permanently tattooed with an identification number that is then recorded with the Jockey Club, the organization that has historically maintained pedigrees and other industry records in this country. Since then, more than one million North American Thoroughbreds have been tattooed. This practice, combined with later advances in blood-typing, would eventually restore a degree of confidence in racing's integrity and virtually eliminate the vile practice of ringing.

AN ERA ENDS

Although several years remained in the decade, by 1947 it was clear that an era was winding down. American racing lost its definitive hero that season with the passing of Man o' War at age 30. His funeral at Faraway Farm drew thousands and was broadcast by radio and newsreel.

Louis B. Mayer's spectacular Hollywood-style dispersals generated never-before-seen auction prices, while his young stallion *Alibhai was syndicated in 1948 for a record $500,000. An even more important syndication occurred a year later when *Nasrullah was acquired by A. B. Hancock for American stud duty. The influence of this stallion was so incredibly widespread and profound that the breeding industry here was never the same.

In 1949, England's Jockey Club backed down after 36 years and rescinded the despised Jersey Act, by now long outdated and hindering rather than helping the British breeding industry. America thus regained its former stature as a respected source of international bloodstock.

Compared to the aforementioned death, monumental syndications, and legislative act, what occurred in a $3,000 claiming event at Golden Gate Fields on April 20, 1949, may seem insignificant. A filly named Shafter V came home a galloping winner of the second race that afternoon, carrying her tiny apprentice jockey into the winner's circle for the very first time. While Shafter V was to become a mere footnote in racing history, the young man who rode her was destined to be a headliner. His name is William Shoemaker.

Man o' War poses with Samuel Riddle, who bought him in 1918 for $5,000.
Big Red died at the age of 30 in 1947.

*Movie man Louis B. Mayer, shown here with filly Your Hostess, was one of racing's
most flamboyant and successful participants during the 1940s.*

CITATION

THE SPORT OF KINGS IN THE TWENTIETH CENTURY WAS POPULATED with exceptional racehorses whose courage, versatility, and blazing speed embodied the American athletic ideal. Yet, whenever the yardstick of greatness is used to measure the relative merits of those champions, three names inevitably tower above all others: Man o' War, Citation, and Secretariat. Together, this dynamic threesome finished first, second, or third in 84 of 87 career starts, and along the way set or equaled 17 speed records from 1 to 2 miles.

Citation appeared on the racetrack nearly equidistant in time between the two "Big Reds"—27 years after Man o' War's career had finished and 25 years before Secretariat. In looks and running style, Citation was the least flamboyant of the three. Whereas the others were strikingly handsome, well-muscled chestnuts who annihilated their competition in fire-breathing fashion, Citation arrived in a less flashy brown package and won many of his races with almost casual ease.

Nicknamed Big Cy, though his size was in the ballpark of average, he was foaled at Warren Wright's Calumet Farm, in Kentucky, on April 11, 1945. His sire, Bull Lea, was a racehorse of moderate talent, whose genetically quirky fate was to become one of the most successful sires of all time. Citation's dam was the beautifully bred *Hydroplane, imported from England during World War II to join the broodmare band at Calumet—which Wright had named for the baking powder company founded by his father in 1889.

Like all Calumet stock back then, Citation became a racehorse in the hands of Ben and Jimmy Jones, a father-son team riding a fast track to the Hall of Fame. He could have had no better teachers, nor could they have had a superior student. The Joneses sensed early on that Calumet's "Bull Lea brigade" of 1947 was something special indeed, with not one but *three* uniquely talented juvenile offspring of that stallion in the barn—the filly Bewitch and colts Coaltown and Citation, future Hall of Famers one and all. They suspected,

however, that *Hydroplane's son, with his long, flawless stride and eagerness to run, might possess a spark of class seen rarely if ever in a lifetime. That spark was soon ignited. At two, Citation blazed to victory in eight of nine races, his only loss an allegedly orchestrated one to stablemate Bewitch.

As the 1948 classic season approached, Calumet's pair of Citation and late-developing Coaltown looked unstoppable. Though the Jones boys knew which colt was the better, jockey Eddie Arcaro still needed convincing. Coaltown had impressed the eventual Hall of Fame rider with a series of lightning-fast workouts that spring, and Arcaro begged Ben Jones to let him ride Coaltown in the Kentucky Derby. His plea fell on deaf ears. Arcaro was the best jockey in America; Jones wanted him on the best horse. "Citation will win," Jones assured the dubious reinsman. "He can catch any horse he can see, and there's nothing wrong with his eyesight."

Down Churchill Downs's long homestretch, known to many as heartbreak lane, Jones was proven right. Citation sailed past his fleet stablemate as though he were tied to the rail, head up, ears flicking about playfully. After that singular performance, Arcaro was an instant convert to Jones's way of thinking: Citation could beat Coaltown or any other horse at distances "from ten feet to ten miles." All he had to do was look an opponent in the eye and the race was over, winning through intimidation, so to speak.

Citation toyed with, then shut down, three rivals in the Preakness Stakes (Coaltown was not among them), before turning in one of his finest efforts in the Belmont Stakes, the final jewel in America's Triple Crown. "He ran so fast it scared me," exclaimed Arcaro afterward. This legendary rider, renowned for his strength and courage, clung in terror to the flying colt's mane as Citation whipped around the far turn and accelerated almost out from under Arcaro through the final furlongs of the 1½-mile test of courage. Citation triumphed by eight lengths that day and made it look easy.

Before a leg injury sent him to the sidelines, Citation had won 19 of 20 starts in 1948, from 6-furlong sprints to 16-furlong marathons. Had his career ended then, his record would have been stunning: 29 starts, 27 wins, 2 seconds, and world record earnings of $865,150. But the master of Calumet was not wholly satisfied.

Big Cy returned after more than a year away from the racing wars and notched his 16th consecutive victory, establishing a twentieth century American record that would eventually be tied but never broken. Though Citation's heart was as bold as ever, age and injury had taken a heavy physical toll. His winning streak ended and he began to lose more often than he won, several times failing under weights of 130 pounds and more, and finishing second on four occasions to an Irish import named *Noor.

Warren Wright passed away in January of 1951 but remained even in death a part of the Calumet equation—his will stipulated that Citation race on until he surpassed the million-dollar mark in earnings. Thus, in deference to Wright's last wishes but against their better judgement, Ben and Jimmy Jones kept the aging champ in training when he should have been retired. Now and then, Citation treated the public to a thrilling glimpse of what he had once been: he raced a world-record mile in 1:33 ⅗ at Golden Gate Fields and became the sport's first millionaire with his victory in the 1951 Hollywood Gold Cup. After Wright's dreamed-of milestone was passed, the Joneses stripped him of his racing gear, cooled him out, and sent him home forever to Calumet Farm.

Citation was not a failure at stud as has sometimes been implied; he sired a champion filly in Silver Spoon and a classic winner in Fabius. But the immortal spark that had set him so distinctly apart as a racehorse was something he simply could not hand down to his offspring.

America's eighth Triple Crown winner died on August 8, 1970, while 500 miles away his successor to that crown grazed a Virginia pasture at the side of his dam. The torch of true greatness was silently passed on that day from Citation to Secretariat, though this transition would not be recognized for another three years.

Citation was buried near his sire and dam in Calumet's famous horse cemetery. He had outlived Ben Jones by a decade, but Jimmy Jones had another 31 years in which to hold the memory of Big Cy evergreen in his heart. "He could beat anything with hair on it," the old man liked to recall. "He could beat the best sprinters sprinting, the best mudders in the mud, the best fast-track horses on a strip as hard as a basement floor, the best milers at a mile, the best routers at two miles, you name the distance." Perhaps less biased were the sentiments expressed by Jones's Hall of Fame contemporaries, James Fitzsimmons and Max Hirsch. Though they'd never laid a hand on Citation, each regarded him as the best they had ever seen—and they had seen Man o' War.

Citation will win, because

he can catch any horse he can see—

and there is nothing wrong with his eyesight.

—TRAINER BEN JONES BEFORE 1948 KENTUCKY DERBY

STYMIE

STYMIE LOST 96 RACES. BY ALL RIGHTS, THAT STATISTIC ALONE should have denied him any shot at equine immortality. Furthermore, he was not a great weight carrier and had a one-dimensional manner of running that required a long distance and a fast pace in front to set up his closing rush past tired horses. Yet none of that seemed to matter. Racing fans of the mid-1940s simply adored Stymie, none more so than noted turf writer Joe Palmer, whose affection for the horse was contagious. "Stymie is just common folks . . . the most average horse you ever saw," he once wrote, before launching into almost poetic discourse of his attributes and style.

Stymie *did* have style aplenty. Though a somewhat imperfect creature physically, his chestnut coat and distinctive high-headed stance called to mind his legendary ancestor, Man o' War. Like other good ones, his personality was electric. When he stepped onto the racetrack, his demeanor became imperial—head aloft, he seemed to look down at his "subjects" with a dash of disdain and regal amusement.

Despite the presence of Man o' War in his family tree—twice—and his own arrogant posturing, Stymie's immediate relations were humble. He was sired by a total flop and produced from a complete failure; his 10 full- and half-siblings won but a single race among them from 85 starts. Stymie ignored the grim realities of his pedigree, eventually banking $918,485 to reign for a time as the world's richest Thoroughbred. He did it the hard way, over seven hard seasons and through 131 starts, on legs seemingly made of iron.

Stymie was bred in Texas by the King Ranch. He was a tough, disagreeable fellow who did little to endear himself to his first trainer, Max Hirsch. (According to writer Abram Hewitt, Stymie's youthful philosophy was: "Why be difficult when with a little more effort you can be impossible?") Hirsch ran him cheap and cheerfully lost him in his third start for $1,500 to fellow future Hall of Fame trainer Hirsch Jacobs. Stymie would be the claim of a lifetime for Jacobs, arguably the greatest claim of all time.

Jacob calmed the difficult colt by racing him relentlessly. At ages two and three, Stymie started 57 times, winning just seven but improving with each passing month. During his fourth year, the once lowly claimer matured into a champion. He won nine races in 1945, including the Brooklyn, Butler, Westchester, and Grey Lag Handicaps, and the Pimlico and Saratoga Cups, as he developed his patented come-from-behind, high-headed style. From then on, Stymie traveled only in top company, his rivals including 1946 Triple Crown winner Assault and Calumet's grand gelding Armed. He lost often, but generally gave as good as he got, and he was very hard to beat at distances of 1½ miles and beyond.

In 1946, Stymie set a record in the Gallant Fox Handicap and captured a second Saratoga Cup. The following year, he overhauled an international field in Empire City's $100,000 Gold Cup, and tossed the earnings crown back and forth with Assault and Armed before taking it as his own. On July 3, 1948, seven-year-old Stymie became the first horse to earn more than $900,000.

Though he had some memorable moments, Stymie seemed to sour a bit with age. "I think he's bored with racing," Palmer mused after one of the horse's less inspiring efforts. A fractured sesamoid late in 1948 sent him to a Kentucky farm, where he was mated with a few mares before returning to the track in 1949 to try for the mythical million-dollar earnings mark. Unlike Citation two years later, Stymie failed in his attempt.

At age eight, Stymie possessed the muscular, thick-necked physique of a stallion, rather than the sleek lines of a fit racehorse, and he battled chronic lameness. "Some days he acts like he feels good and some days he doesn't," admitted Jacobs. "Most of the time he's just a shadow of the old Stymie." The aging champion lost five consecutive races and added just $7,150 to his bank account before Jacobs finally threw in the towel for him. In November of 1949, Stymie was brought to New York's Jamaica racetrack to bid a poignant farewell to the sport he had been so

Claimed for $1,500 early in his career,
Stymie retired as the world's leading money winner with $918,485.

I'll commence to worry about the weight Stymie is asked to carry when Mr. Campbell starts taking it off of him.

—RACING HALL OF FAME TRAINER HIRSCH JACOBS

much a part of for seven years. Too sore for a rider, he was decked out with pink and green braided ribbons and led down the homestretch to the approving roar of the crowd and the Seventh Regiment Band's rendition of "Auld Lang Syne." There may not have been a dry eye in the stands that day.

Stymie's battling heart gave out 13 years later at the Hagyard Farm, near Lexington, Kentucky. He had not figured to be a great sire, nor was he. His offspring for the most part lacked his class and ability, though many shared his iron constitution. Three of his best, Joe Jones, Paper Tiger, and Rare Treat, started more than one hundred times each during their careers.

The legion of fans Stymie left behind did not recall him as a marginally useful sire, but as the charismatic competitor who had injected a healthy dose of fun into postwar American racing. They remembered, as Palmer did, the proud high carriage of his head in full flight, and how he "came around that turn with his copper mane flying in the wind, making good horses look as if they just remembered a pressing engagement with the quarter pole."

Count Fleet

AUSTRIAN-BORN IMMIGRANT JOHN D. HERTZ EMPLOYED THE strive and succeed philosophy of nineteenth century author Horatio Alger to realize his own version of the American dream, working his way up from newsboy and car salesman to become the entrepreneurial founder of the Yellow Cab (1915) and Hertz Drive-Ur-Self (1923) companies. Beginning in the 1920s on through the 1950s, Hertz was able to enjoy his hard-earned wealth, much of which was funneled directly into the business of racing and breeding Thoroughbreds.

The first really good horse to run for Hertz and his wife, Fanny, was 1928 Kentucky Derby winner Reigh Count. By 1939, however, when Reigh Count had become just another aging, moderately successful stallion, Hertz sent him a tough, cheap sprinting mare named Quickly. The result of this union arrived at the Hertz's Stoner Creek Farm, near Paris, Kentucky, on March 24, 1940.

Initially, Hertz and trainer Don Cameron were not impressed with the seal-brown colt and tried to sell him privately in 1942 for $4,500. He was almost effeminate in build, displayed no special talent in early training, and possessed what they saw as a potentially dangerous temperament. Writer Joe Estes noted that conformationally, "he had little to distinguish him from run-of-the-mill . . . and his pedigree was not bulging with promise."

One who disagreed with Estes was future Hall of Fame rider John Longden, who worked the colt in the mornings and sensed a sleeping giant concealed within the ordinary physical framework. He successfully pleaded with Hertz to retain the son of Reigh Count, who was soon after registered with the Jockey Club under the regal name of Count Fleet.

Hertz's decision at first looked to be the wrong one. It took Count Fleet three starts to break his maiden and six starts to win in relatively minor stakes company. He was then twice beaten by a colt named Occupation, who looked to be his superior in every way.

After that inauspicious beginning, however, things came together fast for Count Fleet; with increasing strength and mental maturity, he rocketed from ordinary to magnificent almost overnight. Cameron nearly fainted one morning when the colt burned 6 furlongs down the Belmont Park straightaway in 1:08 ⅕—nearly 20 lengths faster than the trainer had anticipated. In the Champagne Stakes, Count Fleet sped a 1:34 ⅕ mile, the fastest ever clocked by a two-year-old to that time; and in the Pimlico Futurity, he outran Occupation in track record time for 1 1/16 miles. Count Fleet ended the year as undisputed juvenile king with a 30-length romp in the Walden Stakes.

As a three-year-old in the war year of 1943, Count Fleet flew past infield air raid signs to compile an unblemished 6 for 6 record and in the process became America's sixth Triple Crown winner. His 25-length victory in the Belmont Stakes on an injured ankle must rightfully be recalled as one of the most amazing races ever run. It would also be his final career start.

As Count Fleet's four-year-old season approached, the specter of high weight assignments in the handicap division appealed to neither Hertz nor Cameron. "Let the best horse win—not just the best horse at the weights," the trainer said. When it became clear that the 1943 Horse of the Year would be required to shoulder enormous burdens in 1944, Count Fleet was instead retired to Stoner Creek to stand at stud alongside his sire. He had won 16 of 21 career starts and had never finished worse than third.

Unlike Citation and other greats, Count Fleet passed on his genetic gifts in abundance. Thirty-nine of his offspring became stakes winners, including two horses named 1951 and 1952 Horse of the Year, Counterpoint and One Count. His daughters produced 118 stakes winners—among them the great Kelso—and placed Count Fleet ahead of all American broodmare sires in 1963.

Count Fleet's 25-length Belmont Stakes victory margin in 1943 remained a record for 30 years. Note the sign in background.

Although none could doubt the prepotency of Count Fleet as a progenitor, some have questioned his racing greatness, arguing that he had never been tested by a truly good rival. Maybe, but it is just as possible that his excellence was such that he made "truly good rivals" look mediocre.

The man who knew him best took the latter view. For more than half a century, John Longden insisted that Count Fleet was the best he had ever known. In reference to the Count's remarkable Triple Crown season of 1943: "The horse was never foaled who could beat him."

horse and birth year	starts	wins	seconds	thirds	earnings
ALSAB (horse) 1939	51	25	11	5	$350,015
ARMED (gelding) 1941	81	41	20	10	$817,475
ASSAULT (horse) 1943	42	18	6	7	$675,470
BED O' ROSES (filly) 1947	46	18	8	6	$383,925
BEWITCH (filly) 1945	55	20	10	11	$462,605
BUSHER (filly) 1942	21	15	3	1	$334,035
CAPOT (horse) 1946	28	12	4	7	$347,260
CITATION (horse) 1945	45	32	10	2	$1,085,760
COALTOWN (horse) 1945	39	23	6	3	$415,675
COUNT FLEET (horse) 1940	21	16	4	1	$250,300
DEVIL DIVER (horse) 1939	47	22	12	3	$261,064
GALLORETTE (filly) 1942	72	21	20	13	$445,535
HILL PRINCE (horse) 1947	30	17	5	4	$422,140
*NOOR (horse) 1945	31	12	5	3	$356,940
POLYNESIAN (horse) 1942	58	27	10	10	$310,410
PONDER (horse) 1946	41	14	7	4	$541,075
STYMIE (horse) 1941	131	35	33	28	$918,485
TWILIGHT TEAR (filly) 1941	24	18	2	2	$202,165
TWO LEA (filly) 1946	26	15	6	3	$309,250
WHIRLAWAY (horse) 1938	60	32	15	9	$561,161

important races won	special notes
Preakness S.	Racing Hall of Fame, champion at two and three
Suburban H., Widener H. (twice), etc.	Racing Hall of Fame, Horse of the Year, two-time handicap champion, set or equaled nine track records
Kentucky Derby, Preakness S., Belmont S.	Racing Hall of Fame, Horse of the Year, Triple Crown
Santa Margarita H., Lawrence Realization S., etc.	Racing Hall of Fame, champion at two and four
Washington Park Futurity, Arlington Lassie, etc.	Racing Hall of Fame, champion at two and four
Hollywood Derby, Washington Park H., etc.	Racing Hall of Fame, Horse of the Year, champion at two and three
Preakness S., Belmont S.	Horse of the Year
Kentucky Derby, Preakness S., Belmont S.	Racing Hall of Fame; Horse of the Year; Champion at two, three, and six; Triple Crown
Washington Park H., Blue Grass S., etc.	Racing Hall of Fame, Horse of the Year, champion sprinter, equaled world records for $1\frac{1}{8}$ and $1\frac{1}{4}$ miles
Kentucky Derby, Preakness S., Belmont S.	Racing Hall of Fame, Triple Crown
Suburban H., Brooklyn H., Metropolitan H., etc.	Racing Hall of Fame, two-time handicap champion
Brooklyn H., Metroploitan H., Whitney S., Beldame H.	Racing Hall of Fame, champion at four
Preakness S., Jockey Club Gold Cup	Racing Hall of Fame; Horse of the Year; champion at two, three, and four
Hollywood Gold Cup, Santa Anita H.	Champion at five, defeated Citation four times, set five track or world records
Preakness S.	Champion sprinter
Kentucky Derby, American Derby, Jockey Club Gold Cup, Arlington Classic	
Gold Cup, Brooklyn H., Metropolitan H.	Racing Hall of Fame, champion at four, leading money winner
Pimlico Special, CCA Oaks, Classic S.	Racing Hall of Fame, Horse of the Year
Hollywood Gold Cup, Santa Margarita H., Vanity H.	Racing Hall of Fame, champion at three and four
Kentucky Derby, Preakness S., Belmont S.	Racing Hall of Fame, leading money winner, Triple Crown

chapter 7

Fabulous Fifties

Racing rode high as America's top

spectator sport, but change was in the air.

THE TWO FACES OF 1950s AMERICA WERE AS SEPARATE AND distinct as night is from day. It was, on the one hand, an ebullient era of poodle skirts and hula hoops, Barbie dolls and "The Twist." Americans liked Ike and they *loved* Lucy. There were television sets by the millions and TV dinners, Elvis and Marilyn, a miraculous vaccine against polio, midget transistor radios that could fit in a shirt pocket, and a room-sized piece of futuristic machinery called UNIVAC—the Universal Automatic Computer. This decade was one of the most prosperous ever, with the United States, having no international rivals, dominating the world economy.

The other aspect was not so pleasing. America of the 1950s was transported on a jingoistic, paranoid ride known as the Cold War. The frightening scenery of this decade included intercontinental ballistic missiles, hydrogen bombs, nuclear submarines, Soviet spies, mushroom clouds, and fallout shelters—the combination of which spawned a duck-and-cover generation, terrorized by the prospect of nuclear annihilation and willing to look for a Communist under every rock and in every movie.

Nashua, a media darling, became the first million-dollar syndication in 1955.

The Fifties were, in a word, fabulous for racing. Americans were scared but financially secure. They yearned to escape their worries and were willing to fork over big bucks in pursuit of psychic balm. Horse racing was fortuitously positioned to benefit from this mood. No longer hamstrung by war or economic disaster, horse racing became more than the sport of kings. It was the king of sports—head of one of the country's largest monopolies, with virtually no competition for the gambling dollar outside of Las Vegas, then in its infancy. Racing enjoyed a decade-long celebration during which it was crowned the most popular of spectator sports.

If racing had been popular in the 1940s, America's appetite for it now seemed utterly insatiable. In this era before off-track betting, attendance and handle records were established almost annually. In 1949, 19.7 million patrons wagered $1.4 billion on horse racing; by 1959, those figures were 33.5 million and $2.5 billion. Purses generated by increasing pari-mutuel betting created new earnings records across the board, for horses, jockeys, owners, trainers, fillies, two year olds, in just about every imaginable category. Records for sales, syndications, stud fees, and insurance payoffs also came tumbling down.

FINANCIAL EXCESS

It was all about money in the 1950s, and the four-legged embodiment of the dollar sign was Calumet's great Citation. Though well past his prime, Citation returned to racing at age six in 1951 to fulfill the late Warren Wright's final wish for him—that he become the world's first equine millionaire.

That magnificent milestone hinted at what was to come. Purses continued to inflate, from $50 million distributed nationally in 1950 to $93.7 million 10 years later. In 1940, the Santa Anita Handicap had been the lone American race worth $100,000; in 1957, 34 six-figure events were on the calendar. By decade's end such opportunities enabled Nashua and Round Table to join Citation in the millionaire's club, with several others poised for membership.

SIGNS OF THE TIMES

1951 A poll shows that 70 percent of Americans believe Soviets want to rule the world

1952 Among communicable diseases, polio is the number one killer of children

1955 100 Southern senators and congressmen sign petition against school desegregation

1956 Television sets sell at a rate of 20,000 a day

1960 90 percent of American homes have a television set

In decade J. Edgar Hoover states that 33 percent of the world population is part of a Communist conspiracy

A fast-food restaurant offers uranium burgers and sundaes

Average starting salary for high school graduates is $65 per week

10 million record players, with prices averaging $47, are sold annually

Calumet champion Citation ended his legendary career in 1951
as the world's first equine millionaire.

In 1957, Bill Hartack (center), shown here with Hal Price Headley (left) and trainer A. Hultz (right), broke his own earnings record by becoming the first to ride winners of $3 million in a season.

HORSE SIGNS OF THE TIMES

1951 Santa Anita Maturity is the world's richest race, paying out $144,325 to the winner

1951–1960 Purse distribution increases from $55 million to $94 million

1953 Garden State Stakes is the world's richest race, paying out $151,282 to the winner

*Royal Charger commands record advertised stud fee of $10,000

1954 $86,000 Keeneland July yearling breaks a 26-year-old American record

1955 Nashua becomes the first $1 million syndication

1957 Jockey Club foal registrations top 10,000 for first time

More than earnings escalated during this time. In 1951, Lloyds of London paid off a whopping $250,000 premium on critically injured Your Host, who would survive to sire the great Kelso. Preakness Stakes winner Bally Ache was not so fortunate—his untimely death in 1960 resulted in a $1 million insurance payoff.

In 1953, *Royal Charger commanded an unheard of fee of $10,000. Nashua became the first million-dollar syndication three years later. In 1954, a yearling son of *Nasrullah brought $86,000 at Keeneland's July sale, eclipsing the 26-year-old American record of $75,000. In 1956, jockey Bill Hartack became the first to ride winners of $2 million in a single season; he topped $3 million the following year.

At the time, the 1950s must have seemed like days of pure glory for the Thoroughbred industry. However, the clarity of hindsight allows us to see that they were much more than that. The decade marked a subtle turning point for American racing, a bridge between its sporting past and commercialized future. Some of the industry's most confounding issues, such as medication, unsoundness, and disintegration of the handicap division, were born in this decade.

Every so often a horse such as Alsab, Needles, or Silky Sullivan comes along . . . reminding academicians and mystics alike that lightning doesn't care where it strikes.

—TURF WRITER CHARLES HATTON

WINDS OF CHANGE

By the mid-1950s, American racing was huge, with nearly 100 recognized racecourses in operation. Affluent tracks began to compete aggressively for big-name runners and did so by offering enormous purses and lenient weight assignments. Thus, a trainer found himself with choices not available before. If he felt his horse was unfairly weighted for a specific race, he could easily seek competition elsewhere.

To keep top horses in their races, some racing secretaries instituted the limited handicap wherein a 130-pound ceiling was set for races at a mile and beyond. (At his record-breaking best, 1956 Horse of the Year Swaps never carried more than 130 pounds.) While horsemen generally approved of this system, it undeniably robbed the sport of drama. The era of heroic weight carriers was not over by 1960, but its days were surely numbered.

Furthermore, with so much money available at alternate sites, stables could select from a veritable smorgasbord of racing options, while effectively ducking and dodging difficult rivals. Divisional leaders met head-to-head less frequently—another excitement-draining trend that would accelerate in years to come.

Tom Fool even has muscles in his eyebrows!

—*RACING HALL OF FAME JOCKEY TED ATKINSON ON TOM FOOL*

LEADING TRAINERS

Preston Burch
Racing Hall of Fame. Trained 1950s champions Sailor and Flower Bowl; also trained 1951 Preakness winner Bold.

James P. Conway
Racing Hall of Fame. Trained 1950s champions Grecian Queen and Pucker Up.

Elliott Burch
Racing Hall of Fame. Trained 1959 Horse of the Year Sword Dancer. See also 1960s.

James Fitzsimmons
Racing Hall of Fame. Leading money trainer 1955. Trained 1955 Horse of the Year Nashua, 1957 Horse of the Year Bold Ruler; and champions High Voltage and Misty Morn. See also 1920s, 1930s, 1940s, 1960s.

John M. Gaver
Racing Hall of Fame. Leading money trainer in 1951. Best of era: 1953 Horse of the Year Tom Fool. See also 1940s.

Hirsch Jacobs
Racing Hall of Fame. Leading money trainer in 1960. Trained champion Hail to Reason. See also 1940s, 1960s.

Ben Jones
Racing Hall of Fame. Leading money trainer in 1952. Trained 1952 Kentucky Derby winner Hill Gail. See also 1940s.

H. A. "Jimmy" Jones
Racing Hall of Fame. Leading money trainer in 1957. Trained Kentucky Derby winners Iron Liege (1957) and Tim Tam (1958). See also 1940s.

LEADING TRAINERS

Robert H. "Red" McDaniel
Leading trainer by wins five times in the decade (1950–1954). In 1953, he was the first to top 200 wins in a season (211).

Mack Miller
Racing Hall of Fame. Trained 1950s grass champions *Assagai and *Hawaii. See also 1970s.

William Molter
Racing Hall of Fame. Leading money trainer four times in 1950s. Trained 1958 Horse of the Year Round Table and 1954 Kentucky Derby winner Determine.

Mesach Tenney
Racing Hall of Fame. Trained 1955 Horse of the Year and Kentucky Derby winner Swaps. See also 1960s.

Harry Trotsek
Racing Hall of Fame. Leading money trainer in 1953. Trained 1954 Preakness winner Hasty Road and champion grass horse *Stan.

Sylvester Veitch
Racing Hall of Fame. In decade, he trained 1951 Horse of the Year Counterpoint and turf champion Career Boy.

William C. Winfrey
Racing Hall of Fame. Trained 1954 Horse of the Year Native Dancer and 1950s champions Bed o' Roses and Next Move. See also 1960s.

Tom Fool was the undefeated handicap star of 1953.

*The California duo of Swaps and Bill Shoemaker paired up for numerous
record-breaking victories in the 1955–1956 season.*

*Calumet Stable's Lucille Wright (later Mrs. Gene Markey), shown here with trainer Jimmy Jones (right)
and jockey Steve Brooks (left), continued to win coveted racing trophies after her husband's death in 1950.*

TWO-YEAR-OLDS

To this point in history, horsemen tended to regard juvenile racing as a means to an end, a route used to develop young Thoroughbreds into real racehorses. Other than Belmont Park's Futurity Stakes and a few other races, big money opportunities for youngsters were strictly limited.

The 1950s, however, witnessed a growing interest in early competition—particularly after the spectacular 1953 debut of the world's richest race, a $270,000 vehicle for two-year-olds called the Garden State Stakes run at Garden State Park, in New Jersey. From then on, tracks began to explore this uncharted territory with enthusiasm, and juvenile earnings records were routinely blown away. In 1957, a colt named Jewel's Reward banked a record $349,642, while Idun sailed past Top Flight's long-held filly standard. One year later, First Landing flirted with $400,000.

By 1959, at least a dozen juvenile races offered purses of $100,000 or more. Although many owners were grateful for early returns on investment, others thought it was a disturbing trend. Critics argued that two-year-old racing was becoming an unhealthy obsession within the sport. They worried that an increased emphasis on speed and precocity would change the way we breed our horses and eventually drain American bloodlines of their stamina and soundness.

A QUESTION OF SOUNDNESS

Injuries have always been a sad byproduct of the sport of racing, but the daunting procession of high-profile breakdowns during the 1950s eventually created a queasy feeling within the racing community. Hail to Reason, Tim Tam, Swaps, *Turn-to, Your Host, Bally Ache, Venetian Way, Lavender Hill, White Skies, Prince John, and Dark Star were among the casualties. Suddenly, our horses—with the exception of such ironclad runners as Round Table— did not look as rugged as they once had. Writer Frank Talmadge Phelps noted with concern that "when so many of a country's leading performers give way so early, there are grounds for suspicion that something may be wrong with our racing and breeding program."

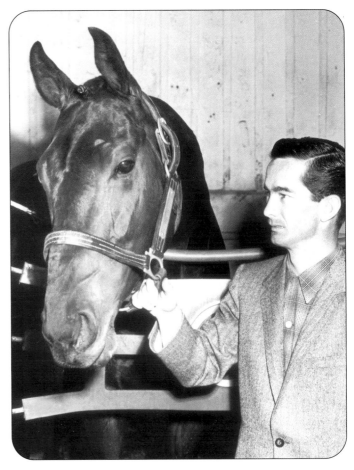

Round Table, shown here with jockey Bill Shoemaker, was an American turf star of the late 1950s.

*Captain Harry Guggenheim owned Cain Hoy Stable,
which was an industry leader in the 1950s.*

Perhaps not coincidentally, the term *phenylbutazone* entered into the industry lexicon at the end of the era, in 1960. This new drug, employed to ease the aches and pains of racing, would explode sensationally into the national headlines eight years later.

THE BRIGHTER SIDE

If viewed from a certain angle, indeed the fifties were fabulous. Despite the cornucopia of problems brewing, racing was a popular betting sport, and it had the marquee names to draw crowds. Citation opened the 1950s. Kelso closed them. In between came a memorable parade of Racing Hall of Famers.

The enormous power of a new medium called television propelled racing into the spotlight as never before. The first equine superhero of the TV age was a compelling individual named Native Dancer, the "Gray Ghost of Sagamore." He was sheer brilliance on the hoof, winning 21 of 22 starts for his young owner-breeder, Alfred G. Vanderbilt. He carried up to 137 pounds successfully, and his only defeat was by a heartbreaking head in the 1953 Kentucky Derby.

Native Dancer's contributions to American racing go far beyond his talents as evidenced by a marvelous statistical record. "His development as a star coincided with the growth of regular telecasting of Saturday feature races," Phelps wrote after the colt's retirement in 1954. "His gray color and consistently winning habits made him easy for the most casual televiewer to recognize. Through this electronic medium, he became a regular and welcome guest in the homes of millions who might never have thought of visiting a racetrack. How many friends he made for racing…will never be known."

In 1953, Native Dancer was scheduled to meet older champion Tom Fool in a highly touted match hailed by many as the race of the century. To the disappointment of the masses, the great event never took place. Native Dancer suffered a stone bruise and was retired, leaving Tom Fool to breeze virtually uncontested through 10 races that season, winning them all under an average impost of 129 pounds.

*A stretch-run injury in the 1958 Belmont Stakes likely denied
the Calumet colt Tim Tam a Triple Crown sweep.*

LEADING JOCKEYS

Eddie Arcaro
Racing Hall of Fame. Leading money rider in 1952 and 1955. Won 1951 Kentucky Derby on Hill Gail. Rode champions Nashua, Bold Ruler, and Sword Dancer in this decade. Retired in 1961 with 4,779 wins.

Steve Brooks
Racing Hall of Fame. Rode 4,451 winners, many in the 1950s. Rode champions Citation, Bewitch, Two Lea, and Round Table. Leading money rider of 1949 when he won the Kentucky Derby on Ponder.

Eric Guerin
Racing Hall of Fame. Regular rider for champion Native Dancer. Won the 1947 Kentucky Derby with Jet Pilot and the 1954 Belmont Stakes with High Gun. He scored 2,712 career victories.

William Hartack
Racing Hall of Fame. Leading money rider in 1956–1957. First to ride winners of $2 million and $3 million in a season (1956, 1957). Won two of his five Kentucky Derbys in this decade on Iron Liege (1957) and Venetian Way (1960).

John Longden
Racing Hall of Fame. Won many important West Coast races of this era. Rode champions Swaps and T. V. Lark. Retired in 1966 as world's top-winning jockey with 6,032 wins.

Ralph Neves
Racing Hall of Fame. Won more than 3,700 races and ranked annually among leading West Coast riders. Rode champion Round Table.

Bill Shoemaker
Racing Hall of Fame. Leading money rider five times in this decade. Leader by wins four times. In 1953, he became the first to ride more than 400 winners in a season. Won the Kentucky Derby with Swaps (1955) and *Tomy Lee (1959).

SWAPS AND NASHUA

As Native Dancer and Tom Fool exited the stage, a prodigiously talented pair of opposites assumed their places in the limelight. Quirky, quick-tempered, and lazy, Kentucky-bred Nashua was bred and owned by American racing royalty William Woodward Sr. (and later his son, William Woodward Jr.) and conditioned by octogenarian Hall of Famer James "Sunny Jim" Fitzsimmons. The son of *Nasrullah was blue-blooded establishment all the way. Swaps, on the other hand, was a free-running upstart out of the Far West. He raced for breeder Rex Ellsworth and was trained by Ellsworth's childhood pal Mesach Tenney. Both were derisively referred to in the Eastern press as cowboys, which, in fact, they were. But they were horsemen as well, and they turned a chronically sore-footed colt into a classic winner, a multiple world record setter, and one of the best racehorses ever seen in America.

Swaps can beat Nashua at any distance from a half-mile to two miles.

—SWAPS'S RACING HALL OF FAME TRAINER, MESACH TENNEY

Nashua can beat Swaps doing anything.

—NASHUA'S RACING HALL OF FAME TRAINER, "SUNNY JIM" FITZSIMMONS

Nashua and Swaps met twice and split decisions, Swaps winning the 1955 Kentucky Derby and Nashua the $100,000 Washington Park match race. No one would ever really know who was best, though opinions abounded. Together they lit up the racing world of the mid-1950s, winning or placing in 50 of 55 starts, banking $2,137,465 between them, and establishing numerous records from 6 to 16 furlongs.

A WORTHY ENCORE

What could 1957 possibly offer as an encore to such brilliance? At first it seemed, not much. The two-year-old crop of 1956 was referred to by one disenchanted scribe as "one of the poorest seen in years." When Bold Ruler, Round Table, and *Gallant Man materialized the following season as three-year-olds, the crop was quickly redefined as vintage.

Round Table was the only one of the three future Racing Hall of Fame members who did not win a 1957 classic. The Kentucky Derby belonged to Calumet long shot Iron Liege after jockey Bill Shoemaker erred in standing up on *Gallant Man a sixteenth-mile from the finish line. Bold Ruler captured the Preakness Stakes, and *Gallant Man redeemed Shoemaker in the Belmont Stakes. But no-nonsense Round Table lasted the longest and ultimately achieved the most in his 66-race career.

The smallish son of *Princequillo was made of pure iron, winning 43 races and more than $1.7 million, stripping Nashua of the money title in 1958. Just as Native Dancer's career had coincided with early television, Round Table came in on the ground floor of big-time American grass racing—and he became our first truly great turf performer.

THE NEXT GENERATION

Time marched on in the 1950s, as it inevitably does, and racing lost important leaders and legends. William Woodward Sr., A. B. Hancock Sr., Samuel Riddle, Louis B. Mayer, and Dr. Charles H. Strub passed on after long and distinguished lives. Others were gone too soon. William Woodward Jr.'s

NECROLOGY

1951 Samuel D. Riddle, 89. Leading owner of 1925, owned Man o' War

Elizabeth Daingerfield. Noted stallion manager, managed Man o' War's stud career

J. K. L. Ross, 75. Leading owner in 1918–1919; raced Sir Barton, first American Triple Crown winner

1952 Elizabeth Kane, 82. Managed Nursery Stud, raised Man o' War

Joe Palmer, 48. Legendary turf writer

1953 William Woodward, 77. Master of Belair Stud, bred and raced Triple Crown winners Gallant Fox and Omaha, chairman of the Jockey Club

Thomas Carr Piat, 53. Owner-breeder, president of the Breeders' Sales Co.

Henry Carnegie Phipps. Co-owner of Wheatley Stable

1954 John B. Campbell, 77. Legendary racing secretary, handicapper

Major Louie A. Beard, 65. Managed stud operations for Whitney family, helped establish Keeneland, Grayson Foundation

Grantland Rice, 73. Renowned sports columnist

*Bull Dog, 27. Leading sire of 1943, three-time leading broodmare sire

*La Troienne, 28. Foundation broodmare, dam of eight stakes winners

NECROLOGY

1955 William Woodward Jr., 35. Owner of Racing Hall of Fame member Nashua

1956 Harry F. Sinclair, 80. Owned Rancocas Stable, leading owner three times

1957 Arthur B. Hancock, 81. Owner of Claiborne Farm, leading breeder five times

Louis B. Mayer, 72. Noted owner-breeder; imported *Alibhai and *Beau Pere

Evan Shipman, 53. Legendary columnist for the Daily Racing Form

Tom Smith, 78. Racing Hall of Fame trainer of Seabiscuit and Kentucky Derby winner Jet Pilot, leading trainer by money won in 1940 and 1945

1958 Dr. Charles H. Strub, 73. Founder of Santa Anita Park

*Blenheim II, 31. Leading sire of 1941, sire of Whirlaway and others

1959 War Admiral, 25. Racing Hall of Fame, 1937 Triple Crown, leading sire of 1945, two-time leading broodmare sire

*Nasrullah, 19. Leading sire five times, sire of Bold Ruler and Nashua

1960 Benjamin F. Lindheimer, 69. Executive director of Arlington and Washington Parks, rebuilt Illinois racing

Hyperion. Great English racehorse and sire

*Bold Ruler (right) won a battle-to-the-finish with *Gallant Man (left) in the 1957 Wood Memorial.*

bizarre death at the hand of his wife, who reportedly mistook him for a prowler, made for lurid headlines in 1955. That same year, five-time winningest American trainer Robert "Red" McDaniel, 44, saddled a winner at Golden Gate Fields, then moments later jumped to his death off the San Francisco Bay Bridge. Four-time leading money-winning trainer Bill Molter was just 50 when his heart gave out. And racing journalism lost three of its finest in untimely fashion—Lexington *Leader* reporter and author Joe Palmer (48), *Thoroughbred Record* editor Neville Dunn (52), and *Daily Racing Form* columnist Evan Shipman (53).

The bell tolled aplenty for the equine element as well: Whirlaway, Gallant Fox, Twilight Tear, Busher, Discovery, War Admiral, *Nasrullah, *Bull Dog, and *Alibhai were among those who died in the 1950s.

What about that generation waiting in the wings for their own moments on stage? Analysts and experts dismissed them with a shrug. Carry Back, they said, was not bred with classics in mind, but the son of undistinguished parents named Saggy and Joppy would win two of them in 1961—the Kentucky Derby and Preakness Stakes. And no one thought much of an ordinary-looking bay gelding with troublesome stifles who managed only to break his maiden in 1959. Nothing in his past performance line or modest physical exterior could prepare the world for the 1960s phenomenon that was Kelso.

When a horse is ready to run, I run him often. There's no use leaving his race on the training track.

—*Five-time leading trainer R. H. "Red" McDaniel*

The contention isn't that everything is all right in racing. If there is any industry involving millions of dollars and thousands of men in which everything is all right, it ought to be stuffed and put on exhibition.

—JOE PALMER, 1953

Leading trainers Bill Molter (left) and R. H. "Red" McDaniel (right) topped training lists in the 1950s.

SWAPS

THE BIRTH OF NOT ONE BUT TWO SUPREMELY GIFTED RACEHORSES marked the fortuitous year of 1952. Brilliant though they both were, Nashua and Swaps were also diametric opposites—in temperament, appearance, racing style, and ownership. Nashua could be lazy and difficult; Swaps's work ethic was flawless. While one required urging to give his best, the other could scarcely be restrained. Nashua was a solid bay owned by the blue-blooded Woodward family; Swaps was a bright chestnut surrounded by plainspoken cowboys. Both, however, possessed unearthly talent, and as long as history is written, this unlikely pair will race together, side by side.

Swaps's owner was an Arizona cattleman named Rex Ellsworth, and his trainer was Ellsworth's lifelong friend, Mesach Tenney. With Tenney's help, Ellsworth had parlayed an $800 trailer full of low-bred Depression-Era horses into one of the most successful Thoroughbred empires the West would ever know.

Ellsworth bought land in the 1940s near the Southern California town of Chino and there developed an austere facility that would later be derided by many a clever journalistic pen. Rather than emulating Kentucky's picturesque white-planked fencing, Ellsworth surrounded his paddocks with V-mesh wiring strung from six-foot creosoted posts. Appearance was not the point; safety and functionality were.

Because his wallet could not at first accommodate the purchase of top bloodlines and performance, Ellsworth relied on knowledge of conformation to develop his program. By the late 1940s, he had money enough to go big time. His first major acquisition was of Irish-bred *Khaled, a talented son of Hyperion for whom he paid $160,000. Ellsworth admittedly had no special plan for him—he sent about every mare he had to *Khaled, including a nonwinner with a bad ankle named Iron Reward. Her chestnut colt arrived in 1952, and after swapping name ideas back and forth with Tenney, Ellsworth gave him the unpretentious moniker of Swaps.

Iron Reward's son represented Ellsworth's ideal: He was long, tall, and wide, with lightning-strike quickness and feline agility. Swaps showed potential

at two, winning three races and ranking 46th of his generation on the Experimental Handicap. His second season was something else entirely.

Although Swaps suffered intermittently from an abscessed foot, which Tenney packed with lanolin and penicillin and covered with a protective pad, this did not prevent the colt from launching a nine-race winning streak that rocketed him from obscurity to superstardom.

In the spring of 1955, Swaps headed east to prepare for the Kentucky Derby. When Tenney noticed a Churchill Downs security guard snoozing on the job, he promptly dropped his own bedding in Swaps's stall, thus eliciting incredulous headlines of "Cowboy Sleeps with Horse!!" This marked the start of an enduring hate-hate relationship between Ellsworth and the press. The no-nonsense cowboy style of horsemanship employed by Ellsworth and Tenney was interpreted by some journalists as cruel, though neither man would debate the issue—a fact that frustrated friend and California writer Oscar Otis. "They *weren't* cruel," he would exclaim years later. "What got everybody down on them was that they treated Swaps the same as a (lead) pony. To them, a horse was a horse."

Swaps strode forth on Derby Day a composed, well-mannered individual, glowing with good health, and proceeded to turn the Eastern racing establishment upside down by galloping away from Nashua in near-record time. In so doing, he followed Morvich as only the second California-bred horse in 81 years to be draped with Derby roses.

The Derby winner shipped home to California after that, a decision that outraged traditionalists who felt he was obligated to try for a Triple Crown sweep. Ellsworth could care less what they thought or said. "Those races just didn't mean that much to us then," he explained in a 1991 interview. "But if we *had* run in the Triple Crown, he would have won it by yards. No question about it."

Nashua captured the Preakness and Belmont Stakes, while Swaps commenced to shatter records and beat top older runners out West. A first attempt on grass in Chicago's American Derby resulted in a 1³⁄₁₆-mile national record.

Match races were still in vogue during the 1950s, and the public clamored for one between Swaps and Nashua. Such an event was ultimately arranged for August 30, 1955, at Washington Park, with a $100,000 winner-take-all purse.

Rumors of oozing blood and crippling pain had floated all year concerning Swaps's bad foot—his was the "most famous heel since Achilles," wrote one turf wag. Reality was not quite so dire, though prior to the match with Nashua, Swaps gouged a rock deep into his foot and fell instantly lame. Ellsworth wanted a postponement, but it was Washington Park's closing day and the track had invested a fortune in promoting the race. So Swaps ran, head cocked awkwardly to one side, bravely matching strides with Nashua until the pain became unbearable. He lost by six lengths.

Swaps never again crossed paths with Nashua, which was too bad. In 1956, Swaps was even better than he had been the year before, winning 8 of 10 races and setting or tying speed records from 1 to 1⅝ miles in 7 of them. He was simply electrifying. Under 130 pounds in the Inglewood Handicap, he theoretically busted a world record by clocking an inconceivable 1:32 ⅗ internal mile while "under stout restraint," according to the official race chart. His final time of 1:39 for 1¹⁄₁₆ miles would not be broken for more than a quarter of a century.

Years later, Hall of Fame jockey Bill Shoemaker would recall Swaps's performance in the 1956 Sunset Handicap as his spine-tingling best. One might reasonably assume that a horse with speed such as Swaps had would burn out over a 13-furlong marathon. Instead, he fought Shoemaker with such exuberance that his rider's powerful arms and back ached from restraining him. The time? Another world record.

On October 9, 1956, in a routine workout at Garden State Park, Swaps's career came to an uncharted end. A nearby rider described hearing a snap that sounded like a pistol shot, then observed a sudden hitch in the champion's normally fluid stride. X rays revealed linear fractures of a hind cannon bone for which a light cast was applied. While recovering in his stall, Swaps somehow managed to reinjure himself, thus transforming a treatable situation into a potentially mortal one. It was Nashua's trainer James Fitzsimmons, of all people, who saved his life. The old horseman rigged up a sling that forced Swaps to keep weight off the injured limb.

A half-interest in the 1956 Horse of the Year had earlier been sold for $1 million to John Galbreath, who bought the remaining half from Ellsworth in 1957 for another cool million. Swaps resided at Galbreath's Darby Dan Farm, in Kentucky, before moving in 1966 to Spendthrift Farm, where he stood for the remaining years of his life alongside his old foe Nashua.

As a sire, he left behind a Kentucky Derby winner in Chateaugay, two champion fillies, and a spate of sons who ultimately failed to keep his name alive in the male line. Swaps died and was buried at Spendthrift in 1972. Thirteen years later, his remains were reinterred in the Kentucky Derby museum garden at Churchill Downs, scene of his most famous victory.

In 1981, the *Thoroughbred of California* magazine asked its readers to rank the best state-bred runners of all time. Swaps was the overwhelming winner. "He's the greatest racehorse California has ever seen, 10 lengths better than anybody else, maybe 15," one fan wrote. "He was larger than life—he was like Man o' War to me," penned another. Terms such as *immortal, awesome, amazing,* and *incomparable* flowed like fine wine in the recalling of California's own Big Red. Despite the appearance of Cal-bred stars such as Tiznow, Snow Chief, and General Challenge in subsequent generations, it is likely that any future survey would net the same result. Swaps is long gone in a physical sense, yet he lives on.

Our only excuse was Swaps.

—EDDIE ARCARO ON NASHUA'S 1955 KENTUCKY DERBY LOSS

BOLD RULER

APRIL 6, 1954, IS A SPECIAL DATE IN THE WORLD OF THOROUGHBRED breeding, for on that night, Bold Ruler and Round Table arrived almost simultaneously in the foaling barn at Claiborne Farm. Like Nashua and Swaps of the previous generation, Bold Ruler and Round Table were very different from one another: the former was high-strung and fragile, the latter, stolid and indestructible. Yet both were truly great, on the racetrack and in the stud.

Bred by Mrs. Henry Carnegie Phipps's Wheatley Stable, Bold Ruler became one of a seemingly endless procession of runners honed to greatness by fabled horseman James Fitzsimmons. Though Bold Ruler's pedigree was high fashion—he was by leading sire *Nasrullah, out of stakes-winning Miss Disco—Claiborne master A. B. "Bull" Hancock remembered him as an unimpressive "skinny foal with a hernia." He outgrew the scrawniness and developed into a fine tall fellow, deep through the heart, though a bit plain-headed. As a youngster, Bold Ruler was a nervous stall pacer who worried the weight right off his large frame and who was prone to accidents and ailments. He had back problems, leg problems, mouth problems, and even alleged cardiac problems. He injured ankles, muscles, and cannon bones, sliced his tongue almost in half on a tie chain, and whacked a hock resoundingly against the side of his stall. In Fitzsimmons's caring hands, Bold Ruler overcame it all.

With slashing early speed, Bold Ruler at two ran the legs off almost everybody and looked like a world-beater as the calendar year flipped to 1957. Hall of Fame conditioner Jimmy Jones knew well what he was witnessing in Bold Ruler as the classic season loomed. "He's the best I've seen since Citation," the Calumet Stable trainer told an interviewer. "He scares me when I see him work. He scares me when I see him run. He just plain scares me!"

Bold Ruler reduced track records in the Flamingo Stakes and Wood Memorial that spring, beating rising star *Gallant Man in the latter.

Fitzsimmons dismissed fast times as unimportant. "All I want is to win if I can, and get the horse back safe." That was a tall order with this particular colt.

Favored for the Kentucky Derby, Bold Ruler was frustrated by jockey Eddie Arcaro's attempt to curb his early speed—pressure on the bit hurt his tongue; he refused to exert himself and finished fourth behind Iron Liege, *Gallant Man, and Round Table. Having learned from that disaster, Arcaro opted to turn him loose in the Preakness two weeks later. He won. "Bold Ruler knows more about running than I do," the jockey explained afterward. "Just let him run and he'll get the job done."

Bold Ruler subsequently got the job done under 130 pounds in the 1-mile Jerome Handicap; smashed Roseben's 51-year-old Belmont Park 7-furlong record in the Vosburgh Handicap, again with 130; and picked up 133 and 136 pounds respectively to win the 1 1/16-mile Queen's County and Benjamin Franklin Handicaps. His great speed was indisputable, though some—including his trainer—wondered how far he could sustain it.

That question was answered in the 1 1/4-mile Trenton Handicap, a tremendous contest for which only three future Racing Hall of Fame members were entered. When the gates opened, Bold Ruler took off as though jet-propelled, leaving *Gallant Man and Round Table scrambling helplessly in the dust. His easy victory over two of the best horses in training ensured his claim on the 1957 Horse of the Year title.

In 1958, Bold Ruler seemed less fretful and more amenable to being rated off his former fiery pace. He ran seven times under crushing weights—winning twice with 133 pounds, twice with 134, and once packing a 135-pound load, after which Arcaro sarcastically queried: "What will they put on him next? I guess my agent will have to ride him." In the 1 1/4-mile Suburban Handicap, Bold Ruler conceded 18 to 29 pounds to good rivals and won, revealing at last the true depth of his heart.

He scares me when

I see him work.

He scares me when

I see him run.

He just plain

scares me!

—TRAINER JIMMY JONES ON BOLD RULER

He retired in 1959 to Claiborne Farm, where his success was immediate: Eight stakes winners, including champion Lamb Chop, emerged from his first crop of 17 foals, which set the trend for Bold Ruler's glorious future at stud. During the 1960s and early 1970s, he became the single most dominant force in American breeding, leading the general sire list eight times—more than any stallion since Lexington a century before. He eventually sired 82 stakes winners, 11 champions, and one immortal of the turf.

Bold Ruler was just 17 when death whisked him away on July 12, 1971, after a yearlong battle with cancer. Waiting in the wings that summer were several good ones as yet unnamed, among them the aforementioned immortal, Secretariat.

Wheatley Stable's Mrs. Henry Carnegie Phipps
leads in her homebred champion Bold Ruler.

NATIVE DANCER

TELEVISION WAS THE AMERICAN CRAZE OF THE 1950S, AN electronic marvel every bit as epoch-making then as the Internet would be 40 years later. When the minimum wage was 75¢, people eagerly forked out $200 to $400 for the privilege of owning this miraculous box of pleasure. By 1953, an estimated 25 million families could huddle together on an afternoon or evening in front of their Magnavox to watch flickering black-and-white images of Ed Sullivan or Ozzie and Harriet.

Alfred Vanderbilt's Native Dancer was an important part of this mid-1950s revolution—both a beneficiary of it and a benefactor. He was later ranked by *TV Guide* magazine as one of the towering television icons of that era, alongside Ed Sullivan and Arthur Godfrey. Native Dancer was, simply put, the right horse at the right time.

He was a big, powerful, charismatic colt whose gray coat made him easy to recognize in a field of browns and chestnuts. Neophyte television viewers were transfixed by the grainy images of this light-colored blur streaking from behind and under the wire first in race after race. For the first time in its two hundred–year history, horse racing could draw from a potential fan base of millions rather than thousands, and Native Dancer made the most of it as he galloped his way into the heart of America.

He was known as the Gray Ghost of Sagamore for his owner's Maryland farm, though he was foaled in Kentucky on March 27, 1950. A young horseman named Bill Winfrey

welcomed this spirited colt into his barn in 1952 and meticulously guided him through a 9 for 9 season during which he eclipsed Top Flight's old juvenile earnings record and set a world record for 6½ furlongs down the Belmont Park straightaway.

As a white-hot favorite for the 1953 Kentucky Derby, Native Dancer continued his winning ways at three, though not without mishap. One morning at Santa Anita, he brought Winfrey and Vanderbilt to the brink of heart failure by tossing his rider and cavorting merrily through the stable area. In a conversation overheard that spring, Vanderbilt was asked what rival Kentucky Derby contender worried him most. "Native Dancer," was his reply.

Vandderbilt was right to worry. On Derby Day, the gray colt was bumped hard and ridden erratically. According to one disgusted observer, jockey Eric Guerin "took him everywhere on the track except the ladies' room." His closing rush fell inches short of catching 25 to 1 long shot Dark Star, thus marking the only loss in an otherwise magnificent 22-race career. The Dancer redeemed himself in the Preakness and Belmont Stakes, taking both by a neck margin, ears laced back in determination. He later added the Withers, Dwyer, and Travers Stakes (each at 1 to 20 odds), the Arlington Classic by nine lengths, and the American Derby to his list of credits, before a bruised foot ended his season.

He took that colt everywhere on the track

except the ladies' room.

—COMMENT ON ERIC GUERIN'S LOSING RIDE ABOARD NATIVE DANCER IN 1953 KENTUCKY DERBY

Native Dancer was ranked by TV Guide as one of the towering television icons of the 1950s.

Winfrey brought the big gray back for a brief 1954 campaign during which he carried up to 137 pounds and went 3 for 3—good enough for Horse of the Year honors. Another foot bruise stopped him permanently, and with a bankroll of $785,240, Native Dancer retired as the fourth most affluent Thoroughbred of all time.

Native Dancer was sent to Sagamore Farm, where he became a mighty sire. Though he lost the one race that mattered most during his own Hall of Fame career, he went on to exert a profound genetic influence on the Kentucky Derby. Two of his sons finished first in that classic—Kauai King in 1966 and Dancer's Image in 1968 (though the latter was disqualified due to a drug infraction). By the turn of the millennium, the blood of Sagamore's Gray Ghost had flowed through the veins of no fewer than 17 Kentucky Derby winners, a number that increases almost annually.

One might argue that although he never led an American sire list, Native Dancer was one of the two or three most important native-born stallions of the mid- to late twentieth century. Certainly, his name will survive as long as there is horse racing, through his paternal grandson Mr. Prospector and maternal grandson Northern Dancer. Television's first equine hero died following intestinal surgery on November 17, 1967. Like Bold Ruler, Native Dancer was gone too soon.

horse and birth year	starts	wins	seconds	thirds	earnings
BALD EAGLE (horse) 1955	29	12	5	4	$692,946
BEWITCH (filly) 1945	55	20	10	11	$462,605
BOLD RULER (horse) 1954	33	23	4	2	$764,204
BOWL OF FLOWERS (filly) 1958	16	10	3	3	$398,504
CITATION (horse) 1945	45	32	10	2	$1,085,760
*GALLANT MAN (horse) 1954	26	14	4	1	$510,355
HAIL TO REASON (horse) 1958	18	9	2	2	$328,434
HIGH GUN (horse) 1951	24	11	5	4	$486,025
HILL PRINCE (horse) 1947	30	17	5	4	$422,140
KELSO (gelding) 1957	63	39	12	2	$1,977,896
NASHUA (horse) 1952	30	22	4	1	$1,288,565
NATIVE DANCER (horse) 1950	22	21	1	0	$785,240
NEEDLES (horse) 1953	21	11	3	3	$600,355
NEXT MOVE (filly) 1947	46	17	11	3	$398,550
PARLO (filly) 1951	34	8	6	3	$309,240
REAL DELIGHT (filly) 1949	15	12	1	0	$261,822
ROUND TABLE (horse) 1954	66	43	8	5	$1,749,869
ROYAL NATIVE (filly) 1954	49	18	13	3	$422,769
SILVER SPOON (filly) 1956	27	13	3	4	$313,930
SWAPS (horse) 1952	25	19	2	2	$848,900
SWORD DANCER (horse) 1956	39	15	7	4	$829,610
TIM TAM (horse) 1955	14	10	1	2	$467,475
TOM FOOL (horse) 1949	30	21	7	1	$570,165

important races won	special notes
Washington, D.C., International (twice), Metropolitan H., Widener H., Suburban H., etc.	Champion at five
Vanity H., etc.	Racing Hall of Fame, concluded her career in this decade
Preakness S., Suburban H., etc.	Racing Hall of Fame, Horse of the Year 1957, champion sprinter 1958
CCA Oaks, Frizette S., Gardenia S., Acorn S., Spinster S.	Champion at two and three
Hollywood Gold Cup	Racing Hall of Fame, became first equine millionaire in 1951
Belmont S., Hollywood Gold Cup, Travers S., Jockey Gold Cup, Metropolitan H., etc.	Racing Hall of Fame
Hopeful S., Sapling S., Sanford S., Tremont S., Youthful S., etc.	Champion at two
Belmont S., Jockey Club Gold Cup, Brooklyn H., Metropolitan H., etc.	Champion at three and four
Preakness S., Jockey Club Gold Cup, etc.	Racing Hall of Fame; Horse of the Year 1950; champion at two, three, and four
Jockey Club Gold Cup	Racing Hall of Fame, five-time Horse of the Year, won 31 stakes, set or equaled nine American and track records
Belmont S., Preakness S., Washington Park Match Race, Jockey Gold Cup, Futurity S.	Racing Hall of Fame, Horse of the Year 1955, champion at two and three
Belmont S., Preakness S., Travers S., Futurity S., etc.	Racing Hall of Fame, Horse of the Year 1952 and 1954
Kentucky Derby, Belmont S., Florida Derby, Sapling S., Hopeful S., etc.	Racing Hall of Fame, champion at two and three
Beldame H. (twice), Ladies H., Vanity H., etc.	Champion at three and five
Alabama S., Firenze H., Beldame H., Delaware Oaks, etc.	Champion at three and four
CCA Oaks, Beldame H., Kentucky Oaks, etc.	Racing Hall of Fame, champion at three
Santa Anita H., United Nations H. (twice), etc.	Racing Hall of Fame; Horse of the Year 1958; set or equaled 15 world, American, and track records
Spinster S., Top Flight H., Black Helen H., Arlington Matron, etc.	Champion at three and four
Santa Anita Derby, Vanity H., Cinema H., etc.	Champion at three
Kentucky Derby, Hollywood Gold Cup, etc.	Racing Hall of Fame; Horse of the Year 1956; set or equaled nine world, American, and track records
Belmont S., Jockey Club Gold Cup, Woodward S. (twice), Suburban H., Travers S., etc.	Racing Hall of Fame
Kentucky Derby, Preakness S., Florida Derby, Flamingo S., etc.	Racing Hall of Fame, champion at three
Suburban H., Brooklyn H., Metropolitan H.	Racing Hall of Fame, Horse of the Year 1953, champion at two, champion sprinter at four, New York Handicap Triple Crown

chapter 8

Racing at the Crossroads

Horse racing became big business in

the 1960s at the expense of sport.

*In the race of the decade, the 1967
Woodward Stakes, Damascus easily
defeats Buckpasser and Dr. Fager.*

$\mathcal{T}$HE 1960s OPENED PEACEFULLY FOR THE UNITED STATES WITH smooth economic sailing for middle and upper classes, and youthfully charismatic President John F. Kennedy setting America on a course to the moon. But the serenity was an illusion that would soon dissipate in a firestorm of race riots, labor strife, social protests, assassinations, mass murders, and war—the most unpopular ever waged by America. Bizarre contrasts marked the era, juxtaposing images such as that of Alabama Governor George Wallace defiantly blocking a schoolhouse door with others of flower children who espoused love and viewed life through groovy, wire-framed glasses.

MICROCOSM

As always, horse racing mirrored the larger world in which it existed. Economically, things were hopping for those at the top, but woe to those at the bottom. Purses for the best horses and leading stables continued to swell. In 1967, Damascus banked a single-season record of $792,941. That same year, North America's earnings per runner averaged barely $3,300—approximately half what it then cost to keep a horse in training for 12 months. The seeds were sown for discontent.

Like other industries of the 1960s, racing experienced labor strikes, some of them violent. Horsemen demanded bigger purses, pari-mutuel workers wanted more pay, and backstretch employees went on strike for better working conditions. And young horsewomen sought the right to compete as jockeys. They were not burning bras on the feminist front line, but they fought and ultimately won this bitter gender battle of their own.

THE QUESTION OF MEDICATION

The Thoroughbred industry shared America's growing concern over the use and abuse of drugs, a problem that would become a public relations nightmare for racing before decade's end. The public already perceived horse racing as a sport in which its athletes were sometimes "doped." Events of the 1960s would only make matters worse.

In 1961, to head off such negative perceptions and to convey a sense that the sport was policing itself, the National Association of State Racing Commissioners recommended a general ban on all "drugs, narcotics, anesthetics, or analgesics . . . and even water itself if used for a derogatory purpose." Within a year, every racing state had outlawed the race-day use of the popular anti-inflammatory medication phenylbutazone (bute), which was really little more than aspirin. The first high-profile bute case was not long in coming. In 1962, a colt named Crimson Satan tested positive after winning Delaware Park's Leonard Richards Handicap. The former juvenile champion was placed last and his trainer suspended.

SIGNS OF THE TIMES

1963 U.S. postage costs 5¢ for first ounce

1964 A gallon of gas costs 30¢

   60 percent of the adult population smokes

1965 25 percent of all milk sold is delivered to homes by milkmen

1968 U.S. postage rate is raised to 6¢

   The cost of a Hershey candy bar doubles to 10¢

1969 250,000 antiwar protesters march in Washington, D.C.

Late 1960s The terms *love-in, flower power, flashback, groovy, far out, turn-on,* and *hippies* gain popular usage

1970 National unemployment rate is 5.5 percent

I'm the happiest hillbilly hardboot in the world!

—*JOCKEY DON BRUMFIELD, AFTER WINNING THE 1966 KENTUCKY DERBY ON KAUAI KING*

Backstretch turmoil was not uncommon in the 1960s. Here Racing Secretary Tommy Trotter tries to lead a horse to the track during a 1969 stable employee strike at Aqueduct.

Dancer's Image, the 1968 Kentucky Derby winner, was subsequently disqualified for being illegally medicated.

Far more lasting damage to racing occurred six years later when the talented Dancer's Image raced with a sore ankle and crossed the line first in the Kentucky Derby. Within hours, chemists found traces of bute in his postrace urine sample, causing him to become the most famous disqualification in American racing history. The battle over the 1968 Derby's outcome was waged in courts for years before runner-up Forward Pass's name was finally inscribed on the trophy.

Although bute and other therapeutic medications subsequently gained legal status in most racing locales, the unsavory image of a doped Kentucky Derby winner proved a black eye forever on the sport of kings and sparked a debate on prerace medication that continues to this day.

CASH COW

The issue of excessive taxation of racing rivaled medication for sheer thorniness in the 1960s. Lawmakers in financially distressed states and cities came to an eye-opening realization at about this time. Since horse racing had provided states with millions in tax revenue over the years, they asked themselves, why not more?

Legislators began to perceive racing not as a sport but as a cash machine that could solve their fiscal woes. For example, takeout from pari-mutuel payoffs in New York doubled in 1965, with the state getting 80 percent of added revenue—state and local government the remaining amount. This, of course, meant less profit for bettors, who thereafter began a slow, disgruntled exodus from Big Apple tracks. "There is a limit to the amount of taxation to which horse racing can be subjected," New York Racing Association President James Cox Brady warned New York Governor Nelson Rockefeller in 1965. "We think it has been reached."

I defy anybody to pick a flaw in Buckpasser.

—DR. MANUEL GILMAN, NYRA VETERINARIAN

OFF-TRACK BETTING (OTB) IS PROPOSED

The subject of off-track betting in New York first came up in the early 1960s, with Mayor Robert Wagner promoting it because of its tax-generating potential. Wagner's legislative rivals opposed the concept, and OTB became a political football that would be kicked around for nearly a decade. Racing folk watched uneasily. New Hampshire was already introducing a lottery sweepstakes tied into a major horse race but with little financial benefit to horsemen. The idea of politicians with no particular concern for racing overseeing an OTB system in New York seemed downright scary. Turf writer Frank Talmadge Phelps summed up the racing community's sentiments in 1963: "The feeling of horsemen is one of revulsion at the reducing of the noble Thoroughbred sport to the level of any other gambling device, to be tolerated only because of the taxes it pays."

State legislatures were not the only predators. Late in the decade, proposed federal tax changes threatened to stop the flow of capital into livestock-based industries such as racing. The American Horse Council was formed in response, uniting representatives of many different breeds to combat the assault.

And this wasn't all. Gradually increasing public interest in other sports and entertainment forms had racing scrambling for solutions. The sport's answer was a "more is better" philosophy, with extended racing calendars, night racing, Sunday racing, more races per card, longer race meetings, and often overlapping dates. But even as year-round racing became the norm in some regions, the sport began losing ground. National attendance declined in 1967 for the first time since World War II, despite nearly 100 added racing days. During the 1960s, total racing days increased 35 percent while average daily attendance declined 3 percent.

He is the leading capitalist of the equine world, yet he not only walks around in his shabby coat of uncertain hue but often has as many as 14 holes in each of his shoes.

—*TURF WRITER DAVID ALEXANDER ON KELSO*

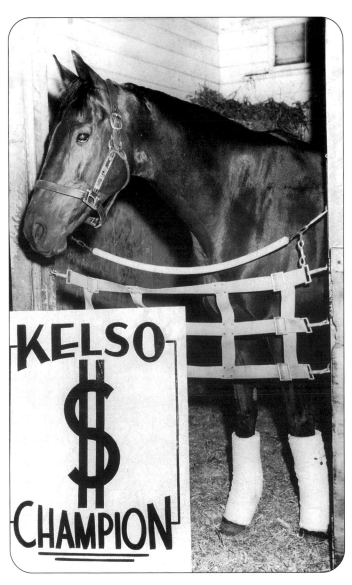

Kelso retired in 1964 as a five-time Horse of the Year recipient and one of the most popular racehorses of the era.

KELSO

Against this chaotic and disquieting backdrop, the steady, rhythmic hoof beats of the greatest American stayer since the 1860s pounded on and on. Kelso—and others like him—ultimately redeemed this troubled era and made it one of the most remarkable in more than two hundred years.

Allaire duPont's Kelso developed from a small unsung juvenile into a 16-hand racing machine who seemed unstoppable as he tore through the handicap ranks from 1960 through 1964. He was one of those extraordinary geldings who come along once in a human generation or so, endowed with mythological strength, speed, and stamina, and who is built to last. Unlike comparatively meteoric superstars of the classic division, Kelso stuck around long enough to make plenty of friends for himself and for racing. He received fan mail by the bagful all the many years of his long life.

Kelso was beloved for good reason. In seven seasons, he won 39 races, earned more than any Thoroughbred to that time, and was voted Horse of the Year in five consecutive seasons. He carried huge weights (winning twice with 136 pounds) and sprinted when asked to, but he truly relished a distance of ground. Five times Kelso won the Jockey Club Gold Cup when that race was a heroic 2-mile test of heart. (It has since been shortened to 1¼ miles.) He swept the New York handicap Triple Crown, eclipsed time records, and won on turf in top company though he vastly preferred dirt.

When a flying dirt clod caught him in the eye in the 1964 Stymie Handicap, Kelso gave up the racetrack for a more genteel life as riding horse and hunter. He was sorely missed by hardcore New York racetrackers. "Hell," exclaimed one upon news of his retirement, "it just won't seem like Saturday if Kelso's not around!"

Kelso was not alone in illuminating the 1960s—Carry Back made for equally terrific editorial copy. By an unknown sire out of a $300 mare, with conformation defects and not especially attractive, Carry Back epitomized Jim Fitzsimmons's classic remark that "it's what you *can't* see that matters most." That intangible carried this ordinary-looking bay to victories in the 1961 Kentucky Derby and Preakness Stakes, put $1.2 million into his account, and assured him a future place in the Racing Hall of Fame.

GREAT RUNNERS, GREAT MOMENTS

A number of grand performers appeared after Kelso's retirement, among them Arts and Letters, Majestic Prince, Nodouble, and Fort Marcy. But truth be told, the remaining years of the decade could best be described thusly: Buckpasser, Damascus, Dr. Fager. *Great* is a word too easily bandied about, but it can be applied to each of these three without apology. It might even be argued that three such runners have never trod the track at the same moment in history, before or since.

Together, Buckpasser, Damascus, and Dr. Fager started 85 times and compiled a 64-13-5 record. Their only unplaced finishes came in Buckpasser's first race; when Dr. Fager was disqualified from first to fourth in the 1967 Jersey Derby; and when Damascus broke down in his final start. They packed enormous weights and routinely obliterated time records. Each was a legend before he ever left the track.

I'd have been just a statistic if not for Carry Back. He changed our lives. We had two daughters, but came to regard Carry Back as our son.

—OWNER-TRAINER JACK PRICE

*The Cinderella horse Carry Back with
owner Katherine Price and trainer Jack Price.*

On conformation, pedigree, and performance,
some regarded Buckpasser as perfection itself.

Racing Hall of Fame trainer Eddie Neloy conditioned Buckpasser and other good ones.

Ogden Phipps's Buckpasser was nobly bred and physically flawless, perfection that translated into racetrack performance. In 1965, this son of Tom Fool was the first juvenile to bank more than $500,000; at three he became the youngest millionaire. He won 15 races in a row, clocked a world record mile of 1:32 ⅗, and carried up to 136 pounds. Despite a full field in the 1966 Flamingo Stakes, at Hialeah Park, Buckpasser proved such an intimidating presence that the track made the race a betless exhibition. He won, of course, and that running was thereafter known as the Chicken Flamingo.

Edith Bancroft's Damascus emerged as a superstar in 1967, winning two classics and then stunning Buckpasser and Dr. Fager by 10 lengths in the Woodward Stakes—an event some termed the race of the decade. He won more money in 1967 than any horse had ever earned in a season, and he triumphed twice in 1968 under 134 pounds.

Every sport has its stars. Buckpasser was a star that never missed a curfew, never had a contract dispute, and always showed up for training.

—*RACING HALL OF FAME TRAINER EDDIE NELOY*

Tartan Farms's Dr. Fager was the most flamboyant of them all. Florida-bred of solid though unfashionable lineage, he became a whirlwind force unto himself. He was a wild-running free spirit, maniacally competitive, impossible to rate, and possessed of fantastic raw talent that brought him to the wire first in 19 of 22 starts, from 5½ to 10 furlongs on dirt and on grass, cracking speed records along the way, with up to 139 pounds on his back. In 1968, he packed 134 pounds and burned a world record 1:32⅕-mile that would stand for more than a decade. Beyond his juvenile season, only Damascus and Buckpasser finished ahead of Dr. Fager.

If such superior weight carriers are still being bred, racing is not likely to recognize them. Cigar's 1995–1996 Horse of the Year titles came under average weights of 122.5 and 126.7 pounds. Buckpasser, on the other hand, averaged 130.6 pounds in 1967, and Dr. Fager 133.3 in 1968. They lent a spicy excitement to racing that is unparalleled today.

THE FEMININE SIDE

Fillies of the 1960s deserve special mention because there were plenty of good ones on racing's landscape. Cicada, Old Hat, Affectionately, Straight Deal, Tosmah, Politely, Gamely, and Shuvee averaged a hardy 56 career starts, and not one ran fewer than 39 times. Dainty Cicada mowed down Bewitch's distaff money record in 1962 en route to a career total of $783,674. In 1965, Moccasin became the first juvenile filly to take Horse of the Year honors. Dark Mirage in 1968 was first to sweep New York's Filly Triple Crown.

Affectionately and Ta Wee packed weight like no other fillies of the modern era. The former hauled 137 pounds to victory in the 1965 Vagrancy Handicap, more than any American female had successfully carried since Pan Zareta in 1916. In 1970, Ta Wee toted an average of 136 pounds. Dr. Fager's little sister lugged 130 pounds or more seven times that year, winning five, including Aqueduct's Interborough Handicap under 142 pounds.

He could have done it in :30 and change—he was six lengths within himself.

—*TRAINER JOHN NERUD ON DR. FAGER'S WORLD RECORD 1:32 ⅕ MILE UNDER 134 POUNDS*

Angel Cordero Jr. (left) with Barbara Jo Rubin,
one of the pioneer female jockeys of the late 1960s.

Hollywood Park's Goose Girl presented a traditionally acceptable image of women in the mid-1960s.

LEADING TRAINERS

Elliott Burch
Racing Hall of Fame. Leading money trainer in 1969. Trained 1969 Horse of the Year Arts and Letters, 1970 Horse of the Year Fort Marcy, and champion Bowl of Flowers. See also 1950s.

Hirsch Jacobs
Racing Hall of Fame. Leading money trainer in 1965. Trained champions Affectionately and Straight Deal in this decade. See also 1940s, 1950s.

Horatio Luro
Racing Hall of Fame. Trained two Kentucky Derby winners in the 1960s: Decidedly in 1962 and Northern Dancer in 1964.

James Maloney
Racing Hall of Fame. Trained 1960s champions Lamb Chop and Gamely.

Eddie Neloy
Racing Hall of Fame. Leading money trainer in 1966, 1967, and 1968. In 1966, he became the first to saddle winners of $2 million in a season. Trained five 1960s champions: Buckpasser, Successor, Queen of the Stage, Impressive, and Vitriolic.

LEADING TRAINERS

John Nerud
Racing Hall of Fame. In decade, he trained 1968 Horse of the Year Dr. Fager and champion Ta Wee.

Woody Stephens
Racing Hall of Fame. Trained 1960s champions Bald Eagle and Bold Bidder. See also 1970s, 1980s.

Mesach Tenney
Racing Hall of Fame. Leading money trainer in 1962 and 1963. Trained 1963 Preakness winner Candy Spots and major winners Olden Times and Prove It. See also 1950s.

Frank Whiteley Jr.
Racing Hall of Fame. Trained 1967 Horse of the Year Damascus. See also 1970s.

William C. Winfrey
Racing Hall of Fame. Leading money trainer in 1964. Trained 1960s champions Bold Lad and Queen Empress. See also 1950s.

Jack Van Berg
Racing Hall of Fame. Leading trainer by wins in 1968, 1969, and 1970. See also 1970s, 1980s, 1990s.

Women were in the news as well. While Bella Abzug, Betty Friedan, and Gloria Steinem stressed broader feminine causes, such as equal pay for equal work, Diane Crump and Barbara Jo Rubin were fighting centuries of industry chauvinism to earn the right to ride as jockeys. At Hialeah Park in February 1969, after several boycotts by male riders and much ill-natured jesting in the press, Crump became the first woman to compete in a pari-mutuel race at an American track. In 1970, she downed another sacred barrier as the first female to ride in the Kentucky Derby. And at Charles Town, West Virginia, on February 21, 1969, 19-year-old Rubin became the first of her sex to experience the joy of victory in an officially recognized race. She later plied her skills in the big leagues of New York.

THE MARKET

The effects of inflation on racing were apparent throughout the 1960s. In 1955, Nashua had been the first $1,000,000 stallion syndication. A decade later, that number no longer raised eyebrows. Graustark was syndicated in 1966 for a record $2,400,000, upped in 1967 by Raise a Native at $2,625,000. Within months, Buckpasser became the record-breaker at $4,800,000 but was quickly surpassed by *Vaguely Noble's $5,000,000 syndication in 1968. Nijinsky II topped the decade in 1970 at $5,440,000.

Auction prices were also heating up. In 1961, America sold its first six-figure yearling at $130,000. The $200,000 mark was attained in 1966 and passed in 1967 with the $250,000 sale of future Kentucky Derby winner Majestic Prince. In 1968, a filly brought $405,000, a record that was obliterated when Crowned Prince commanded $510,000 two years later.

It's nice of him to retire and get out of my way.

—BILL SHOEMAKER, 1962, ON EDDIE ARCARO

BITTERSWEET MOMENTS

The 1960s experienced sad times unrelated to the economics of the sport. Four legendary American trainers—Ben Jones, "Sunny Jim" Fitzsimmons, Max Hirsch, and Hirsch Jacobs—died during the decade. Twelve equine Racing Hall of Fame members, including the great Citation and Native Dancer, also passed on, along with such leading owners and breeders as Hal Price Headley, Isabel Dodge Sloane, Elizabeth Graham, and Mrs. Henry Carnegie Phipps.

Racing is Darwinian in nature—only the fittest survive over time. Unfortunately, the best are not always toughest. Sir Gaylord broke down on the eve of the 1962 Kentucky Derby, for which he would have been favored. Graustark was 7 for 7 before a fracture stopped him in the 1966 Blue Grass Stakes. Raise a Native stunned clockers in a flawless 1963 juvenile campaign that ended with a bowed tendon. *Forli had run his unbeaten streak to eight when a leg injury sent him to stud. Champion fillies Dark Mirage and Lamb Chop did not survive their injuries.

I admire the Turf writers, because it must be tough to write about something you know nothing about.

—*JOCKEY BILL HARTACK*

LEADING JOCKEYS

Braulio Baeza
Racing Hall of Fame. Leading money rider four times in the 1960s. Rode Chateaugay to win the 1963 Kentucky Derby. Also rode 1960s champions Buckpasser, Damascus, Dr. Fager, and Arts and Letters.

Don Brumfield
Racing Hall of Fame. Won the 1966 Kentucky Derby with Kauai King. Also rode 1960s champions Forward Pass and Old Hat. Won 4,573 races in his 35-year career.

Walter Blum
Racing Hall of Fame. Top winning jockey in 1963 and 1964. Rode 4,382 career winners, including champions Affectionately and Gun Bow.

Earlie Fires
Leading apprentice jockey in 1965. Career winner of more than 6,000 races. Scored major 1960s victories aboard In Reality, Dike, and Abe's Hope.

Avelino Gomez
Racing Hall of Fame. Leading rider in 1966 by wins. Seven-time leading Canadian rider. Won 4,081 career races. Rode 1960s champions Affectionately, Ridan, and Crimson Satan. Died in a 1981 racing accident.

William Hartack
Racing Hall of Fame. Scored three of his five career Kentucky Derby victories in this decade with Decidedly (1962), Northern Dancer (1964), and Majestic Prince (1966). Rode 4,272 career winners.

Don Pierce
Rode 3,560 career winners. Won the Santa Anita Handicap four times. Piloted Hill Rise, Physician, and Pink Pigeon to important 1960s victories.

LEADING JOCKEYS

John L. Rotz

Racing Hall of Fame. Rode 2,907 career winners, including the 1962 Preakness with Greek Money. Rode 1960s champions Dr. Fager, Ta Wee, Roman Brother, Silent Screen, and Carry Back. He was the top-winning stakes rider in 1969–1970.

William Shoemaker

Racing Hall of Fame. Leading money rider four times in this decade. Won the 1965 Kentucky Derby with Lucky Debonair. Rode 1960s champions Damascus, Buckpasser, and Northern Dancer.

Ron Turcotte

Racing Hall of Fame. During 1960s, he had the mount on champions Damascus, Arts and Letters, Northern Dancer, Dark Mirage, Tom Rolfe, Fort Marcy, and Lady Pitt.

Jorge Velasquez

Racing Hall of Fame. Leading rider by wins in 1967, leader by money won in 1969. In this decade, he rode champions Fort Marcy and *Hawaii.

Robert Ussery

Racing Hall of Fame. Finished first in back-to-back Kentucky Derbys in 1967 and 1968 with Proud Clarion and Dancer's Image, though latter was disqualified. Rode 3,600 career winners.

Manuel Ycaza

Racing Hall of Fame. Swept the 1968 New York Filly Triple Crown with champion Dark Mirage. Also rode 1960s champions Dr. Fager, Damascus, Gamely, Top Knight, Lamb Chop, and Never Bend.

Legendary trainer Jim Fitzsimmons (left) and
Mrs. Henry Carnegie Phipps, owner of
Wheatley Stable, died during this decade.

CHANGING GAME

Arguably, the most controversial moment of the decade was delivered by vote of the New York Legislature on April 8, 1970, that plainly illustrated just how dependent states had become on tax dollars from racing. Sixty-two springtimes earlier, that same governmental body had handed the sport a near-fatal blow with passage of the moralistic Agnew-Hart Antiwagering Law. Morality was not on the legislative menu of 1970; in fact, the current action represented a 180-degree turn in mindset and intent from 1908. The idea of making more money off racing led to the passage of an off-track betting bill, paving the way for city operated OTB parlors to open in 1971. It was a move that emphasized gambling over sport, eventually distancing bettors from horses while hurting on-track attendance and handle.

So, the game was changing. There would be superstars in the future, but none like Kelso, who could reliably draw standing-room-only crowds to the racetrack for a Saturday afternoon of outdoor fun. That era had ended

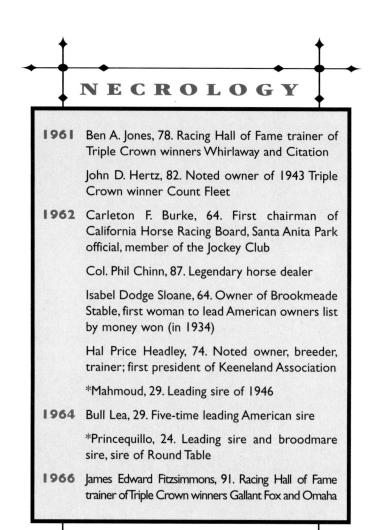

NECROLOGY

1961 Ben A. Jones, 78. Racing Hall of Fame trainer of Triple Crown winners Whirlaway and Citation

John D. Hertz, 82. Noted owner of 1943 Triple Crown winner Count Fleet

1962 Carleton F. Burke, 64. First chairman of California Horse Racing Board, Santa Anita Park official, member of the Jockey Club

Col. Phil Chinn, 87. Legendary horse dealer

Isabel Dodge Sloane, 64. Owner of Brookmeade Stable, first woman to lead American owners list by money won (in 1934)

Hal Price Headley, 74. Noted owner, breeder, trainer; first president of Keeneland Association

*Mahmoud, 29. Leading sire of 1946

1964 Bull Lea, 29. Five-time leading American sire

*Princequillo, 24. Leading sire and broodmare sire, sire of Round Table

1966 James Edward Fitzsimmons, 91. Racing Hall of Fame trainer of Triple Crown winners Gallant Fox and Omaha

If I didn't have a quarter and that horse was mine, I wouldn't sell him for a billion dollars.

—*TRAINER JOHN LONGDEN ON MAJESTIC PRINCE*

NECROLOGY

1966 Elizabeth Graham, 81. Leading owner of 1945, owned Maine Chance Farm

1967 Native Dancer, 17. Racing Hall of Fame, among leading sires

1968 Earl Sande, 69. Racing Hall of Fame jockey

Marshall Cassidy, 76. Executive secretary of Jockey Club and a developer of the modern starting gate

1969 Max Hirsch, 88. Racing Hall of Fame trainer of Assault, Sarazen, Gallant Bloom, and others

1970 Citation, 25. Racing Hall of Fame, Triple Crown winner, first equine millionaire

Hirsch Jacobs, 66. Racing Hall of Fame trainer

Louis Feustel, 86. Racing Hall of Fame trainer of Man o' War

Mrs. Henry Carnegie Phipps, 87. Owner of Wheatley Stable; bred and raced seven champions, including Bold Ruler

Jockey-turned-trainer John Longden admires his star pupil, 1969 Kentucky Derby-Preakness Stakes winner Majestic Prince.

KELSO

ON THURSDAY, APRIL 4, 1957, AS BOLD RULER, *GALLANT MAN, and Round Table prepared to battle it out for Triple Crown supremacy, an event of seemingly little import took place in Paris, Kentucky, far from the madding crowd. The foaling crew at Claiborne Farm attended that day to a young Count Fleet mare as she gave birth to a leggy brown son of Your Host. Maid of Flight's foal was just one of 10,793 Thoroughbreds born in America that year, yet he was also one-in-a-million.

Mrs. Allaire duPont named her colt Kelso. As his plain appearance and strong-willed attitude were not the raw material of a future stallion prospect, she gelded him early and sent him racing under the gray and yellow silks of her Bohemia Stable. He won only once as a juvenile, a painfully slow 6-furlong affair that did nothing to foreshadow what was to come.

No one can really explain why one horse attains immortality, while another of similar DNA is fated for obscurity. Whatever the cosmic reasoning, the genetic attributes of numerous great ancestors seemed to converge with laser accuracy into Kelso's unassuming form. When turned over in 1960 to ex-jockey-turned-trainer Carl Hanford, Kelso's extraordinary abilities were awakened and unleashed with a fury upon an unexpecting world.

Kelly, as he was called, was no equine Clark Gable—writer Jack Mann once noted that "his particular beauty occurred, rather than existed." Kelly had, however, been blessed with an extraordinary inner serenity, though Hanford believed his champion could get nasty if pushed too hard. Fortunately, Kelso rarely required pushing.

In his own sphere, this brown gelding became as wildly popular as the Beatles, who appeared on the scene at roughly the same time. Like that foursome from England, Kelly could draw a screaming crowd, although his was a far tougher audience. His admirers were not hysterical teen girls but

distinctly unsentimental New York bettors, whose grudging respect he earned furlong-by-furlong as the years rolled by. Kelso eventually became a weekend routine for many New Yorkers, who trekked by the thousands to Big Apple racetracks just to see him. It is no coincidence that in Aqueduct's century of existence, 5 of its 14 biggest crowds showed up on days when Kelso was scheduled to appear.

It has been said that no horse stayed so good for so long as did Kelso. Indeed, between 1960 and 1964, he conducted himself with honor at the very apex of his sport. Five times the Horse of the Year crown rested on his brow; five times he won the 2-mile Jockey Club Gold Cup, the country's most demanding test of courage. Kelso's flawless stride, described by the great turf journalist David Alexander as "symphony in motion," carried him to victory in 31 stakes and handicaps over several generations of champions and enabled him to set or equal time records over every imaginable surface, be it dirt, grass, or sloppy mud.

Though his angular frame did not bespeak strength, Kelso was one of the great weight carriers of the 1960s. Thirteen times he won with 130 pounds or more, twice with 136. Hanford would accept no assignment higher than that, for fear of breaking him down.

Under Hanford's loving care, Kelso was a sound racehorse in an era when that commodity was becoming ever harder to find, and he was as honest as the day was long. He ran without hood or blinkers because he did not require them—his mind never strayed from the task at hand. In addition to his perennial parade in the Jockey Club Gold Cup, Kelso's many triumphs read like a grocery list of major North American races: the Woodward Stakes (three times), Whitney Stakes (three times), Suburban Handicap (twice), Metropolitan Handicap, Brooklyn Handicap, Gulfstream Park Handicap, Discovery Handicap, and the Lawrence Realization, to name a few.

It seemed for a while that Kelso was drinking from his own private Fountain of Youth. At age seven, long after most of his contemporaries were retired or slowing down, he claimed the world's money crown while setting an American 2-mile record in his fifth consecutive Gold Cup; whipped the world's best grass horses in the Washington, D. C., International en route to a 1½-mile American turf record; and at Saratoga, equaled the fastest 1⅛ mile ever run in this country. Not bad for an old man.

Alas, age ultimately had its way with him. Kelso began his eighth year on a philanthropic mission, making nonracing appearances to raise funds for industry research. He was a particular favorite with school children, who formed a fan club in his honor and showered him with correspondence for many years afterward. In competition, however, Kelso no longer possessed the relentless power of his youth, but what author Kent Hollingsworth described as "mature greatness." Never was this more evident than in the 1965 Stymie Handicap, which he won by eight lengths despite being half-blinded by a dirt clod.

Surprisingly, Kelso returned at nine to finish fourth in his only start—a 6-furlong dash against horses who could not have warmed him up only a season or two before. When X rays revealed a hairline fracture in his right foreleg, the old warrior went home for good to Woodstock Farm, in Maryland, just $22,000 shy of the $2-million earnings mark he had been in quest of. Fourteen long years of steadily inflating purses came and went before Affirmed and Spectacular Bid supplanted him atop the world money roster and passed that mythical milestone.

In retirement, Kelso was genteelly employed as Mrs. duPont's riding horse, though eventually he was turned out simply to enjoy the good life with a former stakes winner named Sea Spirit, better known as Pete.

On October 15, 1983, the five-time Horse of the Year returned to the racetrack for a final public appearance, appropriately to benefit the Thoroughbred Retirement Foundation. It was a warm, breezy autumn day at Belmont Park, when Kelly stepped onto the track to lead the parade to post for the Jockey Club Gold Cup. The sight of the ancient gelding walking slowly and with dignity down the homestretch over which he had roared with

Kelso became a weekend routine for many New Yorkers, who trekked to Big Apple racetracks by the thousands just to see him.

such magnificence two decades before must have sent a chill up many a spine and put a tear in many an otherwise dispassionate eye. He was greeted along the rail by thousands of cheering, pushing, elbowing, so-called unsentimental New Yorkers, each maneuvering for a better view of their old friend—each knowing it would be the last time.

Perhaps the excitement of the day was too much for the aging champion, or maybe after 26 years he had simply reached the natural end of his life's journey. Kelso made the four-hour van ride from Belmont Park back to Woodstock Farm, and there died the following day.

NORTHERN DANCER

LIKE KELSO, NORTHERN DANCER WAS AN UNLIKELY EQUINE hero, and he was another who gave meaning to James Fitzsimmons's well-worn axiom: "It's what you *can't* see that matters most." Indeed, not many could have perceived future greatness in this bay son of Nearctic who arrived on May 27, 1961, at the Windfields Farm of Canadian industrialist E. P. Taylor. His pedigree exuded class—he was from the first crop of a Canadian Horse of the Year, out of a stakes-class daughter of the great Native Dancer, yet somehow he looked more like a quarter horse than a Thoroughbred, and his short legs did not inspire confidence.

Windfields offered its yearlings for private sale back then, but in 1962 nobody wanted Northern Dancer for his $25,000 asking price. Taylor therefore sent him along to Hall of Fame trainer Horatio Luro, who eyed the pony-sized colt critically, observed his irritating propensity for dumping riders during morning training, and recommended a surgical procedure that would deny him a reproductive future. Fortunately, Taylor nixed the suggestion.

Small he may have been—he never inched much above the 15-hand mark—but Northern Dancer turned out to possess heart and talent enough for three much larger horses. Still, his small stature made him the focus of good-natured media ribbing as the 1964 classics approached. The master of such derision was *Los Angeles Times* columnist Jim Murray, who that spring penned a series of wicked one-liners at Northern Dancer's expense. "You wouldn't pick him over a burro if you placed them side-by-side," he wrote. "He doesn't look big enough to keep up with the traffic on a bridle path. . . . He's the kind of colt, if you saw him in your living room, you'd send for a trap and put cheese in it. . . . His legs are barely long enough to keep his tail off the ground—he probably takes 100 more strides than anyone else in a race. But," Murray acknowledged, "he's harder to pass up than a third martini."

Even Bill Shoemaker, who knew what Northern Dancer was capable of, opted instead for a Californian named Hill Rise as his Kentucky Derby mount. Northern Dancer had the last laugh in this game of musical jockeys, along with newly recruited coconspirator Bill Hartack, who had the privilege of guiding him to his record-breaking Derby victory.

Northern Dancer's race record was impressive—he ultimately won 14 of 18 starts and $580,647, but it was eclipsed by the hysteria surrounding his subsequent stud career. He retired in 1965 to Windfields Farm, in Canada, sired 10 stakes winners and a champion from 21 first-crop foals, moved south in 1968 to the farm's Maryland division, and there became a legend within the span of his own lifetime.

His statistics as a stallion are almost inconceivable. While his second-crop son Nijinsky II tore up the European tracks en route to 1970 Horse of the Year status, Northern Dancer was syndicated into 32 shares for a $2.4-million valuation. In 1981, that syndicate declined a $40-million offer for the then 20-year-old stallion. Three years later, a single breeding to Northern Dancer sold for $1 million with no guarantee of a live foal. Such was his fame; even an old halter bearing his nameplate once sold for $620 at a charity auction.

In 1987, Northern Dancer was pensioned after siring a world-record 146 stakes winners and 23 champions. The book was far from closed on his career as a progenitor, however. He left behind a battalion of top class sons, who picked up his genetic torch and carried it proudly to positions of influence around the world. In America during the final decade of the twentieth century, sons and grandsons of Northern Dancer led the general sire list in 9 of 10 years.

Just as spectacular was Northern Dancer's transformation of the yearling market of the 1970s and 1980s. He became the most commercially successful stallion of all time and generated profound international interest in

His legs are barely long

enough to keep his tail off

the ground. He probably

takes a hundred more

strides than anyone else

in the race, but he's

harder to pass up than

a third martini.

—Los Angeles Times *sports writer* Jim Murray
on Northern Dancer

Northern Dancer became the most commercially successful stallion of all time and generated profound interest in American breeding.

American breeding. At the apex of his popularity, between 1978 and 1989, 149 Northern Dancer yearlings sold at auction for $159,422,432—an average of $1.1 million. "They're collectibles, just like artwork," marveled one consignor/agent. Sheikh Mohammed bin Rashid al Maktoum of Dubai, who engaged in bidding wars with England's Robert Sangster for some of the most expensive Northern Dancers during those years of wild extravagance, once justified his willingness to spend millions for these unproven babies by stating simply: "If you want to breed, you need this blood." For his part, Sangster acknowledged the existence of only two kinds of horses: "Northern Dancers...and the rest."

DR. FAGER

IT WAS THE THIRD WEEK OF JULY 1966, AND WHILE NASA's *Gemini 10* shot into orbit from the Kennedy Space Center, in Florida, a rocket of a very different kind was launched several hundred miles to the north at Aqueduct racetrack. "Don't bet against him," trainer John Nerud had warned in reference to a certain tall, long-legged bay then awaiting his first start in the Tartan Stable barn. "If he can do what I think he can do, don't *ever* bet against him." *Gemini 10* required 70 hours and 46 minutes to get the job done while Dr. Fager's mission was accomplished in 1 minute and 5 seconds. People did bet against him that day—he went off at 10 to 1 odds—but never again in three years would they doubt him.

Dr. Fager was bred in Florida by 3M Company chairman William L. McKnight, owner of Tartan Farms. He was sired by Rough 'n Tumble, out of a $6,500 claiming mare given to McKnight by some of his employees as a birthday present. Named for the neurosurgeon who had saved Nerud's life, Dr. Fager was worked behind a sulky in early training, then was packed off to conquer the world.

If *the best* is an untestable term for describing a racehorse, *one of the best* would surely seem apropos when describing Dr. Fager. In three seasons of racing, he did it all—he sprinted and stayed, packed stupendous weights, outran extraordinary rivals, and smashed speed records almost at will. His greatness came wrapped in a difficult, eccentric package. He was headstrong and arrogant, utterly disdainful when asked to ration his blazing speed, wanting only to fly with wild abandon every time he stepped onto a racetrack. In this free-wheeling manner, he finished first in 19 of 22 starts; only future Hall of Famers Damascus and Buckpasser and champion two-year-old Successor were good enough—or lucky enough—to finish in front of him. "He's not a horse, he's a *machine*," regular rider Braulio Baeza used to say. To rival jockey Bill Boland, who was convinced Dr. Fager could carry 145 pounds and beat any horse in the world at up to 1 mile, Dr. Fager was a freak.

Dr. Fager was good at two, great at three, phenomenal at four. He never carried less than 130 pounds in 1968 and won 7 of 8 starts, including the

Suburban Handicap over arch rival Damascus with whom he split decisions in four epic meetings over a two-year period. As Dr. Fager's career wound down that fall, he treated American race goers to three of the most amazing horse races ever witnessed by any generation anywhere in the world. It was the ultimate grand finale.

In the Washington Park Handicap on August 24, Dr. Fager ran the fastest dirt mile in history, 1:32 ⅕—under 134 pounds. On September 11, he tried grass for the only time in the United Nations Handicap, gave 16 pounds to turf champion Fort Marcy and to Australasian wonder horse *Tobin Bronze—and beat them. And on November 2, an unprecedented 139 pounds was loaded onto his back for the 7-furlong Vosburgh Handicap—which he won in record time.

Dr. Fager retired with fanfare as 1968 Horse of the Year, champion sprinter, champion grass horse, champion older male, and as the world's ninth equine millionaire. Earlier, he had been partially syndicated as a stallion prospect for $3.2 million, with some of racing's biggest names involved in the deal, including Phipps, Hancock, Whitney, duPont, Mellon, and Vanderbilt.

Dr. Fager entered stud at Tartan Farms in 1969 with great fanfare and high expectations, but unfortunately, his career as a stallion was not a long one. On the night of August 5, 1976, he showed signs of abdominal distress; within hours, at age 12, he died from a torsion to the large colon.

The loss of Dr. Fager in the prime of life was tragic, not only because of his iconic status as a racehorse, but for his future contributions to America's breeding industry. A year posthumously he stood alone at the head of the national sire list. Dr. Fager's 265 foals included 35 stakes winners and 3 champions. Some became top sprinters while others loved the grass. They were talented, multi-dimensional runners of class and ability, though none of them approached the untouchable standard set by their sire. His greatness could not be duplicated.

Dr. Fager wanted only to fly with wild abandon every time he stepped onto a racetrack.

horse and birth year	starts	wins	seconds	thirds	earnings
ACK ACK (horse) 1966	27	19	6	0	$636,641
AFFECTIONATELY (filly) 1960	52	28	8	6	$546,659
ARTS AND LETTERS (horse) 1966	23	11	6	1	$632,404
BUCKPASSER (horse) 1963	31	25	4	1	$1,462,014
CARRY BACK (horse) 1958	62	21	11	11	$1,241,165
CICADA (filly) 1959	42	23	8	6	$783,674
DAMASCUS (horse) 1964	32	21	7	3	$1,176,781
DARK MIRAGE (filly) 1965	27	12	3	2	$362,788
DR. FAGER (horse) 1964	22	18	2	1	$1,002,642
FORT MARCY (gelding) 1964	75	21	18	14	$1,109,791
GALLANT BLOOM (filly) 1966	22	16	1	1	$535,739
GAMELY (filly) 1964	41	16	9	6	$574,961
GRAUSTARK (horse) 1963	8	7	1	0	$75,905
GUN BOW (horse) 1960	42	17	8	4	$798,722
KELSO (gelding) 1957	63	39	12	2	$1,977,165
MAJESTIC PRINCE (horse) 1966	10	9	1	0	$414,200
MOCCASIN (filly) 1963	21	11	2	4	$388,075
NATIVE DIVER (gelding) 1959	81	37	7	12	$1,026,500
NORTHERN DANCER (horse) 1961	18	14	2	2	$580,647
SHUVEE (filly) 1966	44	16	10	6	$890,445
STRAIGHT DEAL (filly) 1962	99	21	21	9	$733,020
TA WEE (filly) 1966	21	15	2	1	$284,941
TOSMAH (filly) 1961	39	23	6	2	$612,588

1961 – 1970

important races won	special notes
Hollywood Gold Cup, Santa Anita H.	Racing Hall of Fame; Horse of the Year at five in 1971; between 1968 and 1970 compiled 19-12-5-0, $243,341 record
Top Flight H., Spinaway S., etc.	Racing Hall of Fame, champion at two and five, champion sprinter
Belmont S., Travers S., Jockey Club Gold Cup, Woodward S., etc.	Racing Hall of Fame, Horse of the Year at three
Jockey Club Gold Cup, Suburban H., Woodward S., Brooklyn H.	Racing Hall of Fame; Horse of the Year at three; champion at two, three, and four; NWR mile in 1:32 ⅗
Kentucky Derby, Preakness S., Florida Derby, Metropolitan H., etc.	Racing Hall of Fame, champion at three
Acorn S., Mother Goose S., etc.	Racing Hall of Fame; champion at two, three, and four; leading money-winning distaffer
Belmont S., Preakness S., Woodward S., Jockey Club Gold Cup, etc.	Racing Hall of Fame, Horse of the Year at three
Kentucky Oaks, Delaware Oaks, etc.	Racing Hall of Fame, champion at three, New York Filly Triple Crown
Suburban H., United Nations H., Hollywood Gold Cup	Racing Hall of Fame; Horse of the Year at four; champion sprinter, grass horse, older horse; NWR mile 1:32 ⅕
Washington, D.C., International (twice)	Racing Hall of Fame, co-Horse of the Year at six, champion grass horse twice
Santa Margarita H., Spinster S., Matchmaker S., Gazelle H., etc.	Racing Hall of Fame, champion at two and three
Santa Margarita H., Beldame S. (twice), Vanity H., Alabama S., etc.	Racing Hall of Fame; champion at three, four, and five
Bahamas S., Arch Ward S.	
Metropolitan H., Narragansett Special, Woodward S., Brooklyn H., Charles H. Strub S., etc.	Racing Hall of Fame
Jockey Club Gold Cup S. (five times), etc.	Racing Hall of Fame, five time Horse of the Year (1960–1964)
Kentucky Derby, Preakness S., Santa Anita Derby, etc.	Racing Hall of Fame
Gardenia S., Matron S., Spinaway S., Selima S., Alcibiades S., Test S., etc.	Co-Horse of the Year at two
Hollywood Gold Cup (three times), Los Angeles H. (twice), etc.	Racing Hall of Fame, won 34 stakes
Kentucky Derby, Preakness S., Queen's Plate, Florida Derby, etc.	Racing Hall of Fame, champion at three
CCA Oaks, Jockey Club Gold Cup, etc.	Racing Hall of Fame, champion at four and five, leading distaff money winner, New York Filly Triple Crown
Spinster S., Delaware H., Santa Margarita H., Hollywood Oaks, Ladies H., etc.	Champion at five
Vosburgh H., Fall Highweight H. (twice), etc.	Racing Hall of Fame, two-time champion sprinter
John B. Campbell H., Barbara Fritchie H., Frizette S., Arlington Classic, Beldame S., etc.	Champion at two and three

The Age of Titans

Several of the century's greatest racehorses emerged in this decade and gave the sport a much-needed boost.

Spectacular Bid's 1980 Woodward Stakes marked the first American walkover in a major race in 31 years.

IN SOME RESPECTS, THE DECADE OF THE 1970S WAS ONE OF THE century's most satisfying periods for American Thoroughbred racing. Great runners and big money energized the era and propelled it to the border of fiscal insanity. Purses continued their upward climb, producing new equine millionaires and even a pair of horses who surpassed $2 million by decade's end. The bloodstock market was turbocharged as well, with million-dollar yearlings, broodmares, and horses in training passing through the auction rings of America—plus a $22 million stallion syndication that was simply spectacular. Foreign buyers attended marquee sales in ever-increasing numbers, paying homage to the fact that America's Thoroughbred industry had come of age. By the 1970s, it was undeniably the mother lode of top international racing stock.

Television coverage of horse racing was also on the rise due to an unprecedented explosion of megastars. After a quarter-century of classic frustration, fans basked in the unlikely glow of *three* Triple Crown winners in a six-year span: Secretariat, Seattle Slew, and Affirmed. That terrific trio shared the 1970s limelight with a mighty supporting cast that included Forego, Ruffian, and Spectacular Bid.

Yet, even as the sport soared to new heights on the towering performances of Secretariat—even as the modern Big Red adorned covers of *Time* and *Newsweek,* as seven-figure yearlings were hammered down before awestruck audiences, as Ruffian shattered record after unbelievable record—something essential was slipping away. One racing scandal after another hit the newspapers and television broadcasts, and more lenient medication rules lessened the public's estimate of the sport.

A TIMELY HERO

America's age of innocence, if one ever had existed, was long past by 1973. The country had been hardened by the deceit of Watergate, nightly televised images of the Vietnam War, and the horror of the Munich Olympics, where 11 Israeli athletes were murdered by terrorists. Through it all, racing struggled under its own heavy load of negative publicity.

Americans have always looked for inspiration in times of national stress, often finding it in a charismatic leader or a notable athlete. This time, that uplifting spirit arrived on four legs with a flowing chestnut tail. It has been said that Secretariat appeared at the precise moment when America and racing needed him most. A transcendent, larger-than-life figure bursting with almost supernatural vitality, he streaked across racing's stage in 1972 and 1973, leaving behind an impression of pure greatness unrivaled since Man o' War. If Buckpasser had defined perfection in the 1960s, Secretariat redefined it in every possible way. Still, there were doubters. The Meadow Stable colt had garnered a rare Horse of the Year title at the age of two in 1972, but distance then remained a question mark for any offspring of the brilliant Bold Ruler.

Of course, furlongs meant nothing to Secretariat. After he won the 1973 Kentucky Derby in record time (1:59 ⅖, a mark that still stands) and the Preakness Stakes with consummate ease (also probably a record even though the timing was botched), even skeptics began sensing a possible Triple Crown sweep—the first since Citation's 25 years before. Could it still be accomplished? Statistically, the feat would be far more difficult to

SIGNS OF THE TIMES

1970s The terms *stagflation, organic, recycling, toxic waste, acid rain, ozone layer,* and *oil spills* enter popular lexicon

1971 First-class postal rate is 8¢

Cigarette ads are banned on TV and radio

1974 National speed limit is lowered to 55 miles per hour after the previous year's Arab oil embargo

Word processing machines begin replacing typewriters

1975 First-class postal rate is increased to 10¢

Dow Jones Industrial Average bottoms out at 570

1980 Inflation and interest rates reach near-record highs

achieve than it was in 1948: Citation was one of 5,800 foals registered by the American Jockey Club in 1945; Secretariat was one of 24,367 registered in 1970.

On June 9, 1973, one of the greatest horse races seen anywhere, at any time or place, was run at Belmont Park. Dismissing doubters and ignoring statistics, Secretariat squandered the classic hopes of four rivals in the 1 ½-mile Belmont Stakes. He shot past them all with the emphatic power of a high-speed locomotive, accelerating on turns as was his fashion, and motoring home under a feathery hand ride from jockey Ron Turcotte, who looked back in wonder as the field receded to a speck on the horizon, 31 lengths behind. The timer confirmed just how amazing Sectretariat's performance was: His time of 2:24 was 2⅗ seconds—11 lengths—faster than the existing world record.

Secretariat proved mortal—4 times in 21 starts he did not cross the finish line first—but he was surely heroic in an age of few heroes. During a scandal-plagued era of growing cynicism, this titan, owned by a woman, Penny Chenery, at a time of the growing women's liberation movement, brought to his sport a much-needed dose of positive publicity. He was, indeed, a symbol of all that was good in American racing.

Forego, three-time Horse of the Year, was one of America's last great weight carriers.

He's the kind of horse that if he wants to go left and you want to go right, you go left.

—FOREGO'S GROOM, DON MOORE

AN ALL-STAR SUPPORTING CAST

Secretariat did not stand alone in the spotlight. In this decade, 22 future Racing Hall of Fame members campaigned, including 6 from that remarkable 1970 foal crop. Among them was Forego.

A gigantic tyrant early on, Forego proved such a menace to those around him that he was gelded at two, yet he forever remained an opinionated and not particularly lovable character. So massive that he could barely fit into a starting gate and plagued with troublesome ankles, Forego possessed a heart to match his frame and an intense desire to win that could never be doubted. Three times Horse of the Year in the mid-1970s, Forego won 34 races, including 14 of Grade 1 stature, and 24 times he carried 130 pounds or more—winning 13 races with up to 137 pounds. Trainer Frank Whiteley Jr. called him the last great American weight carrier, and perhaps he was right. In 1978 when Forego's legs could no longer handle the weight and rigors of racing, he was retired, as popular as Kelso had been a decade before.

While Forego's popularity matured over the years, Ruffian's star rose and set in a matter of months and after a handful of races. No horse of the 1970s touched the heart of America more than this big, near-black filly with unearthly talent. She cruised unbeaten through 10 starts, winning by a combined 83 lengths while rewriting stakes records with ludicrous abandon. After her 1975 Filly Triple Crown sweep, Ruffian became the distaff half of a "battle of the sexes" publicity stunt at Belmont Park, with Kentucky Derby winner Foolish Pleasure her male counterpart. An estimated television audience of 18 million bore witness to one of racing's great modern tragedies when she broke down irreparably 3 furlongs into the race.

The most notable ongoing equine rivalry of the late twentieth century was staged in 1977 and 1978 between Affirmed and Alydar, two names so often written and spoken in tandem. Not much separated them on the racetrack, although Affirmed compiled the better head-to-head record, finishing ahead of Alydar in 8 of 10 meetings, including the epic 1978 Triple Crown races. Most of Affirmed's victories over his nemesis, however, were by slim margins of a head, nose, or neck.

HORSE SIGNS OF THE TIMES

1971–1980	Twelve yearlings sell for $1 million or more
	Sixteen new equine millionaires emerge
1971	National purse distribution tops $200 million
1977	American foal registrations exceed 30,000 for the first time
1978	Average earnings per American runner is $4,951
1980	National yearling sales average is $29,683, quadruple that of a decade earlier

The intense 1977–1978 rivalry between Affirmed and Alydar thrilled American racing fans.

Seattle Slew did not stand out on the catalog page at the 1975 Fasig-Tipton Kentucky July sale, where he commanded a relatively modest $17,500 bid—two days before another more fashionably bred yearling, across town but a world apart, fetched 40 times that amount at Keeneland's elite auction. Racing is full of ironies—the $715,000 yearling never raced while the bargain colt turned out to be among the best of all time.

Seattle Slew, a sturdy bay son of Bold Reasoning, was purchased by a youthful group of owners who would be popularly dubbed "the Slew crew." Although conventional wisdom has it that Slew's true greatness was not revealed until he had survived a brutally demanding four-year-old season, in 1977 he zoomed gloriously into the record books as the first undefeated American Triple Crown winner.

The era closed with yet another performer for the ages. The Triple Crown eluded Spectacular Bid, but not much else did between 1978 and 1980. The steel-gray colt described by trainer Bud Delp as "the best to ever look through a bridle," reigned as record-breaker of the decade, with nine track, American, and world standards to his credit. There is even room to argue that Bid rather than Forego was the last great American weight carrier—he won five consecutive races in 1980 under imposts of 130 to 132 pounds and then scared off all rivals when dropped to 126 for the weight-for-age Woodward Stakes. That event represented the first major American walkover in 31 years.

Good Stories and Record Breakers

Despite the ever-present problems, there were plenty of good racing stories in the 1970s, several involving the Kentucky Derby. The nation was captivated in 1971 by the fairy tale Kentucky Derby and Preakness triumphs of Canonero II, a $1,200 yearling who had honed his racing talent in the mountains of Venezuela. Three years later, a record 163,628 fans packed Churchill Downs to witness Cannonade's triumph in the centennial Derby. And in 1980, Genuine Risk became only the second filly in 106 years to wear the blanket of roses.

LEADING TRAINERS

Lazaro Barrera
Racing Hall of Fame. Won Eclipse Awards in 1977, 1978, 1979, and 1980. Trained 1978 Triple Crown winner Affirmed, 1976 Kentucky Derby winner Bold Forbes, and champions It's in the Air and J. O. Tobin. See also 1980s.

Dale Baird
Leading trainer by wins four times in this decade. In 1973, he became the first to saddle 300 winners in a season (305). See also 1980s.

Grover "Buddy" Delp
Won Eclipse Award in 1980. Trained champion and 1979 Kentucky Derby winner Spectacular Bid.

H. Allen Jerkens
Won Eclipse Award in 1973. In 1970s, he trained Onion and Prove Out to defeat Secretariat. Trained later champion Sky Beauty.

LeRoy Jolley
Racing Hall of Fame. Trained two Kentucky Derby winners in this decade: Foolish Pleasure (1975) and Genuine Risk (1980). Also trained 1970s champions Honest Pleasure and What a Summer.

Lucien Laurin
Racing Hall of Fame. Won Eclipse Award in 1972. Trained 1973 Triple Crown winner Secretariat and 1972 Kentucky Derby winner Riva Ridge.

Frank Martin
Racing Hall of Fame. Trained 1970s champion Autobiography and major winner Sham. Leading trainer in New York most of the decade.

Mack Miller
Racing Hall of Fame. Trained 1970s Grade I winners Halo, Tentam, and Winter's Tale. Later trained 1993 Kentucky Derby winner Sea Hero. See also 1950s.

LEADING TRAINERS

Woody Stephens
Racing Hall of Fame. In decade, he trained champion fillies Smart Angle, Sensational, and Heavenly Cause. See also 1960s, 1980s.

Billy Turner
Trained 1977 Triple Crown winner Seattle Slew.

Jack Van Berg
Racing Hall of Fame. Leading money trainer in 1976. Leader by wins three times. In 1976, he became the first to saddle 400 winners in a season (496). See also 1960s, 1980s, 1990s.

John Veitch
Trained 1970s champions Our Mims, Davona Dale, and major winner Alydar. See also 1970s.

Sherrill Ward
Racing Hall of Fame. Won Eclipse Award in 1974. Trained champion Forego to Horse of the Year titles in 1974 and 1975.

Charlie Whittingham
Racing Hall of Fame. Won Eclipse Award in 1971. Trained 1971 Horse of the Year Ack Ack and champions *Cougar II and Turkish Trousers. See also 1980s, 1990s.

David Whiteley
Trained 1970s champions Revidere, Waya (Fr), and Just a Game (Ire).

Frank Whiteley Jr.
Racing Hall of Fame. Trained champion Forego to 1976 Horse of the Year title and champion Ruffian. See also 1960s.

Charlie Whittingham, the Bald Eagle,
was a leading trainer in the 1970s.

On the breeding side, Bold Ruler's lengthy reign as America's premier sire was winding down. He died of cancer in 1972, leaving the field open for Raise a Native and Northern Dancer—and their descendents. As the decade closed, offspring of Northern Dancer began to dominate the sale arenas; in 1980, 13 yearlings by Windfields Farms's "little pony" averaged more than $500,000, and the roof would come off in ensuing years. Another future heir appeared on the racetrack in 1973. Though not as accomplished as same-crop contemporaries Secretariat and Forego, this Raise a Native son, Mr. Prospector, carved a name for himself as a fine sprinter. An even brighter future awaited him at stud.

Jockey records tumbled throughout the 1970s due to dramatically higher purses and more races. In 1973, Sandy Hawley passed the once unthinkable 500-win milestone in a single season, but his record was short-lived—within a year, 19-year-old Chris McCarron bettered it.

The 1970s signaled the dramatic rise of top Hispanic jockeys, with none more prominent than Laffit Pincay Jr., who in 1973 rode winners of a

Nelson Bunker Hunt with his dual-continent champion, Dahlia, the first distaff millionaire.

We've come up here— two Indians and a black— with a horse nobody believed in, and we're destroying 300 years of American racing tradition, dominated by the flower and cream of your society.

—Don Pedro Baptista, owner of 1971 Kentucky Derby winner Canonero II

record $4 million. Seventeen-year-old sensation Steve Cauthen, riding the first half of the year as an apprentice, crossed the $6 million mark in 1977, only to be surpassed by Pincay in 1979 as the world's first $8 million jockey.

Among trainers, the torch of leadership was passed from the late Eddie Neloy and Hirsch Jacobs to Charlie Whittingham and Laz Barrera, whose West Coast–based stables also hailed the arrival of California as a centerpiece of American racing. Together, Whittingham and Barrera captured eight of the decade's 10 money titles.

Equine earnings inflated impressively in the 1970s. In 1979, Affirmed and Spectacular Bid were the first to bank $1 million in a season and subsequently ended their careers as the first $2 million earners. Distaffers Dahlia, Susan's Girl, and Allez France added their names to an expanding list of equine millionaires, which numbered 26 at the close of 1980.

Auction prices also escalated throughout the era, with broken records in all categories. In July 1976, a son of Secretariat was sold at Keeneland for $1.5 million—the first seven-figure yearling in history. Although that colt—Canadian Bound—never amounted to much, future superstars and leading sires Nureyev and Storm Bird were among the other million-dollar yearlings of the 1970s.

Most amazing of all were the soaring values of top stallions and stallion prospects. Secretariat's record $6.08 million price tag had seemed mind-boggling in 1972 but was small potatoes by 1980 when Spectacular Bid was syndicated for $22 million.

Tarnished Reputation

Money does not buy everything, and it certainly does not buy a good name. During this period, racing lost some of its integrity as judged by the court of public opinion. While horse racing had long been regarded as a vehicle for shenanigans because of its association with gambling, aggressive media coverage in this era brought such chicanery into sharp focus.

Systematic efforts to fix races were frequently exposed in the 1970s. Among the most infamous was the 1977 Lebon-Cinzano ringer case in which a South American champion, Cinzano, ran under the name of a less-talented stablemate, won a $16,000 claimer at Belmont Park, and paid $116. The scam was foiled by chance when someone recognized Cinzano as the winner. That same year, the Jockey Club launched the first stage of its comprehensive blood-typing identification program, which would go a long way toward eliminating equine switching, whether intentional or accidental.

The 1970s also showcased the sleazy antics of convicted race-fixers Tony Ciulla and Con Errico, whose 1980 federal trials revealed widespread corruption within the sport. Most of their schemes involved bribing jockeys to throw races, usually in exacta or triple wagering events.

Many blamed the epidemic of scandal on the coinciding rapid growth of gimmick wagers such as trifectas, quinellas, and twin doubles. Famed Racing Secretary Frank E. "Jimmy" Kilroe lamented in 1977:

> The trifecta has provided motivation for 90 percent of the scandals by which our sport has been beset. It is a device to which racetracks, hard put to show a profit with state governments going off with an unconscionable share of pari-mutuel revenue, have resorted as a lure for patrons in search of sudden wealth.
>
> Consider the simple arithmetic of exotic betting. While 20 percent of tickets in an average win pool pay off, that drops to 5 percent with the exacta. If it's four times as difficult to pick a race 1-2 as to pick the winner, how much more so must it be to pick it 1-2-3, especially when there are malign forces whose interest it is that you do not?

Racing did not sit idly by in the face of such corruption. The Thoroughbred Racing Protective Bureau, created in 1946 by the Thoroughbred Racing Associations to police the sport, worked diligently through the 1970s, investigating matters related to possible race-fixing—from possession of illegal electrical devices to bribery and extortion. In 1975, those investigations resulted in 929 fines, suspensions, and denials of licenses. Despite such efforts, the abhorrent acts of a few continued to overshadow the vast law-abiding majority in racing and contributed to a slow unraveling of the sport's fabric of credibility.

LEADING JOCKEYS

Braulio Baeza
Racing Hall of Fame. Won Eclipse Awards in 1972 and 1975. Rode 3,140 career winners, including 1970s champions Susan's Girl, Key to the Mint, Foolish Pleasure, Honest Pleasure, Numbered Account, Wajima, and Optimistic Gal.

Steve Cauthen
Racing Hall of Fame. Won three Eclipse Awards. Leading money rider in 1977; first to top $6 million in a season. At 17, he rode Affirmed to the 1978 Triple Crown sweep. Nearly 2,800 wins in the United States and abroad.

Angel Cordero Jr.
Racing Hall of Fame. Leading money rider in 1976. Won two of his three Kentucky Derbys in this decade with Cannonade (1974) and Bold Forbes (1976). Also rode champion Seattle Slew.

Sandy Hawley
Racing Hall of Fame. Won Eclipse Award in 1976. Leading rider by wins in 1972, 1973, and 1976. First to top 500 wins in a season (1973). Nine-time leading Canadian rider.

Chris McCarron
Racing Hall of Fame. Won Eclipse Awards in 1974 and 1980. Leading rider by wins in 1974, 1975, and 1980, setting a record in former year of 546. Leading money rider in 1980.

LEADING JOCKEYS

Laffit Pincay Jr.
Racing Hall of Fame. Won Eclipse Awards in 1971, 1973, 1974, and 1979. Five-time leading money rider in this decade. First to top $4 million in single-season earnings (1973). First to top $8 million (1979).

Bill Shoemaker
Racing Hall of Fame. In this decade, he rode champions John Henry, Forego, and Spectacular Bid.

Ron Turcotte
Racing Hall of Fame. Won the 1973 Triple Crown on Secretariat and the 1972 Kentucky Derby with Riva Ridge. Two-time leading stakes rider by wins. Rode 3,032 winners before becoming paralyzed in a 1978 racing accident.

Jacinto Vasquez
Racing Hall of Fame. Regular rider of champion Ruffian. Won 1975 and 1980 Kentucky Derbys on champions Foolish Pleasure and Genuine Risk.

Jorge Velasquez
Racing Hall of Fame. Rode 1970s champions Alydar, Spectacular Bid, Chris Evert, Our Mims, Davona Dale, Lord Avie, and Desert Vixen.

The Affirmed team was comprised of teen jockey sensation Steve Cauthen (center), Affirmed's owner Louis Wolfson (left), and trainer Laz Barrera (right).

He'll be the last of the great weight carriers.

—*TRAINER FRANK WHITELEY ON FOREGO*

OTHER PRESSING ISSUES

Race-day medication remained a 1970s newsmaker, although nothing so surreal occurred as the disqualification of a Kentucky Derby winner. Several incidents brought notice to the issue, including champion Riva Ridge's strangely listless behavior before the 1972 Monmouth Invitational Handicap—and subsequent fourth-place finish at 3 to 10 odds. Post-race tests revealed the presence in his system of a tranquilizer for which his respected trainer was not held responsible. Also at this time, animal-rights activists went on the warpath over a perceived correlation between medications and increased breakdowns, a situation that soon drew unwelcome attention from the federal government.

In 1980, the Corrupt Horse Racing Practices Act was put before Congress, with a plan to outlaw all medications, criminally penalize violators,

It's becoming increasingly difficult in this age of analgesics to give a foal sound parents, and it is surprising some of them live down their pedigrees to win at all.

—*TURF WRITER CHARLES HATTON*

NECROLOGY

1971 Bold Ruler, 17. Racing Hall of Fame, eight-time leading sire

James Cox Brady, 63. Vice chairman, steward of the Jockey Club, a founder of Monmouth Park and the American Horse Council

Charles W. Engelhard, 54. Raced Nijinsky II

Captain Harry F. Guggenheim, 81. Owner of Cain Hoy Stable

Eddie Neloy, 50. Racing Hall of Fame trainer of Buckpasser

Marion H. Van Berg, 75. Racing Hall of Fame trainer, leading owner by wins 14 times

George D. Widener, 82. Chairman of the Jockey Club, breeder of more than 100 stakes winners

1972 Arthur B. "Bull" Hancock Jr., 62. Owner of Claiborne Farm, four-time leading North American breeder

Willie Knapp. Racing Hall of Fame jockey, rode 4,185 winners

*Ribot, 20. Undefeated European champion, among the leading sires

Swaps, 20. Racing Hall of Fame, five-time world record holder

1973 Christopher T. Chenery, 86. Owner of Meadow Stud and Secretariat

Count Fleet, 33. Racing Hall of Fame, Triple Crown winner

Two Lea, 27. Racing Hall of Fame, dam of champion Tim Tam

NECROLOGY

1974 Isidor Bieber, 87. Four-time leading owner with Hirsch Jacobs

Robert Kleberg Jr., 78. Owner of King Ranch

1975 Mrs. Charles Payson, 72. Co-owner of Greentree Stable

Ruffian, 3. Racing Hall of Fame, Filly Triple Crown winner

1976 Dr. Fager, 12. Racing Hall of Fame, world record miler

Hail to Reason, 18. Champion, leading sire of 1970

Johnny Loftus, 80. Racing Hall of Fame jockey, rode Man o' War

Tom Fool, 27. Racing Hall of Fame, sire of Buckpasser

1978 Buckpasser, 15. Racing Hall of Fame, leading broodmare sire

Preston Burch, 93. Racing Hall of Fame trainer

William L. McKnight, 90. Owner of Tartan Farms

1979 Prince John, 26. Stakes winner, leading broodmare sire

Sigmund Sommer, 62. Leading North American owner of 1971 and 1972

1980 Avelino Gomez, 51. Racing Hall of Fame jockey, rode 4,081 winners

Hoist the Flag, 12. Champion, among the leading sires

Admiral Gene Markey, 84. Master of Calumet Farm from 1950 to 1980

and turn drug-testing authority over to an arm of the United States Department of Justice. The proposed legislation was clearly unacceptable to industry leaders, who fought to retain control of their sport's destiny. They won this battle—the act languished and eventually disappeared—but the problems it outlined lived on as the warm glow of Secretariat, Slew, Affirmed, and Bid faded into memories.

NEW GAMBLING

Through good times and bad, racing's path was changing, due in part to the 1971 introduction of off-track betting in New York. As racing days in the Big Apple shot up in number between 1971 and 1980, attendance went down. Aqueduct Racetrack declined from its 1971 daily average of 27,531 to 14,767 by decade's end—a 46.4 percent slide. Belmont Park also hit the attendance skids. A commission was appointed to study New York racing, and after some analysis one panel member bluntly observed: "Belmont Park with 60,000 people is an exciting place; with 5,000 it is a graveyard." New York Racing Association (NYRA) records indicate that ballooning off-track handle siphoned more than attendance from New York tracks. Off-track betting wagers finally exceeded money wagered on track in 1977; the gap would widen thereafter.

In 1975, the Thoroughbred industry glimpsed the future when the nonracing state of Connecticut opened a state-of-the-art facility called Teletrack. This new facility provided patrons with theater seating, a 24- x 32-foot screen, and a setting in which they could comfortably watch and wager on New York races imported live via satellite signal. Teletrack was, of course, a precursor of the 1980s phenomenon of simulcasting, which in turn was the model for full-card simulcasting in the 1990s. In anticipation of a wave of new wagering options, Congress passed the 1978 Interstate Horseracing Act, allowing for legal betting between agreeing parties in different states.

By 1980, racing had come to yet another crucial crossroad, with a choice between maintaining the ways of the past or embracing technological innovations of the future. The latter option was chosen to accompany the sport of kings into the complex world of the late twentieth century.

The grandstand of the famed New Jersey track, Garden State Park, was destroyed by fire in 1977.

It was horse racing without horses . . . sanitized racing without the feel and essence of racing—but most assuredly, with the essence of gambling.

—TURF WRITER WILLIAM RUDY ON CONNECTICUT'S TELETRACK

Racing's future arrived in 1975 with the opening of the Teletrack wagering facility, in New Haven, Connecticut.

SECRETARIAT

FOR 50 YEARS, AMERICA MEASURED THE GREATNESS OF ITS racehorses against a solitary yardstick known as Man o' War. Each year, hopes soared as another young champion appeared on racing's horizon, and each year, hopes quietly died. The big red superstar of 1920 remained a towering colossus of near perfection, the best of the very best.

Perfection is what Americans yearned for in 1972, when relentless war, political scandal, and Olympic murders stripped them of their idealism. In this murky season of death and corruption, a balm was needed to soothe a collective wounded soul, and that summer it was found in a golden colt who loved to run. Man o' War's lonely vigil at the top was over. "He was the only honest thing in this country at the time," author George Plimpton later recalled of Secretariat, who in pedigree, looks, and performance, came as close to flawless as seemed possible in a mortal world.

Secretariat was foaled in Virginia on March 30, 1970, at the Meadow Stud of C. T. Chenery, and his career was capably managed by Chenery's daughter, Penny. As a son of Bold Ruler from a *Princequillo mare, his lineage paired classy speed with rugged stamina, both of which he would prove to have inherited in abundant measure. Trainer Lucien Laurin was privately dubious when the colt first appeared in his barn. The muscular chestnut moved with the metaphorical power of a locomotive, the speed of a

comet, and the grace of Baryshnikov: to the aging horseman, Secretariat seemed too good to be true. But he was real enough, and larger than life—a horse of destiny.

Between July 4, 1972, and October 28, 1973, Secretariat illuminated the American sporting scene as no horse had since Man o' War. He graced the covers of *Newsweek, Time,* and *Sports Illustrated* and drew standing-room-only crowds to the racetracks like a living, breathing magnet. He was syndicated for record millions and became the first American Triple Crown winner since Citation 25 years before.

Secretariat lost his first start after being banged around early and shoved into the rail. From then on, *he* would be the aggressor, demoralizing all rivals in his next 10 races. So impressive was Secretariat in 1972 that he was voted America's Horse of the Year, the rarest of honors for a two-year-old. In some corners, hushed comparisons were being made between the new Big Red and the old.

Measurements taken of Secretariat as a three-year-old confirmed what most already knew: he was a perfect racing machine. The tape put him at 16.3 hands, an inch taller than Man o' War at a similar age, and he measured three inches more around the girth than had the original Big Red—indicating profound heart and lung capacity.

I've never seen perfection before.

Secretariat's only point of reference is himself.

—TURF WRITER CHARLES HATTON ON SECRETARIAT

In pedigree, looks, and performance, Secretariat came as close to flawless as seemed possible in a mortal world.

I am in absolute awe of him.

—OWNER PENNY CHENERY ON SECRETARIAT

SECRETARIAT continued

He would need every millimeter of that capacity to carry him through the most amazing Triple Crown ever witnessed.

Despite his outstanding record at two, doubts remained in 1973. Bold Ruler's offspring to that point had shown speed aplenty, but not much interest in staying a classic distance early in their three-year-old seasons. Secretariat's clockings that spring only fueled the suspicion that he would not stay far. He blistered 3 furlongs one morning in :32 ⅗, faster than the track record and equaled Belmont Park's 1:33 ⅖ mile standard in the Gotham Stakes. How on earth could he sustain such speed for an additional ¼ or ½ mile?

He proved his mortal status by finishing second in the Wood Memorial with an abscessed mouth. On Kentucky Derby Day, however, Secretariat silenced doubters forever. The momentum from his mighty acceleration forced him wide on the famed turns at Churchill Downs, after which he straightened out, shifted into yet another gear, and sprinted away from a splendid colt named Sham and a future legend named Forego—in record time. Far from tiring as many had suggested he would, Secretariat actually ran the fastest final ½ mile in Derby history.

The Preakness came next, a similar story, and then the Belmont Stakes. In that now historic race, Secretariat blew out of the gate like an animal possessed and with each bounding leap demolished the classic dreams of his would-be challengers. Ron Turcotte sat immobile in the saddle as his mount barreled around the final turn and into the homestretch, at which point the jockey glanced back to look for their competition. He would have needed a telescope to find them. "Secretariat is moving like a tremendous machine!" announcer Chick Anderson shouted as Turcotte loosened a notch on the reins and asked for more. The big colt responded like no horse ever had, passing under the finish line 31 lengths in front while smashing the American record for 1½ miles. Turf journalist Charles Hatton had seen all the greats of 50 years, but could scarcely believe what he had witnessed that day. "I've never seen perfection before," he wrote. "Secretariat's only point of reference is himself."

Secretariat ran without his usual brilliance twice later that year, finishing second both times. (Some called it the curse of the Ws, for his three 1973 losses came in the Wood Memorial, Whitney, and Woodward Stakes.) In the Marlboro Cup that autumn, he found redemption while setting yet another American record at the expense of his champion older stablemate Riva Ridge. Secretariat's final two starts were on grass; he won them both.

With 16 victories in 21 races and earnings of $1,316,808, Secretariat retired in 1974 to Claiborne Farm, in Kentucky, where he resided until his death 15 years later. He did not become a great sire—that would have been impossible considering how high the bar had been set for him—but he did get 56 stakes winners, including a Horse of the Year and a double-classic winner.

Claiborne had historically been a private facility, but public demand was such after Secretariat's arrival that the Hancock family opened its gates to visitors. It was the right thing to do. Admirers streamed through those gates for years thereafter, posing proudly next to their idol as thousands of cameras clicked away. With good-natured dignity, head high, and ears to the fore, Secretariat inevitably struck a regal pose as if to say this is what greatness looks like.

Monuments and statues have since been constructed to honor the 1973 Triple Crown winner, and he has been the idealized subject of innumerable books and poems, paintings and essays. But the most touching tributes are the more personal ones, those that reside between the covers of scrapbooks and photo albums of ordinary Americans.

While flipping through such an album many years from now, one might happen across a color-faded snapshot of a big red stallion with a beaming human standing at his side, hand resting tentatively on a massive shoulder—somebody's grandfather, perhaps, or great-grandmother. And transcending time and poor image quality, this horse who meant so much to so many, will still convey as he had in life an aura of indescribable grace, a sense of destiny fulfilled.

Secretariat's defining moment in the 1973 Belmont Stakes.

RUFFIAN

"FOR ALL SAD WORDS OF TONGUE OR PEN, THE SADDEST WERE these: 'It might have been.'" So wrote poet John Greenleaf Whittier, who, had he lived a century later, could have penned that poignant line with Ruffian in mind. For a fleeting few months during the mid-1970s, this nearly black filly was everything of which dreams and legends are made, before fate cast her as a tragic heroine in one of racing's darkest moments.

Ruffian was bred and owned by Mr. and Mrs. Stuart Janney, trained by Hall of Fame horseman Frank Whiteley Jr., and like Kelso, Secretariat, and Bold Ruler, she was foaled at Claiborne Farm, that launching pad for so many twentieth century equine greats. She was a giant, literally and figuratively— physically larger than most of her sex, and faster than any of either gender. *Sports Illustrated* eventually ranked her 53rd among the top 100 female athletes of the twentieth century alongside Jackie Joyner-Kersee, Billie Jean King, and Mia Hamm. Ruffian was the only four-legged member of that elite list.

Soundness was not a hallmark of her bloodline, but every other vital quality was, and Ruffian made the most of that. Her unearthly speed transformed routine morning workouts into record-breaking exhibitions of wonderment; in the afternoons, her raging competitive spirit propelled her to 10 consecutive victories by a combined 80 lengths, setting or equaling records in every one of them, from 5½ furlongs to 1½ miles. There seemed no limit to what she could do, except, perhaps, sprout wings and fly, and surely in her eagerness to run she might have tried even that.

Trainer Whiteley was living a dream with the big filly, but it was an uneasy one with the potential to segue into a nightmare at any moment. Ruffian had no mercy to spare for her racetrack victims, nor was she likely to spare any for herself if the unthinkable ever happened. This Whitely knew, and it terrified him.

After Ruffian had crushed her opposition in the New York Filly Triple Crown of 1975, the Janneys agreed to a July 6 match race at Belmont Park against an exceptional colt named Foolish Pleasure. Because the women's liberation movement was then in full bloom, the boy-girl angle of the contest was much ballyhooed, and it was predictably promoted as the battle of the sexes. Ruffian, who was more than an inch taller and 65 pounds heavier than her Kentucky Derby–winning rival, was made the 2 to 5 favorite by an overflowing on-track crowd while 18 million television viewers tuned in, many, no doubt, hoping to witness a repeat of tennis star Billy Jean King's 1973 trouncing of Bobby Riggs. Hall of Fame jockey Eddie Arcaro predicted they'd "burn from the start." He was right. The pair left the gate like simultaneous bolts of lightning and for nearly ½ a mile it was the race one waits a lifetime to see—champion versus champion, battling furiously for the lead.

Ruffian's dark nose had pushed in front at the precise moment when her trainer's worst nightmare was realized. Both jockeys heard it, a sharp, clear sound like a board snapping in two. The filly stumbled, then instinctively grabbed the bit and ran on, as she was bred to do, as Whiteley feared she would. Any chance she had of surviving the injury to her right fore ankle was lost in those precious seconds when she ignored her rider's desperate pleas to stop.

Dr. Jim Prendergast was among those who fought and failed to save her in the agonizing hours that ensued. "She only knew one way—her way, and that was her undoing," he explained sadly. "The same thing that made her win, made her die." Ruffian was buried on July 8 in the Belmont Park infield, her handsome black head facing toward the finish line she had crossed so triumphantly only weeks before. In 1976, the Ruffian Stakes was inaugurated as tribute to this great filly who had been unbeatable but, alas, not indestructible, and who many still consider the best of all time.

The great filly Ruffian went 10 for 10 before her tragic breakdown in a 1975 match race.

The same thing that made her win, made her die.

—JIM PRENDERGAST, D.V.M.,
ON RUFFIAN'S TRAGIC END

SEATTLE SLEW

THE APPEARANCE OF A PARTICULAR DARK BAY COLT IN THE Fasig-Tipton Kentucky auction ring on July 19, 1975, did not spark unusual interest. He was good-sized, but not especially attractive, and was from a then unproven sire and dam. Veterinarian Jim Hill nevertheless saw something he liked in the sturdy son of Bold Reasoning and bid $17,500 to acquire him for Mickey and Karen Taylor, a young couple from Washington State. Thus began one of racing's most remarkable fairytale stories.

Seattle Slew was initially unimpressive. Trainer Billy Turner would recall him in those early days of training as a "big, ugly duckling," explaining why the colt was nicknamed Baby Huey, for a goofy, diapered cartoon duck of the 1950s. The name did not fit for long.

Within months, Huey had made a startling transformation from clumsy, backward youngster, to a highly concentrated bundle of competitive energy just begging to be cut loose. Hot-blooded and tightly wound, he pranced rather than walked, and his steely determination to run faster than anybody else became evident in every aggressive, hard-pounding stride he took. Slew exploded into the headlines late in 1976, winning all three of his races—including a soaring 10-length triumph in the Champagne Stakes that earned him a juvenile championship.

Excitement around the Turner barn escalated dramatically after he uncorked a record-blitzing 7-furlong sizzler in his 1977 Hialeah debut. "He's so good, it's scary," the trainer was heard to comment as Derby time approached. Author Walter Farley paid Slew a literary compliment as well, likening him to the fictional Black Stallion's intensely brilliant son, Satan.

During that unforgettable spring, Seattle Slew achieved something even the great Secretariat had not: He became America's first undefeated Triple Crown winner, sweeping the Derby, Preakness, and Belmont Stakes with varying degrees of ease, for his seventh, eighth, and ninth consecutive victories. But despite that amazing achievement, the Slew bandwagon remained half empty. Among the nonbelievers was ex-riding great Eddie Arcaro who felt Slew had beaten nothing of merit in the Triple and acknowledged him only as "the best of an ordinary lot." Others, such as trainer John Russell, disagreed. "Whether this crop is good, bad, or ordinary is irrelevant," Russell argued, "because Seattle Slew is in a class by himself."

Slew met defeat for the first time that summer in California's Swaps Stakes, a demanding test close on the heels of his rigorous Triple Crown campaign. He did not race again for 10 months, though in the interim he was crowned Horse of the Year and syndicated for a record $300,000 a share.

At four in 1978, Seattle Slew finally gained the respect he so richly deserved. In history's only meeting between American Triple Crown winners, he dominated the younger Affirmed every step of the way in the 1⅛-mile Marlboro Cup and finished just ⅖ of a second off Secretariat's world record. In the Woodward Stakes, Seattle Slew ran the fastest 1¼ miles ever recorded at Belmont Park, while outrunning a bona fide star in Exceller. And finally, Slew displayed his heart as never before in the 1½-mile Jockey Club Gold Cup—losing by inches to Exceller after engaging in an exhausting duel down the length of the Belmont stretch. Never again could anyone doubt what Seattle Slew was made of.

If he isn't a racehorse, my name's not Jim Hill.

—JIM HILL, D.V.M., ON SEATTLE SLEW AS A YEARLING

*In 1977, Seattle Slew, shown here with Jean Cruguet up,
became the first undefeated American Triple Crown winner.*

Seattle Slew closed his career with a victory in the Stuyvesant Handicap under 134 pounds, then retired to Spendthrift Farm, in Kentucky, to reside in Swaps's old stall opposite 27-year-old Nashua. Slew was later moved to Three Chimneys Farm, where the robust stallion survived to a ripe old age and carried the Bold Ruler male line proudly into a new millennium.

Over the years, the former $17,500 yearling became one of the most sought-after market sires the industry has ever known, with offspring selling at auction for as much as $4.2 million. There was good reason for his popularity: Unlike many superior racehorses, Seattle Slew bestowed an abundance of riches upon his many offspring—speed, class, heart, versatility, and will to win. His more than one hundred stakes winners included several important stallions in their own rights, sires who have done their part in passing on the miraculous genetic spark of Seattle Slew to the next generation and beyond.

TOP RUNNERS

horse and birth year	starts	wins	seconds	thirds	earnings
ACK ACK (horse) 1966	27	19	6	0	$636,641
AFFIRMED (horse) 1975	29	22	5	1	$2,393,818
ALYDAR (horse) 1975	26	14	9	1	$957,195
BOLD 'N DETERMINED (filly) 1977	20	16	2	0	$949,599
BOLD FORBES (horse) 1973	18	13	1	4	$546,536
CHRIS EVERT (filly) 1971	15	10	2	2	$679,475
*COUGAR II (horse) 1966	50	20	7	17	$1,172,625
DAHLIA (filly) 1970	48	15	3	7	$1,489,105
DAVONA DALE (horse) 1976	18	11	2	1	$641,612
DESERT VIXEN (filly) 1970	28	13	6	3	$421,538
EXCELLER (horse) 1973	33	15	5	6	$1,674,587
FOOLISH PLEASURE (horse) 1972	26	16	4	3	$1,216,705
FOREGO (gelding) 1970	57	34	9	7	$1,938,957
GENUINE RISK (filly) 1977	15	10	3	2	$646,587
LA PREVOYANTE (filly) 1970	39	25	5	3	$572,417
RIVA RIDGE (horse) 1969	30	17	3	1	$1,111,497
RUFFIAN (filly) 1972	11	10	0	0	$313,428
SEATTLE SLEW (horse) 1974	17	14	2	0	$1,208,726
SECRETARIAT (horse) 1970	21	16	3	1	$1,316,808
SPECTACULAR BID (horse) 1976	30	26	2	1	$2,781,608
SUSAN'S GIRL (filly) 1969	63	29	14	11	$1,251,668
WAJIMA (horse) 1972	16	9	5	0	$537,837

important races won	special notes
Hollywood Gold Cup, Santa Anita H., etc.	Racing Hall of Fame, Horse of the Year at five, champion sprinter and older horse
Kentucky Derby, Preakness S., Belmont S., etc.	Racing Hall of Fame, Horse of the Year at three and four, champion at two, won American Triple Crown
Florida Derby, Flamingo S., Travers S., Blue Grass S., Champagne S., etc.	Racing Hall of Fame
Coaching Club American Oaks, Spinster S., Kentucky Oaks, etc.	Racing Hall of Fame
Kentucky Derby, Belmont S., Wood Memorial S., Saratoga Special S., etc.	Champion at three
La Canada S., Hollywood Special S., etc.	Racing Hall of Fame, champion filly at three, won Filly Triple Crown
Santa Anita H., Sunset H., Century H., Californian S. (twice), etc.	Champion grass horse
Washington, D.C., International, etc.	Racing Hall of Fame, twice England's Horse of the Year, champion grass horse in U.S., first distaff millionaire
Fantasy S., Kentucky Oaks, etc.	Racing Hall of Fame, champion filly at three, won Filly Triple Crown
Beldame S. (twice), Monmouth Oaks, etc.	Racing Hall of Fame, champion at three and four
Hollywood Gold Cup, Jockey Club Gold Cup, Hollywood Invitational H., etc.	Racing Hall of Fame
Kentucky Derby, Suburban H., Hopeful S., etc.	Racing Hall of Fame, champion at two
Woodward H. (twice), Brooklyn H. (three times), etc.	Racing Hall of Fame, Horse of the Year three times
Kentucky Derby, Ruffian H., Demoiselle S., etc.	Racing Hall of Fame, champion at three
Selima S., Frizette S., etc.	Racing Hall of Fame, Canadian Horse of the Year at two, champion filly in U.S. at two, 12 for 12 as juvenile
Kentucky Derby, Belmont S., Brooklyn H., etc.	Racing Hall of Fame, champion at two and four
CCA Oaks, Mother Goose S., Acorn S., etc.	Racing Hall of Fame, champion filly at two and three, won Filly Triple Crown
Kentucky Derby, Preakness S., Belmont S., etc.	Racing Hall of Fame; champion at two, three, and four; first undefeated American Triple Crown winner
Kentucky Derby, Preakness S., Belmont S., etc.	Racing Hall of Fame, Horse of the Year at two and three, won Triple Crown
Kentucky Derby, Preakness S., Santa Anita H., etc.	Racing Hall of Fame, Horse of the Year at four, champion at two and three
Beldame S., Spinster S. (twice), etc.	Racing Hall of Fame; champion at three, four, and six; won 24 stakes
Marlboro Cup Invitational H., Travers S., Monmouth Invitational H., etc.	Champion at three

The King of Sports

The 1980s belonged to former quarter horse trainer D. Wayne Lukas, who set spectacular money records and then broke them.

WHILE THE PREVIOUS DECADE HAD BEEN DOMINATED BY great racehorses, the 1980s were fueled by big money—in the auction ring, on the track, and in the breeding shed. And as the sport went through a revival spurred by the appearance of three Triple Crown winners in the 1970s, it lured a new breed of racehorse owners, people who sought to strike it rich with the "big horse."

The dream of owning a top racehorse who could be syndicated for millions, or even tens of millions of dollars, took the sport by storm in the early part of the 1980s, a period that saw auction and syndication prices become completely detached from the true economics of racing. This bull market was in part stoked by the founding of the rich Breeders' Cup championship day event in 1984, as well as the institution of several million-dollar bonuses that could be earned by top racehorses. While it all added up to a colossal boom in the Thoroughbred market, no one could have predicted—or even imagined—exactly how high prices for untested yearlings could go before they reached their apex on a hot summer day in Lexington, Kentucky.

It was late afternoon on July 23, 1985. Excitement crackled like an electrical current through the Keeneland sales pavilion as hip number 215 appeared in front of the auctioneer's stand. He was a special colt, son of an English Triple Crown winner, half brother to an American Triple Crown winner, and looking every bit the part. Moments later, when Seattle Slew's half brother by Nijinsky II left the ring, English sportsman Robert Sangster and partners had paid a world record $13.1 million for the privilege of owning him. It was pure and, some might say, reckless speculation. One old-time trainer grumbled after the $13.1 million sale: "He might not outrun ol' Shep." Even master salesman Leslie Combs II wondered aloud if any untried baby was worth millions.

A record had been anticipated, though. Auction prices in America had gone through the roof in the early 1980s, and million-dollar milestones were eclipsed with clocklike regularity, fueled by foreign investors such as Sangster and the Maktoums of Dubai, and the platinum blood of Northern Dancer.

It was a thrilling time for America's Thoroughbred industry, especially for those playing at the top level. In 1984, 40 million-dollar yearlings were auctioned, and the lucky few who sold one of Northern Dancer's 14 sale yearlings that year received an average of $3,320,357. Like big-time stock investors then enjoying one of the strongest bull markets in Wall Street history, many industry leaders were bubbling with optimism; a sudden crash in bloodstock values just did not seem possible.

Sheikh Mohammed was a leading
top-of-the-market buyer in the 1980s.

If you want to breed, you need this blood.

—*Sheikh Mohammed bin Rashid al Maktoum on Northern Dancer*

In a market like this, every story is a positive one. Any news is good news. It's pretty much taken for granted now that the market is going to go up.

—*The* WALL STREET JOURNAL, *AUGUST 26, 1987*

Is the party over?

—*The* WALL STREET JOURNAL, *OCTOBER 26, 1987,*
AFTER 33 PERCENT STOCK-MARKET DECLINE

The $13.1-million son of Nijinsky II, later named Seattle Dancer, sold in 1985 and remains the most expensive auction yearling of all time.

*Northern Dancer's commercial appeal helped fuel
the 1980s bloodstock price boom.*

*There are two
kinds of horses—
Northern Dancers
and the rest.*

—ROBERT SANGSTER, 1983

SIGNS OF THE TIMES

1981 National debt reaches $1 trillion

First IBM personal computer retails for $4,500 and 65,000 are sold within four months

1982 U.S. unemployment reaches 10.4 percent, the highest since 1940

Time's Man of the Year is a computer

1986 Average annual salary is $15,757

1989 U.S. population is 246,819,230

1990 Minimum wage is raised to $3.80 per hour

In decade Average life span is 73.7 years

The terms *power lunch, junk bonds, insider trading, yuppie, punk rock, perestroika, cyberspace, crack, supply-side economics, dress for success,* and *corporate raider* enter popular lexicon

Popular catch phrases include: *Where's the beef? Read my lips, Just say no, I'll be back.*

But numbers overall were not adding up. The top of the market was a fantasyland, experienced by a fortunate few. Elite auction prices carried the national yearling average to a record $41,396 in that watershed year of 1984, encouraging future production of record numbers of foals—more than 50,000 annually between 1985 and 1987—too many, as it turned out, for the market to handle at inflated price levels. Stud fees had also risen sharply in response to sales prices; in 1985, a no-guarantee season to Northern Dancer was auctioned for $1 million.

The day-to-day cost of raising bloodstock zoomed upward along with stallion fees, making Thoroughbred breeding a costly endeavor. When expensively raised yearlings flooded the sales rings of the late 1980s, they were appraised by a far more conservative buying audience than had engaged in the wild bidding wars a few years before. With so many yearlings to choose from, buyers became increasingly selective, and heaven help the individual with a physical flaw or lacking Northern Dancer or Seattle Slew in the male line.

Just as the stock market would crash in 1987, so too would the Thoroughbred market, its fragile underpinnings no longer able to support such a top-heavy frame. Between 1984 and 1990, the average North American yearling sale price tumbled by nearly a third, to $29,377 (and down to $22,748 by 1992), while production expenses remained high. Financial setbacks drove a number of prominent owners and breeders out of the business in the closing years of the 1980s, including the famed Spendthrift Farm, where Triple Crown winners Affirmed and Seattle Slew had once stood at stud. While the stock market regained its lost ground in a matter of months, the bloodstock market required the better part of a decade before another significant upward trend could be noted.

PERIOD OF ADJUSTMENT

The 1980s as a whole will be remembered for the speed of technological advancements—space shuttles, artificial hearts, fetal surgeries, and personal computers. Fifty-two Americans were taken hostage in Iran and a terrorist bomb exploded in the air over Scotland. AIDS emerged from the depths of Africa to travel the globe with devastating effect. The Berlin Wall fell and the Persian Gulf erupted. Such internationally known figures as President Anwar Sadat of Egypt and Prime Minister Indira Ghandi of India were assassinated, while others such as Prince Charles and Lady Diana of England were married in front of worldwide television audiences.

For horse racing, though, the 1980s will be recalled for the instruction they provided in economics and gravity, tough lessons of supply and demand, and how what goes up will come down in due course. It was a period of adjustment and reassessment. Racing maintained its battle with corruption and race fixing—a future Racing Hall of Fame jockey served a year's suspension for alleged involvement in a 1970s bribery scandal. Exotic new designer drugs were detected in testing labs, among them etorphine, widely known as elephant juice, a painkiller far more potent than morphine but a powerful stimulant in minute traces.

So, where was the industry headed at the dawn of the 1980s? After 31 years as the nation's number one spectator sport by attendance, racing slipped to second behind baseball in 1984. Clearly, it was not keeping pace

HORSE SIGNS OF THE TIMES

1980s	232 yearlings sell for $1 million or more
1984	Northern Dancer's 14 sales yearlings average $3,320,357
	North American yearling average peaks at $41,396
1985	Foal registrations top 50,000 for the first time
1986	Foal registrations peak at 51,296
1990	North American purses almost double from 1980
	There are more than 200 equine millionaires
	Two horses have topped $6 million in earnings
	North American yearling average declines to $29,377

Do you have any rules on hay and grain? Because if you don't, don't bother me. I'm not using any drugs. I'm not going to, and I never have.

—*Racing Hall of Fame trainer Mesach Tenney, when stewards updated him on 1980s medication rules*

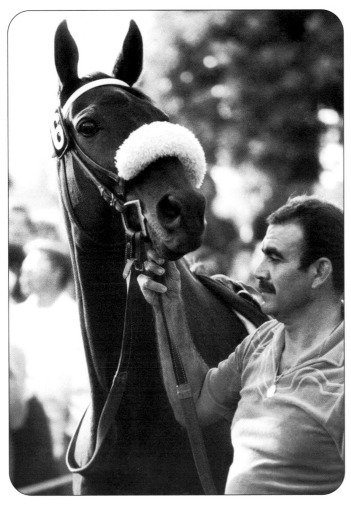

Popular gelding John Henry won two Horse of the Year titles and retired in 1985 with record earnings of $6,591,860.

in an expanding entertainment world of casinos, lotteries, and other sport wagering. Its World War II fan base was aging, and not much was being done to attract a new generation of racing enthusiasts.

The big horses of the 1970s, Triple Crown winners Secretariat, Seattle Slew, and Affirmed, had helped maintain the sport through that decade, but by the early 1980s a decline had become painfully evident. The sport tried to innovate—phone betting in Pennsylvania and intertrack simulcasting in New Jersey were two of several initiatives—but such endeavors appealed primarily to the already converted. New fans remained elusive.

BREEDERS' CUP

In 1982, horseman John Gaines had an idea. A year earlier, the Arlington Million had been inaugurated in Chicago as the world's first $1 million race. Enthusiastically received, it had drawn a field of international grass stars and was won by an all-American hero named John Henry. Could the concept be taken further? Gaines envisioned a single championship day of racing, offering millions of dollars in purse money funded through stallion and foal nomination fees. These races would attract top horses from around the world and showcase the sport in grand fashion before a vast television audience. It would be the Super Bowl of racing, a day on which, as Gaines said, "the sport of kings would become the king of sports."

Development of this idea required unprecedented cooperation among the industry's many factions, but in the end they created a dream day of racing. On November 10, 1984, at Hollywood Park, the Breeders' Cup was born. Seven races worth a total of $10 million were contested, culminating in the $3 million Breeders' Cup Classic. Five North American champions were crowned. More importantly, Thoroughbred racing enjoyed unprecedented exposure that afternoon, with four consecutive hours of coverage on a major television network, NBC. Nearly two decades later, the Breeders' Cup remained one of the sport's great success stories, a shining example of what a good idea and cooperative effort can achieve.

John Henry evolved into an overachiever, being the first to surpass $4 million in earnings,
then $5 million, and finally $6 million in earnings.

I don't care

what color he is.

—OWNER SAM RUBIN, WHEN TOLD

JOHN HENRY WAS A GELDING

BIG MONEY

Purses continued to rise, providing spectacular earnings opportunities. In 1987, Tejano became the first juvenile to earn $1 million, and by 1990 the list of equine millionaires had surged past 200, four of whom had banked more than $4 million. A leading beneficiary of this financial windfall was Dotsam Stable's John Henry, who proved once again that the American Dream was alive and well. He was a gelded son of an obscure sire, not much in the looks department, and a former $1,100 yearling who raced in claiming company before maturity radically improved him.

John Henry evolved into a supreme overachiever; beginning at age five in 1980, he won on dirt and grass everywhere he went, always against the best. John earned two Horse of the Year titles, his second in 1984 when he won four Grade 1 races and $2.3 million—a feat all the more remarkable because he was nine years old at the time. This unassuming bay was the first to surpass $4 million in earnings, then $5 million, and then $6 million, on his way to career earnings of $6,591,860. Cherished by fans in the manner of a Kelso or Forego, it was fitting that in retirement John would belong to the people as a popular main attraction at the Kentucky Horse Park.

Do you suppose we could give some of

my other horses a piece of his heart

while he's not using it to race?

—TRAINER RON MCANALLY ON JOHN HENRY

THE BEST OF THE DECADE

John Henry aside, this decade will not be known for its great runners. Not once in 10 years was the Triple Crown swept, and certainly no male runner of the era compared to the stars of the 1970s or to such luminaries as Damascus and Dr. Fager of the 1960s. In the 1980s, fillies shined brightest. Eight of the decade's thirteen Racing Hall of Fame performers, including two Horse of the Year recipients, one Kentucky Derby winner, and an undefeated champion, were members of the distaff set.

Among the best of this or any era was Ogden Phipps's Personal Ensign, who over three seasons won all of her 13 career starts, including a career-topping nose triumph over Kentucky Derby heroine Winning Colors in the 1988 Breeders' Cup Distaff. The embodiment of equine perfection, Personal Ensign retired sound and in possession of an American record unsurpassed in the twentieth century.

Through the 1980s, all of racing waited eagerly for another Ruffian to come along. Of course that was an impossible dream, but a pair of genuinely wonderful fillies did appear—fantastically talented, almost unbeatable, and, like Ruffian, doomed. Landaluce went an unchallenged 5 for 5 for trainer D. Wayne Lukas, including a 21-length, 1:08 victory in the 1982 Hollywood Lassie Stakes, before a strange and virulent infection claimed her life. Go For Wand's end was far more public, with a nightmarish feel akin to that of Ruffian in 1975. The brilliant three-year-old was struck down at the moment of her greatest glory as she streaked through the stretch of the 1990 Breeders' Cup Distaff, battling for the lead with older champion Bayakoa (Arg). Her gruesome breakdown occurred ½-furlong from home in front of packed stands and a television audience of millions.

Among the era's great distaffers who enjoyed careers unmarred by tragedy were Horse of the Year recipients All Along (Fr) and Lady's Secret; filly Triple Crown winners Mom's Command and Open Mind; Kentucky Derby winner Winning Colors; two-time Breeders' Cup Distaff winner Bayakoa; two-

Arlington Park's grandstand burned to the ground in 1985.

Four years after devastating fire, ultramodern Arlington International Race Course reopened in 1989.

time Breeders' Cup Mile heroine Miesque; and champions Princess Rooney, Life's Magic, Meadow Star, Estrapade, and Royal Heroine (Ire).

Although males of the 1980s lacked the brilliance of their female counterparts, they did provide memorable moments. Ferdinand gave 73-year-old training legend Charlie Whittingham his first Kentucky Derby victory in 1986, and in 1987 that same colt fought to the bitter end to edge Derby winner Alysheba in the Breeders' Cup Classic. The fierce 1989 rivalry between Sunday Silence and Easy Goer must rank well up any list of 1980s highlights, as would Conquistador Cielo's 14-length triumph in the 1982 Belmont Stakes, the first of trainer Woody Stephens's historic five straight wins in that classic. Kentucky Derby winner Spend a Buck drew outrage in 1985 when his owner bypassed the Preakness Stakes for a (successful) shot at a $2.6 million payday in the Jersey Derby at newly reopened Garden State Park. And then there was trainer Carl Nafzger's spontaneous televised description of Unbridled's 1990 Kentucky Derby stretch run for 92-year-old owner Frances Genter, telling her that her horse was winning America's best-known race.

If you go anywhere in America and they find out you're a horse trainer, the only thing they ask you is 'You ever win the Kentucky Derby?'

—*Charlie Whittingham, trainer of two 1980s Kentucky Derby winners*

LEADING TRAINERS

Laz Barrera
Racing Hall of Fame. Trained champions Lemhi Gold and Tiffany Lass in this decade. See also 1970s.

John P. Campo
Trained 1981 Kentucky Derby/Preakness winner Pleasant Colony. Trained earlier champions Protagonist and Talking Picture.

Neil Drysdale
Racing Hall of Fame. Trained Hall of Fame fillies Princess Rooney and Bold 'n Determined, and champion Tasso. See also 1990s.

LeRoy Jolley
Racing Hall of Fame. Trained 1980s champions Manila and Meadow Star. See also 1970s.

D. Wayne Lukas
Racing Hall of Fame. Won Eclipse Awards in 1985, 1986, and 1987. Leading money trainer seven times. Leader by wins four times. Trained Horse of the Year Lady's Secret (1986) and Criminal Type (1990). Trained 1988 Kentucky Derby winner Winning Colors. Trained ten additional 1980s champions. See also 1990s.

Ron McAnally
Racing Hall of Fame. Won Eclipse Award in 1981. Trained two-time Horse of the Year John Henry and champion Bayakoa (Arg) during 1980s. See also 1990s.

Claude "Shug" McGaughey
Won Eclipse Award in 1988. In decade, he trained undefeated champion Personal Ensign and champions Easy Goer, Rhythm, and Vanlandingham. See also 1990s.

LEADING TRAINERS

Carl Nafzger
Won Eclipse Award in 1990. Trained champion and 1990 Kentucky Derby winner Unbridled.

Flint "Scotty" Schulhofer
Racing Hall of Fame. Trained five career champions, including 1980s stars Smile and Fly So Free. See also 1990s.

Woody Stephens
Racing Hall of Fame. Won Eclipse Award in 1983. Trained five straight Belmont Stakes winners (1982–1986), including champions Conquistador Cielo and Swale. Also trained 1980s champions De La Rose, Devil's Bag, and Forty Niner. See also 1960s, 1970s.

Jack Van Berg
Racing Hall of Fame. Won Eclipse Award in 1984. Leading trainer by wins three times. Trained 1988 Horse of the Year/1987 Kentucky Derby winner Alysheba. Also trained 1984 Preakness winner Gate Dancer.

John Veitch
Trained 1980s champions Sunshine Forever and Before Dawn. See also 1970s.

Charles Whittingham
Racing Hall of Fame. Won Eclipse Awards in 1982 and 1989. Trained Kentucky Derby winners Ferdinand (1986) and Sunday Silence (1989). Also trained champions Perrault (GB) and Estrapade. See also 1970s, 1980s.

Wild Again gets decision over Gate Dancer and Slew o' Gold in the inaugural Breeders' Cup Classic.

OTHER HAPPENINGS

True racing greatness may have been hard to find in the 1980s, but it was a decade of happenings nonetheless as the sport continued to grow. Alabama, Minnesota, and Oklahoma opened new racetracks; Texas finally obtained approval for pari-mutuel racing; and Arlington Park and Garden State Park, each destroyed by fire, rose from the ashes in spectacular fashion. Triple Crown Productions was incorporated in 1985 to provide promotional services and bonus money intended to keep classic contenders from going elsewhere for lucrative opportunities, as Spend a Buck's connections had done that spring.

Immigration and Naturalization Service (INS) raids in Southern California apprehended hundreds of illegal immigrants working at racetracks and training centers, causing headaches for those who employed them.

Headline-grabbing stories that came out of such raids revealed a deeper problem within racing: substandard living conditions and an epidemic of alcoholism and drug addiction in the stable areas of America's racetracks.

Trainer D. Wayne Lukas rewrote the record books repeatedly during these years, setting and breaking his own earnings standards, and then breaking them again. Jack Van Berg in 1987 became the winningest trainer of all time with more than 5,000 victories to his credit; a year later Van Berg's best runner, Alysheba, retired as the world's richest racehorse with $6,679,242.

In the saddle, several major milestones were passed. Angel Cordero Jr. became the first $10 million jockey in 1983, and in 1989 young Kent Desormeaux rode a record 598 winners. Julie Krone's Racing Hall of Fame career flowered as the decade opened in 1981; Bill Shoemaker ended his in 1990 after having won a then record 8,789 races.

On the breeding end, in 1985 Spendthrift Farm, near Lexington, became the first Thoroughbred operation listed on the American Stock Exchange, opening at approximately $8 per share. Within a year, the farm faced lawsuits from irate investors and ex-employees, and in 1988 filed for bankruptcy as its stock plunged to 5¢ a share.

An outbreak of Equine Viral Arteritis (EVA), a highly contagious viral infection that causes spontaneous abortions in mares, created a mid-1980s scare on Blue Grass horse farms. The disease threatened the very foundation of the industry's economic well-being and led to the halting of the 1984 breeding season two weeks early by order of the Kentucky commissioner of agriculture.

In 1983, the Aga Khan's European champion Shergar was stolen by armed men in the dark of a February night at Ballymany Stud, in Ireland, causing fear and outrage in the international Thoroughbred community. He was never recovered. Genuine Risk's colt by Secretariat would have been the first offspring of two Kentucky Derby winners but was stillborn on April 4, 1983. The book closed on Northern Dancer's illustrious career as a sire when his

LEADING JOCKEYS

Angel Cordero Jr.
Racing Hall of Fame. Won Eclipse Awards in 1982 and 1983. Leading money rider in 1982 and 1983. Won 7,057 career races. Rode 1980s champions All Along, Slew o' Gold, Chief's Crown, and Gulch. Won the 1985 Kentucky Derby on champion Spend a Buck.

Pat Day
Racing Hall of Fame. Winner of Eclipse Awards in 1984, 1986, and 1987. Leading rider by wins five times in this decade. Won the Breeders' Cup Classic on Wild Again (1984) and Unbridled (1990). Won Preakness twice and the 1989 Belmont Stakes on Easy Goer.

Eddie Delahoussaye
Racing Hall of Fame. Won the 1982 and 1983 Kentucky Derby with Gato del Sol and Sunny's Halo. Rode champion Prince Rooney to win the 1984 Breeders' Cup Distaff. Won the 1989 Breeders' Cup Turf with Prized.

Kent Desormeaux
Won two of his three Eclipse Awards in this decade (1987 and 1989). Top-winning rider of 1987, 1988, and 1989, setting a single-season victory record of 598 in 1989.

Chris McCarron
Racing Hall of Fame. Leading money rider in 1981 and 1984. Won the 1987 Kentucky Derby on Alysheba and the 1986 Belmont Stakes on Danzig Connection. Rode 1980s champions John Henry, Lady's Secret, Sunday Silence, and Precisionist.

last foal arrived in March of 1988. The once-dignified Calumet Farm empire of the late Warren Wright began to crumble publicly with the intrigue-shrouded death of Alydar after a suspicious leg injury in 1990.

Moving headlong into a new era, the industry began electronically storing pedigrees, race records, and other up-to-the-minute information. Statistical research that had once required laborious effort and travel was now available instantaneously with a few clicks of a computer keyboard. The future had arrived.

LEADING JOCKEYS

Laffit Pincay Jr.
Racing Hall of Fame. Leading money rider in 1985. Won the 1984 Kentucky Derby with Swale and three consecutive Belmont Stakes (1982–1984). Also won five Breeders' Cup events in the 1980s.

Jose Santos
Won Eclipse Award in 1988. Leading money rider in 1988, setting a single-season record of $14.9 million. Rode six career Breeders' Cup winners, including champions Fly So Free, Meadow Star, Manila, and Steinlen (1981–1990).

Bill Shoemaker
Racing Hall of Fame. Won Eclipse Award in 1981. Won 8,833 races in his 41-year career that ended in 1990. World's winningest rider, until surpassed by Pincay.

Jacinto Vasquez
Racing Hall of Fame. Rode 5,231 career winners. Rode 1980s champions Princess Rooney, Smile, Manila, and Christmas Past.

Jorge Velasquez
Racing Hall of Fame. Leading 1985 stakes rider by money won. Rode 6,795 career winners, including 1981 Kentucky Derby/Preakness winner Pleasant Colony.

He's taken the lead,

Mrs. Genter. . . .

He's gonna win! . . .

He's a winner, Mrs. Genter,

he won it, he won it!

You won the Kentucky Derby, Mrs. Genter!

—*Trainer Carl Nafzger's description of Unbridled's 1990 Kentucky Derby victory to his 92-year-old owner*

STAGGERING LOSSES

The 1980s did not lack in racetrack tragedy. Top three-year-old Timely Writer broke down fatally in the 1982 Jockey Club Gold Cup. Kentucky Derby winner Swale mysteriously collapsed and died eight days after winning the 1984 Belmont Stakes. Champion Roving Boy's life ended when he broke both hind legs two bounds past the finish line of the 1983 Alibhai Handicap, which he won. And, of course, there was Go For Wand and Landaluce. On the farm, Secretariat succumbed to laminitis at age 19. A number of seemingly indestructible individuals proved mortal: 33-year-old Round Table, 34-year-old *Gallant Man, 29-year-old Northern Dancer, and 26-year-old Kelso all galloped off to greener pastures in the 1980s.

The decade took a particularly harsh toll on industry leaders. Leslie Combs II, Olin Gentry, Eugene Klein, John Hay Whitney, John Gaver, Lucille Markey, Humphrey Finney, Mrs. and Mrs. John Galbreath, E. P. Taylor, Stuart Janney Jr., John W. Hanes, Frank De Francis, Duval Headley, Walter J. Salmen, and James P. Mills were among those to whom we bid farewell—men and women who for decades had built the Thoroughbred business with their money, foresight, and enthusiasm. Such notable losses almost begged the question: Who was left? Who would be the industry masterminds of tomorrow? Who would come up with the good ideas and leadership necessary to navigate the turbulent waters that surely lay ahead? As the 1990s began, the racing industry was searching for answers.

Millions of dollars for horses is too damn much money.

—*LESLIE COMBS II*

NECROLOGY

1981 Majestic Prince, 15. Racing Hall of Fame

1982 Nashua, 30. Racing Hall of Fame

John Hay Whitney, 77. Owner of Greentree Stud

Desert Vixen, 12. Racing Hall of Fame

Landaluce, 2. Undefeated champion

John M. Gaver, 82. Racing Hall of Fame trainer of 73 stakes winners

Lucille Markey, 85. Owner of Calumet Farm

William H. P. Robertson, 62. Author, editor, and publisher of *The Thoroughbred Record*

1983 Exclusive Native, 18. Leading North American sire of 1978 and 1979

Kelso, 26. Racing Hall of Fame, five-time Horse of the Year

1984 James P. Conway, 73. Racing Hall of Fame trainer

Humphrey Finney, 81. Noted horseman and author

James Maloney, 74. Racing Hall of Fame trainer

Swale, 3. Champion, winner of the Kentucky Derby and Belmont S.

Sherrill Ward, 72. Racing Hall of Fame trainer

1985 John A. Morris, 93. Jockey Club steward

Riva Ridge, 16. Racing Hall of Fame, classic winner

1986 Shuvee, 20. Racing Hall of Fame

1987 Duval Adams Headley, 77. Trained 23 stakes winners, bred 29 stakes winners

Don MacBeth, 37. Rode 2,764 winners

James P. Mills, 78. Bred 30 stakes winners

Round Table, 33. Racing Hall of Fame, among the leading sires

NECROLOGY

1988 Dr. Eslie Asbury, 92. Author, bred more than 40 stakes winners

John Galbreath, 90. Owner of Darby Dan Farm, bred and raced Kentucky Derby and English Derby winners

*Gallant Man, 34. Racing Hall of Fame, classic winner

Graustark, 25. Stakes winner of 7 of 8 starts, among the leading sires

John W. Hanes, 95. First chairman of NYRA

Stuart Janney Jr., 81. Bred 24 stakes winners, including Ruffian

Haden Kirkpatrick, 76. Long-time publisher of *The Thoroughbred Record*

Raise a Native, 27. Undefeated champion at two, among the leading sires

Roberto, 19. Champion in Ireland and England, among the leading sires

Susan's Girl, 19. Racing Hall of Fame, three-time Eclipse Award winner, first American-raced distaff millionaire

1989 Frank De Francis, 62. Moving force in Maryland racing

Secretariat, 19. Racing Hall of Fame, American Triple Crown winner

E. P. Taylor, 88. Owner of Windfields Farm, bred more than 320 stakes winners, including Northern Dancer and Nijinsky II

1990 Alydar, 15. Racing Hall of Fame, leading sire of 1990

Leslie Combs II, 88. Master of Spendthrift Farm, noted syndicator and market breeder

Go For Wand, 3. Champion at two and three

Northern Dancer, 29. Racing Hall of Fame, leading international sire

Trainer Woody Stephens leads Swale with jockey Laffit Pincay Jr. up as they celebrate their 1984 Belmont Stakes victory. Eight days later, the double classic winner died following a routine gallop.

JOHN HENRY

THIS IS THE STORY OF A HORSE NOBODY WANTED, AT LEAST IN THE beginning. He was as plain as could be, solid brown with no white ornamentation, and undersized with legs that looked like trouble waiting to happen. His pedigree was maybe a 1 on a 10-point scale—his sire was an obscure $900 stallion, his dam from a family of little merit. Worst of all was his attitude. He came to the track with little enough promise, then had the audacity to reveal himself as a groom-biting, stall-kicking, bucket-smashing terror, possessed of arrogance far beyond what his plebian pedigree should have allowed as tolerable.

He changed hands several times in those early years, selling once for $1,100 and again for $2,200 before being surgically stripped of his manhood and entered five times in claiming company with no takers. Yet, like any true fairytale, this one took a happy turn when the beast in question ended up in the hands of a wizard who, with a horseman's magic wand of patience and knowledge, turned him into a beauty—of sorts.

John Henry was named for the legendary nineteenth century steel-driving man who did not know the meaning of the word *quit*. How apt this name would be, no one could have guessed as this ill-natured gelding was being tossed among owners like a scalding potato. In 1978, he began revealing brief glimpses of a talent previously unnoted, and when New York bicycle importer Sam Rubin looked to stock a one-horse racing stable, it was John Henry who landed in his barn for $25,000. When Rubin later placed him in the care of trainer Ron McAnally, John Henry's fate was sealed.

John's aptitude for grass racing was discovered that year, thus bringing to a screeching halt the gelding's headlong plummet into an abyss of anonymity. In relatively short order thereafter, he was transformed from unwanted claimer into one of the most beloved of American racehorses.

Five-year-old John Henry came into his own in 1980 with six important stakes victories in a row. He was just getting started. By age six, when most top racehorses are either over-the-hill or out to pasture, John had never been better. He won six Grade 1 races that year—four on grass and two on dirt—and the distinctive white shadow roll he wore on his bridle

became a familiar sight at racetracks across America as he bobbed and wove his way through fields in patented come-from-behind fashion. His amazing last second victory in the 1981 Arlington Million would later be immortalized at Arlington International Race Course with a bronze statue of John Henry and The Bart locked in a fierce battle to the finish. It was entitled *Against All Odds*.

The racing public had by now developed a passion for the tough little gelding and couldn't get enough of him. They loved everything about him— his pride, his willingness, his iron heart. They loved how he stopped in the post parade to gaze thoughtfully back at them, and how in competition he invariably gave his best. Even when his best was not good enough, they loved him.

John Henry was popularly acclaimed Horse of the Year in 1981 after which his stature slowly began to slip. John's 1982 and 1983 campaigns were of Grade 1 caliber but did not measure up to that golden season of 1981. He ran less often, won fewer races, earned less money. It looked like Father Time would, after all, overtake this seemingly ageless, indomitable spirit.

Thus, 1984 came as a surprise to just about everyone, and certainly gave cause for celebration among the aged and aging. At nine, John was a veritable Methuselah in racehorse terms. The great Exterminator had been washed up by that point; Kelso was finished; Forego had been retired. John Henry, however, seemed to defy the passage of time—he was better in 1984 than he had ever been at any point in his remarkable life. He won four Grade 1 races that season, banked a whopping $2,336,860, and set or equaled two course records. When asked how this was possible, McAnally shook his head and replied, "Only the Almighty knows." *Daily Racing Form*'s fabled columnist Joe Hirsch likened John's 1984 season to "Pete Rose winning all the batting championships at age 60. Things like that are just not done in sports." While gunning for the inaugural Breeders' Cup Turf that autumn, John proved mortal when he suffered a ligament injury that would eventually end his fairytale career.

John Henry (outside) edges The Bart in the historic first running of the Arlington Million, in 1981.

Horse of the Year is traditionally announced at the annual Eclipse Awards ceremony. Many in 1984 assumed the title would go to a top four-year-old named Slew o' Gold, with one newspaper even announcing in a premature headline that Slew had won. But when Thoroughbred Racing Associations's president Ted Bassett opened the Horse of the Year envelope that night at the Century Plaza Hotel, in Los Angeles, and spoke the words: "Like fine wine," the crowd of racing dignitaries went joyously wild.

Temperamental he may have been, but John Henry was among the few goodwill ambassadors for his sport, and the attention he received from mainstream media outlets put him in a league with Secretariat himself. *Reader's Digest* ran a four-page article on the life of John Henry. *People* magazine named him one of their 25 "most intriguing" personalities of 1984 along with Ronald Reagan and Michael Jackson. John's human-interest appeal stepped far beyond racing's provincial boundaries and into the larger world.

John attempted comebacks at ages 10 and 11, each foiled by flare-ups of the old injury. He was not made of steel, after all. Finally, and with much fanfare, he was sent to live alongside three-time Horse of the Year Forego in the Kentucky Horse Park's Hall of Champions, where fans visited him by the thousands into the new millennium. He was, said Hirsch at a 1985 black-tie dinner honoring John, "the most remarkable horse who ever raced."

John Henry's record was, indeed, amazing. He stayed at the top of his game longer than any outstanding racehorse of the past century, perhaps of any century, winning 39 races, 16 Grade 1 events, two Horse of the Year titles, and four grass championships. He established a world earnings record of $6,591,860 and ultimately found his way into the Racing Hall of Fame. He was that "glorious uncertainty" that the great horseman John Madden spoke of so long ago, the kind who makes racing "the most exciting and exhilarating sport in the world."

PERSONAL ENSIGN

"LADY, WHAT IN HELL ARE YOU DOING NOW? YOU'RE SO FAR behind in the biggest race of your life, that people can't find you with a search warrant. . . . Now you're moving? This late? Who do you think you are, the immortal Person o' War?" So wrote the late, great turf journalist William Leggett in the November 11, 1988, *Thoroughbred Times,* describing Personal Ensign's desperate, seemingly hopeless flight through the final furlongs of the 1988 Breeders' Cup Distaff. The filly who had never known defeat was scrambling madly over a track surface she clearly did not like; and as the finish line loomed ever closer, only a big, gray Kentucky Derby winner stood between her and immortality. With a mighty lunge in the last stride of the million-dollar race, Personal Ensign thrust her bay nose in front of Winning Colors and into the history books, where she will live forever as one of the queens of sport.

Undefeated racehorses are not unusual; countless have retired after winning one start, or two or three. Such records don't prove much beyond exceptional precocity or luck. But Personal Ensign was no flash-in-the-pan. She belonged instead to an extraordinary league of Thoroughbreds, whose very names bring a tingle of pleasure to racing historians—horses such as European champions *Ribot, *Ormonde, and Nearco, flawless performers over extended periods of time. With victories in each of her 13 starts during three seasons of racing, Ogden Phipps's homebred filly, Personal Ensign, ended her career in possession of the longest unbeaten American winning streak since the great Colin 80 years before.

Between 1986 and 1988, Kentucky Derby winners and male champions could not beat Personal Ensign. Nor could track condition, injury, or simple bad luck. She never had an off day, never once decided she wasn't in the mood to run, never threw in an inexplicable clinker, never required an excuse of any kind.

Personal Ensign ran twice at age two in 1986 before a cracked hind pastern put her under the surgeon's knife. Five implanted screws and 11 months later she was back, as good as ever—or better. Four times she raced and won in 1987, but all of those starts were contested at New York's Belmont Park, and cynics began to wonder if she was merely a one-track marvel. They got their answer the following season.

In 1988, trainer Claude "Shug" McGaughey continued to base the now four-year-old filly in the Empire State where she won five important stakes and handicaps—including the Whitney—over top males. Twice, however, Shug took her on the road where she continued her flawless ways in New Jersey's Molly Pitcher Handicap and in the aforementioned Breeder's Cup Distaff at Churchill Downs, thereby silencing the naysayers once and for all.

Unlike the flamboyant Ruffian of 13 years earlier, Personal Ensign walked off the racetrack on four sound legs and into retirement following the Distaff, unbeaten dignity intact. The phenomenal race mare went on to become an equally phenomenal producer—America's 1996 Broodmare of the Year, in fact. This supreme overachiever did everything ever asked of her, and did it better than anybody else of her era, on the racetrack and at the breeding farm. She was a great one.

Who do you think you are, the immortal Person o' War?

—TURF JOURNALIST WILLIAM LEGGETT

Personal Ensign (left) ran down Kentucky Derby winner Winning Colors in the 1988
Breeders' Cup Distaff and retired with a 13 for 13 record.

SUNDAY SILENCE

FATE HAS A CURIOUS SENSE OF HUMOR AS FAR AS HORSE RACING is concerned. It may create unexpected giants in a John Henry or a Kelso, while often turning its back on those born with all the obvious advantages. How else do we explain why some colts worth millions achieve little of lasting note, while a $17,000 auction reject becomes one of racing's great competitors?

Such a story began at the 1987 Keeneland July sale, where four royally bred, beautifully conformed yearlings sold for a combined $11 million. Few in Keeneland's sophisticated crowd that week even noticed destiny's true favorite, a nearly black colt who had scored poorly on the conformation scale and whose pedigree was not high fashion. Their indifference sent him home a $17,000 buy-back from a sale that averaged $400,000. Fate was in an ironic mood, however, for while those multimillion-dollar beauties eventually banked about $110,000 each in racetrack earnings, the unwanted one galloped into the Racing Hall of Fame with a cool $5 million.

Arthur Hancock III had raised the son of Halo at his Stone Farm, near Paris, Kentucky. Though not the official breeder—that honor went to Oak Cliff Thoroughbreds—Hancock ended up with title to the colt following the Keeneland nonsale. After trying again without success to sell him at a 1988 two-year-olds-in-training auction, then nearly losing him in a highway van accident, Hancock persuaded Hall of Fame trainer Charlie Whittingham to buy into the unsellable prospect. This would make all the difference for the colt named Sunday Silence.

A wise, infinitely patient septuagenarian and one of the finest horsemen who ever lived, Whittingham soon recognized what others had missed—this colt could run. Whittingham took his time, running Sunday Silence lightly at two, then in 1989 unleashed a titan on the racing world. He was simply awesome in California that winter. After the colt's devastating 11-length romp in the Santa Anita Derby, Whittingham set his sights on Kentucky and the New York phenomenon Easy Goer.

The two made for great media. They were enormously talented, but physical opposites—Easy Goer, a muscular, red-coated Adonis with a glamour pedigree; Sunday Silence, lean, leggy, and dark as night—a contrast that added spice to an unforgettable classic season. Sunday Silence struck the first blow, weaving erratically through the final furlongs of the Kentucky Derby before dashing under the wire 2½ lengths in front of Easy Goer. In the Preakness Stakes two weeks later, sheer grit carried Sunday Silence to a much narrower victory over the same opponent. Easy Goer's shining moment came on June 10 in the Belmont Stakes, when he breezed home 8 lengths ahead of Whittingham's colt. The great rivalry ended that November in the Breeders' Cup Classic with Sunday Silence holding off Easy Goer in a free-running battle to the wire, thus giving Sunday Silence a 3-to-1 edge. As 1989 Horse of the Year, he had established a single-season earnings record of $4,578,454.

Whittingham was known to compare horses to strawberries—an odd but apt analogy. "You must enjoy them while you can," he said, "because they don't last long." Sunday Silence was proof of this. The champion lasted just 2 starts into his third campaign before a ligament injury ended his career. He had never finished worse than second in 14 starts, and his lifetime bankroll of $4,968,554 placed him third among international money winners, behind only Alysheba and John Henry.

It was a dark day for America's Thoroughbred industry when Sunday Silence was sold in 1990 to a Japanese breeder and sent to live on the island of Hokkaido. The black stallion who had twice been rejected at public auction in the United States became a perennial leading sire and a national icon in the Land of the Rising Sun. Kentucky has had a long tradition of bringing home the world's top stallion prospects to perpetuate their genes in the Blue Grass. Sunday Silence reversed that trend. He was the big one that got away.

Sunday Silence (#8) edged out Easy Goer in the 1989 Preakness Stakes.

horse and birth year	starts	wins	seconds	thirds	earnings
ALL ALONG (Fr) (filly) 1979	21	9	4	2	$2,125,809
ALYSHEBA (horse) 1984	26	11	8	2	$6,679,242
BAYAKOA (Arg) (filly) 1984	39	21	9	0	$2,861,701
CHIEF'S CROWN (horse) 1982	21	12	3	3	$2,191,168
CONQUISTADOR CIELO (horse) 1979	13	9	0	2	$474,328
EASY GOER (horse) 1986	20	14	5	1	$4,873,770
FERDINAND (horse) 1983	29	8	9	6	$3,777,978
GO FOR WAND (filly) 1987	13	10	2	0	$1,373,338
JOHN HENRY (gelding) 1975	83	39	15	9	$6,591,860
LADY'S SECRET (filly) 1982	45	25	9	3	$3,021,325
LANDALUCE (filly) 1980	5	5	0	0	$372,365
LIFE'S MAGIC (filly) 1981	32	8	11	6	$2,255,218
MIESQUE (filly) 1984	16	12	3	1	$2,070,163
OPEN MIND (filly) 1986	19	12	2	2	$1,844,372
PERSONAL ENSIGN (filly) 1984	13	13	0	0	$1,679,880
PRECISIONIST (horse) 1981	46	20	10	4	$3,485,398
PRINCESS ROONEY (filly) 1980	21	17	2	1	$1,343,339
SLEW O' GOLD (horse) 1980	21	12	5	1	$3,533,534
SPEND A BUCK (horse) 1982	15	10	3	2	$4,220,689
SUNDAY SILENCE (horse) 1986	14	9	5	0	$4,968,554
SWALE (horse) 1981	14	9	2	2	$1,583,660
UNBRIDLED (horse) 1987	24	8	6	6	$4,489,475
WINNING COLORS (filly) 1985	19	8	3	1	$1,526,837

important races won	special notes
Washington, D.C., International, Turf Classic, etc.	Racing Hall of Fame, Horse of the Year at four
Kentucky Derby, etc.	Racing Hall of Fame, Horse of the Year at four, champion at three, leading money winner
Breeders' Cup Distaff (twice), Spinster S., etc.	Racing Hall of Fame, champion mare at four and five
Breeders' Cup Juvenile, Marlboro Cup H., Travers S., Blue Grass S., etc.	Champion at two
Belmont S., Metropolitan H., Dwyer S., etc.	Horse of the Year at three
Belmont S., Jockey Club Gold Cup, Travers S., etc.	Racing Hall of Fame, champion at two
Kentucky Derby, Breeders' Cup Classic, Hollywood Gold Cup Handicap, etc.	Horse of the Year at four
Breeders' Cup Juvenile Fillies, Beldame S., etc.	Racing Hall of Fame, champion filly at two and three
Arlington Million, Santa Anita H., etc.	Racing Hall of Fame, twice Horse of the Year, four-time grass champion, won 30 stakes, leading money winner
Breeders' Cup Distaff, Whitney H., Beldame S., etc.	Racing Hall of Fame, Horse of the Year at four
Oak Leaf S., Del Mar Debutante, Hollywood Lassie S., Anoakia S.	Champion at two
Breeders' Cup Distaff, Mother Goose S., Beldame S., etc.	Champion at three and four
Breeders' Cup Mile (twice)	Racing Hall of Fame, champion U.S. grass horse twice
Breeders' Cup Juvenile Fillies, Alabama S., etc.	Champion filly at two and three, won Filly Triple Crown
Breeders' Cup Distaff, Beldame S. (twice), Whitney H., etc.	Racing Hall of Fame, champion at four
Breeders' Cup Sprint, Woodward S., Californian S., Swaps S., etc.	Champion sprinter at four
Breeders' Cup Distaff, Spinster S., etc.	Racing Hall of Fame, champion at four
Jockey Club Gold Cup, Marlboro Cup Invitational H., etc.	Racing Hall of Fame, champion at three and four
Kentucky Derby, Monmouth H., Arlington-Washington Futurity, etc.	Horse of the Year at three
Kentucky Derby, Preakness S., Breeders' Cup Classic, Santa Anita Derby, etc.	Racing Hall of Fame, Horse of the Year at three
Kentucky Derby, Belmont S., Florida Derby, Futurity S.	Champion at three
Kentucky Derby, Breeders' Cup Classic, Florida Derby, etc.	Champion at three
Kentucky Derby, Santa Anita Derby, etc.	Racing Hall of Fame, champion filly at three

ALL WINDOWS SELL

NTRA

Go Baby Go™

NATIONAL THOROUGHBRED

NTRA

NATIONAL THOROUGHBRE

A Revolutionary Ending

After a century of strife and struggle,

significant changes occur in

the sport of kings.

S THE FINAL DECADE OF THE TWENTIETH CENTURY began, horse racing in America found itself in a rather disheartening position. It was no longer the number one spectator sport, no longer capable of drawing huge weekend crowds for anything other than a handful of events, and no longer the only gambling game in town. Its old-time glamour had faded, its bloodstock markets were in disarray, and the sport generally was caught in a cash crunch with costs rising and revenues declining.

Horse racing was born centuries earlier along country back roads, with one man matching his steed against that of another for a friendly wager. The sport matured into a highly organized, big money enterprise, the popularity of which seemed to peak in America during the middle years of this century—and then to slowly wane. By the 1990s, racing was struggling for survival in a crassly commercial, technologically charged culture, where attention spans were short and entertainment options many. But with some creativity and a few rare moments of unanimity, the ancient sport of kings somehow managed to hold on—bloodied yet still on its feet as a new millennium approached.

CHANGE, CHANGES

Every new era brings change, but racing in the 1990s rode a veritable tsunami of the new and different. While some changes were regrettable—such as the continuing decline of on-track attendance—others enabled the sport to adapt. Perhaps the most forceful impact on horse racing in these years came from the dizzying expansion of legal gambling. America's appetite and legislative tolerance for gaming were on the increase during the 1990s as casinos, riverboats, card clubs, all-sports betting facilities, state lotteries, and video poker machines began to appear everywhere.

Racing's leaders generally had neither the will nor the resources to buy into alternative forms of gaming. As a result, racing's share of the United States legal gambling market diminished from a virtual monopoly in the first half of the century to a 9 percent sliver—and dropping—in 1992. It was only a matter of time before certain enterprising members of the racing community adopted an "if you can't beat 'em, join 'em" posture. Led by R. D. Hubbard, Hollywood Park transformed a white elephant clubhouse structure into a card club—a gambling form already permitted under California law.

In the mid-1990s, some tracks facing extinction gained legislative approval for other forms of gambling. Delaware Park, 1½ hours from Atlantic City's casinos, opened a slots pavilion in 1995, a few months after slots had been installed at Prairie Meadows Racetrack, in Iowa. New Mexico and West Virginia also authorized slot machines at the states' tracks in the late 1990s, and some tracks in Louisiana were scheduled to have slots as the new century dawned.

But the major business development in horse racing of the 1990s was full-card simulcasting in which entire racing programs from a track were beamed by satellite to tracks around the country. These expanded pari-mutuel opportunities began slowly with a track offering three or four other betting cards. By mid-decade, though, most tracks had the ability to send and receive signals, and every track or off-track facility became a race book. By the late 1990s, it was not unusual for one track to offer as many as 20 additional signals.

What we are witnessing in American racing today is disgraceful. In order to attract the best horses, racing secretaries are being forced to weight them lightly or kiss them goodbye.

—TURF WRITER KELSO STURGEON, 1991

SIGNS OF THE TIMES

1991 245 Americans out of 1,000 own computers

1999 Dow breaks 10,000 for first time

2000 Average family median income is $50,200

580 Americans out of 1,000 own computers

Unemployment is the lowest in three decades, dropping to 3.9 percent from 7.5 percent in 1991

In decade Average home sells for $121,000, compared to $64,000 in 1980

Minimum wage is raised from $4.25 to $5.15 per hour

The terms *Global warming, Y2K, going postal, on-line, e-mail, Generation X,* and *information superhighway* enter popular lexicon

Popular catch phrases include: *If it doesn't fit, you must acquit; It's the economy, stupid; Been there, done that;* and *Is that your final answer?*

Where a bettor once watched a live race every 25 minutes, he or she could now bet on a race every 3 minutes.

The full-card explosion transformed horse race gambling—potential payoffs often dictated wagers rather than painstaking handicapping of a single race—and it forever altered the sport. At one time, a track and its horsemen had to live or die on money bet on the track's live races. With full-card simulcasting, track revenues were augmented by money bet on other tracks' races and by wagers on its own races at other locations. By mid-decade, off-site wagering accounted for 74 percent of racing's handle, a figure that jumped to 82 percent by 1999. There was a practical upside to this depersonalization of the sport. By making pari-mutuel wagering more accessible to a vastly larger audience, racing's gambling base broadened overall. From this came another advantage. As former Santa Anita Park General Manager Lonny Powell put it, "The world of simulcast and off-track betting has been an outstanding source of purses. At the end of the day, it's not how the bucket is filled. As long as handle grows, that's how the industry will develop."

Handle did grow and so did purses. In 1999, gross North American purse money topped $1 billion for the first time. Spectacular equine earnings records were established as America got its first $3 million fillies and came within a few dollars of witnessing a $10 million earner.

You can't live at the temple of regret in this game. You must always dwell on the positives—the negatives will eat you alive.

—*Trainer D. Wayne Lukas*

One-armed bandits helped save racing at several troubled tracks throughout the country.

Thoroughbred racing and casino gambling have never in the United States been able to coexist at a profit for racing.

—CHARLES W. BIDWILL, PRESIDENT OF SPORTSMAN'S PARK, 1993

Storm Cat reigned supreme with both breeders and buyers.

GO BABY GO!

Full-card simulcasting provided the economic wherewithal for another major change, a national office to promote racing, much as the National Basketball Association had guided the growth of professional basketball. In 1996, Lexington ad executive Fred Pope and breeder John Gaines proposed an industry alliance to revitalize the sport and create a "major league of racing." Their National Thoroughbred Association, an owner-driven organization, was soon swallowed up by the National Thoroughbred Racing Association (NTRA), which was launched with $4 million in start-up funds from Breeders' Cup, Ltd; the Jockey Club; National Thoroughbred Association; and the Keeneland and Oak Tree Racing Associations.

The NTRA opened its league office in April of 1998 and hired Tim Smith as commissioner. Its initial focus was to create a series of national advertising campaigns for racing. The first of these was the famous—or infamous—series of ads featuring actress Lori Petty, wherein an androgynous racing fan paced frantically while clutching mutuel tickets and repeatedly screaming the NTRA tag line, "Go baby go!" This new-wave approach was not what racing's elite had in mind to promote their dignified sport of kings, but apparently it connected with a broader audience. According to surveys, those ads actually succeeded in raising positive public awareness of horse racing.

HORSE SIGNS OF THE TIMES

1992 Racing's share of the gambling market declines from 21 percent in 1982 to 9 percent

Total auction revenues are down for the fifth straight year

1995 Japanese buyers account for 65 percent of total sales at Barretts March auction of two-year-olds in training

Mid-decade Live racing accounts for 42 percent of racing's total handle

1998 Simulcasting accounts for 80 percent of handle

1999 The national yearling auction average rebounds to a record $51,210

The number of annual starters decreases to 68,435 from 86,483 in 1991

Total auction sales reach an all-time record $970 million, up 113 percent from 1990

Televised racing totals 137 hours, up from 94 in 1997

It's hard to die on the racetrack, because you're always trying to hang around for the good thing that runs tomorrow.

—JOURNALIST/COMMENTATOR PETE AXTHELM, WHO DIED IN 1991 AT 47

The world of simulcast and off-track betting has been an outstanding source of purses. At the end of the day, it's not how the bucket is filled. As long as handle grows, that's how the industry will develop.

—*Lonny Powell, then president of Santa Anita Park*

Increased television coverage, beyond the Triple Crown and Breeders' Cup, was also key to promoting racing in the 1990s. The American Championship Racing Series (ACRS) in the early 1990s and later the NTRA Champions series on Fox at the end of the decade showcased important races in entertaining fashion. In 1999, horse racing was allotted 137 hours of major airtime—up nearly one-third from 1997. Also in 1999, full-time racing channels, Television Games Network (TVG) and The Racing Network (TRN), debuted on satellite.

Other industry efforts to promote and/or improve itself included the Thoroughbred Racing Associations's development of the National Pic 6, a multirace wager on races conducted at six tracks across the country, and its ill-conceived hiring of a highly paid racing "commissioner," who possessed little actual authority and achieved virtually nothing of importance during his relatively brief tenure. America's Day at the Races was a promotional vehicle of the Thoroughbred Owners and Breeders Association, offering an annual afternoon of family oriented entertainment at racetracks across the country.

While it was an era of innovation in American racing, results were mixed. The ACRS and NTRA Champions series on Fox were not renewed by their networks; TRA's commissioner was gone within a year; and the long-term viability of NTRA, TVG, and TRN remains to be seen.

MARKET REBOUND

The American bloodstock market continued its cyclical ways, reflecting the economy at large. Auction prices of the early 1990s continued along the same depressing downward path that had marked the closing years of the previous decade. By 1993, however, the pendulum began to swing the other way, sparked by a strengthening U.S. economy, declining unemployment, a soaring stock market, rock-bottom stud fees, and continuing interest in American horses on the part of foreign buyers.

Million-dollar-plus yearlings reappeared in the sales rings in increasing numbers. Yearling averages edged up toward levels of the mid-1980s until a record $51,210 was attained in 1999—almost dead even with the median American family income of $50,200. Total auction receipts of $970 million in 1999 were up 113 percent from 1990, representing yet another all-time record. While the 1985 world yearling record of $13.1 million was not threatened, a decade-high $6.8 million was paid for a Storm Cat colt at the 2000 Keeneland September sale. He was one of 56 yearlings to surpass the $1 million mark that year.

Stallion valuations also headed up. Leading 1999 sire Storm Cat covered 118 mares in 2000 at a $300,000 stud fee, while lightly raced but regally bred Fusaichi Pegasus commanded a record $60 million to $70 million as a stallion prospect.

BEST OF THE ERA

High-priced horses and illustrious pedigrees may have illuminated the sales rings of the 1990s, but, for the most part, they did not dominate the racing scene. In fact, several of the decade's best runners came from relatively modest backgrounds. A trio of sensational grays—Holy Bull, Silver Charm, and Skip Away—and Allen Paulson's marvelous bay Cigar captured the imagination of the racing public. Together they won classics, championships, and $30 million but were sired by stallions who had stood for average reported fees of just $7,800.

It was an exciting classics decade, and despite the absence of a Triple Crown winner, racing got the next best thing each spring between 1997 and 1999. In all three of those years a single standout emerged to generate good will and massive publicity for the sport by winning the Kentucky Derby and Preakness Stakes, only to lose a heartbreaker in the Belmont Stakes. Two of these double-crown winners, Real Quiet and Silver Charm, introduced American racing to a character named Bob Baffert, a white-maned ex–quarter horse trainer who charmed fans and media alike with outrageous humor, forthright comments, and a ridiculous Austin Powers impersonation.

LEADING TRAINERS

Bob Baffert
Won Eclipse Awards in 1997, 1998, and 1999. Leading money trainer in 1998, 1999, and 2000. Trained two Kentucky Derby winners in decade: Silver Charm (1997) and Real Quiet (1998). Also trained champions Silverbulletday and Chilukki.

Warren A. "Jimmy" Croll
Racing Hall of Fame. Trained 1994 Horse of the Year Holy Bull and champion Housebuster.

Neil Drysdale
Racing Hall of Fame. Trained 1992 Horse of the Year A.P. Indy, 2000 Kentucky Derby winner Fusaichi Pegasus, and champions Hollywood Wildcat and Fiji (GB). See also 1980s.

Robert Frankel
Racing Hall of Fame. Won Eclipse Awards in 1993 and 2000. Trained 1990s champions Bertrando, Possibly Perfect, Ryafan, and Wandesta (GB).

Hubert "Sonny" Hine
Trained 1998 Horse of the Year Skip Away.

D. Wayne Lukas
Racing Hall of Fame. Won Eclipse Award in 1994. Leading money trainer five times in decade. Trained Kentucky Derby winners Thunder Gulch (1995) and Charismatic (1999). Trained seven additional champions, including Serena's Song. See also 1980s.

LEADING TRAINERS

Richard Mandella
Racing Hall of Fame. Trained 1993 Horse of the Year Kotashaan (Fr); champion Phone Chatter; and major winners Soul of the Matter, Atticus, Gentlemen (Arg), Siphon (Brz), Sandpit (Brz), and Puerto Madero (Chi).

Ron McAnally
Racing Hall of Fame. Won Eclipse Awards in 1991 and 1992. Trained two-time champion Paseana (Arg) and champion grass horses Tight Spot and Northern Spur (Ire) in decade. See also 1980s.

Claude "Shug" McGaughey
In 1990s, he trained champions Queena, Inside Information, and Heavenly Prize. See also 1980s.

William Mott
Racing Hall of Fame. Won Eclipse Awards in 1995 and 1996. Trained two-time Horse of the Year Cigar and 1990s champions Escena, Ajina, and Paradise Creek.

Flint "Scotty" Schulhofer
Racing Hall of Fame. Trained 1990s champions Lemon Drop Kid and Rubiano. See also 1980s.

Nick Zito
Trained Kentucky Derby winners Strike the Gold (1991) and Go for Gin (1994), champion Storm Song, and 1996 Preakness winner Louis Quatorze.

Sold as a yearling for $4 million, Fusaichi Pegasus was later valued at $70 million.

Most dramatic of the three near misses came in 1999, when a beautiful one-time claimer named Charismatic, trained by D. Wayne Lukas, made a bid for history in the stretch run of the Belmont Stakes only to break down near the finish. Jockey Chris Antley clung to the frightened colt while holding the damaged foreleg off the ground, a quick-thinking act that may have saved the champion's life—and one that provided racing with a poignantly bittersweet moment that would not be soon forgotten.

The era's crowning equine achievement, however, belonged not to a member of the classic set but to an older runner whose early career had branded him as mediocre at best. But like Seabiscuit and John Henry before him, Cigar was a late bloomer who improved with age—and with a major switch in his racing regimen. Though his pedigree said grass, the contrarious colt felt otherwise. After switching from turf to dirt on October 28, 1994, Cigar went on a winning tear that ultimately equaled the great Citation's modern American record for consecutive victories. During a 21-month span through July 13, 1996, the handsome horse started 16 times and won them all.

Cigar's overall record was not that of a truly great runner—he lost 14 of his 32 career starts. But if the many early grass races are expunged from his record, the tally looks quite a bit more impressive: 18 wins, 2 seconds, and 1 third from 22 dirt starts. Upon his retirement in 1996, the son of Palace Music boasted $9,999,815 in earnings, an American record into the new millennium.

Paulson turned down a $30 million offer for Cigar from Japanese interests before accepting a less-lucrative deal to keep the two-time Horse of the Year in the United States for stud duty. It was fruitless bargaining, for the champion proved to be hopelessly infertile. Cigar presently resides at the Kentucky Horse Park near another two-time Horse of the Year, John Henry.

On the distaff side, no race mare of the 1990s could top Bob and Beverly Lewis's Serena's Song. After bearing witness to the tragic breakdowns of Ruffian, Go For Wand, and others, American racing fans were ready for this iron lady, who started 38 times, won 17 stakes—including 11 in Grade 1 company—twice beat top males, and finally retired with filly earnings record of $3,283,388.

LEADING JOCKEYS

Jerry Bailey
Racing Hall of Fame. Won four Eclipse Awards. Leading money rider five times, setting a record $19.5 million in 1996. Won the Kentucky Derby with Sea Hero in 1993 and with Grindstone in 1996. Also won 11 Breeders' Cup races in this decade.

Russell Baze
Racing Hall of Fame. Won special Eclipse Award in 1995. Leading rider by wins for five consecutive years (1992–1996). Rode more than 7,000 winners through 2000, including over 400 stakes.

Pat Day
Racing Hall of Fame. Won Eclipse Award in 1991. Top rider by wins in 1991. Won the 1992 Kentucky Derby on Lil E. Tee. Won the Preakness five times—three in this decade. Rode 11 Breeders' Cup winners through 2000. More than 8,000 career victories.

Eddie Delahoussay
Racing Hall of Fame. Winner of over 6,000 races, including seven Breeders' Cup events through 2000. Won 1992 Classic aboard A.P. Indy.

Kent Desormeaux
Won Eclipse Award in 1992. Won the Kentucky Derby with Real Quiet in 1998 and with Fusaichi Pegasus in 2000. Youngest to ride winners of $100 million in career purse money.

Leading Jockeys

Julie Krone
Racing Hall of Fame. In 1993, she became the first woman to win a Triple Crown event when she was aboard Colonial Affair in the Belmont Stakes. Retired in 1999 as winningest female jockey with 3,545 career victories.

Chris McCarron
Racing Hall of Fame. In 2000, he became racing's all-time money leader with $240 million in purse earnings. Winner of eight Breeders' Cup races through 2000. He had more than 7,000 career victories to turn of millennium.

Mike Smith
Won Eclipse Awards in 1993 and 1994. Leading money rider in 1994. Won eight Breeders' Cup events in the 1990s. Rode champions Skip Away, Lure, and Inside Information.

Gary Stevens
Racing Hall of Fame. Won Eclipse Award in 1998. Leading money rider in 1998. Won two of his three Kentucky Derbys in this decade with Thunder Gulch (1995) and Silver Charm (1997).

Silver Charm and Bob Baffert made an entertaining team.

Cigar and Jerry Bailey thrilled the racing world and beyond with 16 straight wins.

Julie Krone had a Hall of Fame decade.

SURVIVING

Throughout the 1990s, racing had to deal with longstanding problems. Although the decade did not feature as many high-profile tragedies as in the past, there were still too many racetrack injuries and too many unnecessary deaths. When eventual champion Prairie Bayou broke down catastrophically in the 1993 Belmont, the industry was forced, yet again, to confront the confounding issues of soundness and drugs. Medication, legal and otherwise, continued to make news—as it had for decades. On September 1, 1995, New York became the last racing jurisdiction to legalize race-day use of the antibleeding medication furosemide.

A spate of horses testing positive to scopalamine and clenbuterol caused headaches for some of America's leading trainers, all of whom proclaimed innocence. Testing for illegal or excessive medication was becoming more refined—detection down to the smallest particles was possible—and horsemen asked for national standards based on a drug's effectiveness rather than trace findings. They did not get those standards.

Far more evil and certainly more deliberate than the above medication controversies was the insertion of sponges into the nostrils of horses racing at Churchill Downs in 1996. Though not a drug, sponges were clearly used to manipulate performance. The alleged culprit was indicted in 1998.

On a more positive note, quality racing returned to Texas for the first time in half a century. The first two tracks to open, Sam Houston Race Park and Retama Park, struggled initially, but Lone Star Park in the populous Dallas-Fort Worth area was a success from its opening in April of 1997. Tracks also opened successfully in Washington State (Emerald Downs) and Indiana (Hoosier Park), but Colonial Downs, in Virginia, failed to fulfill early expectations. Old Aksarben was razed in Nebraska to make way for an office park, Atlantic City Race Course ran only enough to keep its simulcasting license, and Arlington Park shut down for two years until Illinois passed legislation favorable to racing.

NECROLOGY

1991 Mary Bacon, 43. Pioneer female jockey

Lazaro Barrera, 66. Racing Hall of Fame trainer of Affirmed and Bold Forbes

Horatio Luro, 90s. Racing Hall of Fame trainer

1992 Frances Genter, 94. Owner of 1990 Kentucky Derby winner Unbridled

C. V. Whitney, 93. Legendary owner-breeder of more than 140 stakes winners

Nijinsky II, 25. European champion, sire of 155 stakes winners

Blushing Groom (Fr), 18. Sire of 93 stakes winners

1993 Robert P. Strub, 74. Chairman of the board of the Los Angeles Turf Club

Keene Daingerfield, 82. Respected racing steward and author

William Haggin Perry, 82. Leading owner-breeder

Mesach Tenney, 85. Racing Hall of Fame trainer of Swaps

1994 Warner L. Jones, 78. Owner of Hermitage Farm, breeder of 110 stakes winners

John M. S. Finney, 60. President of Fasig-Tipton Sales Co.

Donald "Bud" Willmot, 77. Owner of Kinghaven Farm, leading owner-breeder in Canada

1995 Damascus, 31. Racing Hall of Fame

Vice Regent, 28. Sire of more than 100 stakes winners

1996 Howard B. Keck, 83. Bred 42 stakes winners

Frank E. "Jimmy" Kilroe, 84. Respected racing official

Stavros Niarchos, 86. International owner

1997 Eddie Arcaro, 81. Racing Hall of Fame jockey

NECROLOGY

1997 Bayakoa (Arg), 13. Racing Hall of Fame

Jim Bolus, 54. Noted author and Kentucky Derby historian

Rex Ellsworth, 89. Leading American owner-breeder, bred Swaps

Thomas Mellon Evans, 86. Owner of Buckland Farm

Forego, 27. Racing Hall of Fame, three-time Horse of the Year

Charles Taylor, 62. Vice president of the Ontario Jockey Club, operator of Windfields Farm

1998 Woody Stephens, 84. Racing Hall of Fame trainer

1999 Kent Hollingsworth, 69. Respected writer and editor

Paul Mellon, 91. Breeder of champions Mill Reef, Arts and Letters, and Fort Marcy

Mr. Prospector, 29. All-time leading sire of 175 stakes winners

Riverman, 30. Sire of 127 stakes winners

Alfred G. Vanderbilt, 87. Noted owner-breeder; member of the Jockey Club

Charlie Whittingham, 86. Racing Hall of Fame trainer

2000 Hubert "Sonny" Hine, 69. Trainer of 1998 Horse of the Year Skip Away

Clement Hirsch, 85. A founder and president of Oak Tree Racing Association

Fred Hooper, 102. Prominent owner-breeder

Lucien Laurin, 88. Racing Hall of Fame trainer of Secretariat.

Allen Paulson, 78. Eclipse Award-winning owner and breeder

Ernie Samuel, 69. Owner of Sam-Son Farms

SNAPSHOTS OF AN ERA

Racing in the 1990s was not all big money, big business, and big controversy. There were other moments to be savored, special Technicolor snapshots that served to remind us of what this sport is really all about. For example, when historic Calumet Farm landed on the auction block in 1992 after years of mismanagement, Henryk de Kwiatkowski paid $17 million to save it, promising that not one blade of grass would be changed. He kept his word. Then there was trainer Claude "Shug" McGaughey's afternoon for the ages, on October 26, 1993, when he saddled five graded stakes winners at Belmont Park; Arazi's amazing flight through the final furlongs of the 1991 Breeders' Cup Juvenile; Arcangues's 134 to 1 triumph in the 1993 Breeders' Cup Classic; Julie Krone's 1993 Belmont Stakes victory aboard Colonial Affair, making her the first woman to ride an American classic winner; Favorite Trick's perfect 9 for 9 juvenile season in 1997; and Jockey Laffit Pincay Jr.'s record 9,000th career win.

So closed a century that had taken us from inkwell and quill pen to computer and the Internet, from horse and buggy to supersonic jets. Racing changed with the times. On the doorstep of a new age, races were being run approximately 30 lengths faster than in 1901; 12 times more foals were being produced each year; the reported high stud fee had gone from $250 to $300,000; *Daily Racing Form* sold for $5 a copy rather than 5¢; and the American earnings title ballooned from $193,550 to $9,999,815. Perhaps it is fitting that the final Breeders' Cup Classic of the twentieth century ended as it did, with Tiznow, the son of a stallion who once stood for $2,500 vanquishing a $70 million rival in Fusaichi Pegasus.

What form the sport of kings will take in the twenty-first century is anybody's guess, though it is certain that the next one hundred years will be no easier than the past one hundred. But survive it will—you can bet on it.

Go baby go!

CIGAR

CIGAR WAS ARGUABLY THE MOST EXCITING RACEHORSE OF THE 1990s: he lasted longer, won more often, carried more weight, and earned more money than almost any other top runner of his era. But what truly set him apart was what he accomplished between October 28, 1994, and July 13, 1996, when he won 16 consecutive races to tie Citation's longstanding twentieth century American record—a remarkable feat some likened to Joe Dimaggio's 56-game hitting streak of 1941.

Cigar's 21-month streak lasted longer than the entire careers of many champions. Although he did not dazzle us with 20-length triumphs and track-scorching speed records, his zest for crossing the finish line first in top company was a pleasure to behold and ensured him a future pedestal in the Racing Hall of Fame.

Foaled in Maryland in April of 1990, Cigar was a son of international turf star Palace Music. He was bred by Gulfstream Aerospace founder Allen Paulson, who reportedly did not appreciate a good cigar but loved to pilot his planes far and fast and named this particular colt for an aeronautical checkpoint in the Gulf of Mexico.

Although his lineage hinted at a future on turf, in reality Cigar preferred the taste of grass to the cushiony feel of it under his galloping feet. Over that springy surface he was unexceptional during the early months of his career, winning just 1 of 11 grass starts. When Bill Mott took over Cigar's training in 1994, he was confounded by the handsome four-year-old who looked so much better than the dismal record he brought with him. Perhaps grass was not his thing, after all. Mott decided to experiment by entering Cigar in a 1-mile dirt race at Aqueduct on October 28. The colt's explosive eight-length victory that afternoon marked the beginning of his transformation from ordinary to extraordinary. Cigar proved to be John Henry in reverse. Whereas the latter's greatness was revealed after a switch from dirt to grass, Cigar's true talents were unveiled when transferred from grass to dirt. On that surface the sky seemed the limit for Paulson's rising star.

In 1995, Cigar blossomed into a major league headliner all over North America—from New York to California to Florida, and beyond—winning everywhere he went. As the triumphs kept coming, a quiet countdown began among close observers of racing, who wondered how long he could go before injury, bad luck, or a faster horse stopped him.

When the media and general public finally caught on to what was unfolding, the quiet countdown became a roar of approval every time Cigar galloped to another victory—in the Donn, Gulfstream Park, Oaklawn, and Massachusetts Handicaps, Pimlico Special, Hollywood Gold Cup, and Breeders' Cup Classic. He won each of his 10 starts in 1994 (stretching his overall winning streak to 12), and established a single-season earnings record of $4,819,800 en route to Horse of the Year honors. Not bad for a horse who a year before had lost 8 consecutive races.

What to do with him now? Industry economics of the late twentieth century dictated that beyond a certain point, top male racehorses—excluding geldings, of course—were more valuable for breeding purposes than for racing. That point generally came after their three-, four-, or five-year-old racing seasons. In the first 30 years of Eclipse Award polling (1971-2000), 17 potential stallion prospects reigned as Horse of the Year (several more than once). Of those, five retired at the age of three; five at age four; and six at age five. Only one raced on as a six-year-old: Cigar.

Allen Paulson possessed a strong sense of history. He knew what a horse like Cigar meant to racing, how priceless he was to an industry in dire need of positive publicity. He also knew that if Cigar stayed sound and at the top of his game—two very big ifs in this high-risk sport—he stood to surpass both Citation's consecutive win streak and Alysheba's all-time earnings record. A curious man as well as a sporting one, Paulson decided to roll the dice and see how far his champion could go in pursuit of both.

Thus it was that instead of courting mares at a Blue Grass farm, six-year-old Cigar stretched his streak to 13 in the Donn Handicap at Gulfstream Park, then traveled 6,000 miles to notch number 14 in the United Arab Emirates' Dubai World Cup. Cigar Mania was by then in full throttle, and the charismatic stallion disappointed no one. In a sporting gesture rare for the 1990s, Mott and Paulson accepted a weight assignment of 130 pounds for Cigar in Suffolk Downs's Massachusetts Handicap, which he won handily—number 15.

He went to Chicago after that for Arlington International's Citation Challenge Invitational, which had been specifically created as a vehicle for his assault on Citation's 46-year-old record. On July 31, again with 130 pounds up, Cigar streaked to victory number 16 and into the history books alongside Big Cy.

Del Mar Racetrack's $1-million Pacific Classic on August 10 was chosen to showcase Cigar's shot at immortality. His arrival that week at Ontario International Airport was a media event, with television news helicopters hovering over the police-escorted 100-mile van ride to the seaside track, where in a few days' time bettors would make him a white-hot 1 to 10 favorite. History, however, would not be made in the Classic. Whether tired from the stress of travel, high weights, and escalating media attention that accompanied his growing fame, or simply worn out in a speed duel with a fleet-footed rival, Cigar could not hold off the final charge of a 30 to 1 long shot named Dare and Go. The quest was over, but what a run it had been.

Cigar was not the same after that; and by late fall, Paulson knew it was time to call it quits. Although he had failed to break Citation's consecutive win streak, Cigar had zoomed past Alysheba's earnings record in breathtaking fashion, becoming the first American racehorse to bank more than $7 million, $8 million, and $9 million, before stopping just $185 short of the $10-million mark.

The post-racing story of Cigar sadly did not go as planned. Paulson sold 75 percent of his two-time Horse of the Year for $25 million and dozens of top mares arrived at Cigar's court in 1997. There was only one problem: By season's end, not a single one of them was in foal to Cigar. A record $25-million infertility policy was paid off, although research continued for some time in a futile attempt to reverse Cigar's problem. Not since Assault in the 1940s had a racehorse of such stature proven so hopelessly, heartbreakingly sterile.

The breeding industry's loss eventually became Kentucky tourism's gain. Rather than sequestering him on a private farm, hidden from public view, Cigar was sent in 1999 to the Kentucky Horse Park and installed in the Hall of Champions across from another two-time Horse of the Year, John Henry. This pair, who won nearly $17 million between them, spent their days thereafter employed as goodwill ambassadors for their sport, annually greeting thousands of visitors who came to pay their respects and recall them as they were in their days of glory.

You'd love to have one

20% as game as Cigar.

—THEN UNIVERSITY OF KENTUCKY BASKETBALL COACH RICK PITINO

Serena's Song

Thoroughbreds are big, strong, and fast, but they are also frighteningly fragile. Between 1975 and 2000, top race fillies in particular had a penchant for rising to meteoric prominence then departing the scene tragically—and far too soon—from catastrophic injuries, viral infections, freak accidents, even in one case from an adverse reaction to a vitamin shot. Ruffian and Go For Wand, Landaluce, Pleasant Stage, and Three Ring were among the wonderful fillies who broke our hearts in that quarter-century slice of history, here one moment and gone in the blink of an eye. So when Serena's Song arrived in the mid-1990s, she seemed made-to-order for a racing public fatigued by tragedy. When once asked what set this filly apart from others of her gender, trainer D. Wayne Lukas replied: "C-L-A-S-S." But it was more than that. Racing's tragic heroines each owned that quality in abundance, while Serena possessed others just as precious: she was durable, sound, and, yes, lucky.

Lukas, who has an unparalleled knack for spotting talent in untried youngsters, acquired the yearling daughter of Rahy at the 1993 Keeneland July yearling sale on behalf of clients Bob and Beverly Lewis. The deep-pocketed international crowd had overlooked her at Keeneland that summer—her $150,000 price was well below average for the sale—but she would prove a rare bargain.

Serena's Song was a stout, muscular filly, and Lukas fretted over her tendency toward fat. But if she carried extra pounds, they did not slow her down. She was precocious enough to win three important California stakes in 1994, though she lost the two-year-old championship by a nose to stablemate Flanders in the Breeders' Cup Juvenile Fillies. Flanders broke down winning that race, but Serena's Song was just getting started.

For three seasons she would be racing's equivalent of the Energizer Bunny, never winding down while finishing first, second, or third in 32 of 38 starts, virtually all in the best of company.

In 1995, Lukas engaged Serena in a fearless campaign as a three-year-old for which he received criticism and to which he replied: "She's hickory tough and thrives on activity." He raced her from one end of the continent to the other that season, over every type of racetrack, from sprints to classic distances. She loved to run hard and on the lead from the start so that good horses had to run their hearts out to catch her if they could.

Most late twentieth century trainers opted to race their good fillies exclusively within their own divisions, where big money was available and where they could avoid generally stronger, faster male rivals. Lukas, however, scoffed at such conservatism where Serena's Song was concerned, and on several occasions openly challenged colts with his tomboy of a filly. Although her front-running speed betrayed her in the waning furlongs of the 1995 Kentucky Derby, she beat the boys in both New Jersey's Haskell Invitational and Kentucky's Jim Beam Stakes—while racing for a cause. The Lewises had pledged a portion of her multimillion-dollar earnings to an organization, coincidentally called Serena's Song, that gave hot air balloon rides to people with disabilities.

Serena continued in top form at age four, winning five more important stakes before retiring sound in November of 1996 with an American distaff earnings record of $3,283,388. "She's done everything she can possibly do. . . . Her place in history is established," crowed Lukas, a master salesman and promoter. But those who had seen her run needed no convincing. They knew without being told that she was one of the best.

At retirement in 1996, Serena's Song became America's leading distaff earner with $3,283,388.

SKIP AWAY

THE 1990s WAS A DECADE OF GREEN AND GRAY FOR THE SPORT of horse racing—green for the explosion in purse values, gray for the coat-color of several of the era's finest runners. Gray is not a mainstream color for American Thoroughbreds, in part because it was long viewed suspiciously by prominent horsemen, who saw it as a weak, unlucky hue and therefore avoided it like the plague. Odd as it may seem, it was not until English Derby winner *Mahmoud's arrival here in the 1940s that gray-coated Thoroughbreds were looked upon as something other than freakish.

Even as the millennium ended, grays were a distinct minority in this country, comprising only about 10 percent of the Thoroughbred population. Yet in the final few years of the twentieth century, three of racing's brightest stars were gray or roan. Holy Bull, Silver Charm, and Skip Away together won seven championship titles and banked a whopping $19,042,489—or $244,134 every time they ran. Richest of them all was Carolyn Hine's Skip Away.

Mrs. Hine's husband, trainer Hubert "Sonny" Hine, had bid $30,000 in 1995 to obtain the son of Skip Trial at a two-year-old auction, only to discover a bone chip in one ankle, after which he argued the price down to $22,500. The chip was never removed and Skippy became one of racing's all-time great bargains. For the Hines, Skip Away became an unexpected phenomenon—his sire was a good racehorse but moderate sire, his dam a mare of fair quality.

In a time of intense national pride, it was worth noting that his bloodlines were about as American as apple pie: not a single imported ancestor populated the first three generations of his family tree. The male line of Skip Away was a strictly domestic affair dating back to the 1920s, while his female side had been here since seventh dam *Herodias arrived on England's flood tide of World War I exportations. As for Skippy's distinctive steel-gray coat, that was a gift from *Mahmoud himself, a fifth-generation ancestor.

Under the fluorescent red and yellow silks of Mrs. Hine, the high-striding gray was easy to spot and easy to love. Skip Away was atypical of most modern day champions, though similar in some ways to Cigar. Both had remained sound and competitive through several seasons and many starts; both carried their class all over North America, and both had toted 130 pounds or more to victory in an era when high weight assignments were seldom given and even more rarely accepted.

The two 1990s champions had something else in common: money, and lots of it. Back in 1951, Citation had become the first equine millionaire, and nearly 30 years elapsed before Affirmed and Spectacular Bid topped the $2-million mark. When purse inflation exploded during the 1980s, John Henry and Alysheba each blazed past $6 million, with the latter establishing a record in 1988 that many thought would be impossible to surpass. But records are, indeed, made to be broken, as Cigar and Skip Away proved within a decade, making a quantum leap to the $6-million plateau without a backward glance and raising the American bar to nearly $10 million.

During his jaunt into the record books, Skip Away won 16 important stakes in seven states and in Canada, including the Breeders' Cup Classic, Hollywood Gold Cup, Woodward Stakes, Pimlico Special, Donn Handicap, Woodbine Million, Haskell Invitational, Gulfstream Park Handicap, and Jockey Club Gold Cup (twice). In the 1998 Massachusetts Handicap, he carried 130 pounds to a track record-breaking victory at 1⅛ miles, then picked up a pound more and won the $500,000 Philip H. Iselin Handicap at Monmouth Park.

Skip Away retired in 1999 to Hopewell Farm, in Kentucky, taking with him earnings of $9,616,360—second only to Cigar in America—and a well-deserved reputation as one of the last great racehorses of the twentieth century.

Skip Away, the 1998 Horse of the Year,
was a popular runner.

horse and birth year	starts	wins	seconds	thirds	earnings
A.P. INDY (horse) 1989	11	8	0	1	$2,979,815
BANSHEE BREEZE (filly) 1995	18	10	5	2	$2,784,798
BEAUTIFUL PLEASURE (filly) 1995	25	10	5	2	$2,734,078
BEST PAL (gelding) 1988	47	18	11	4	$5,668,245
CIGAR (horse) 1990	33	19	4	5	$9,999,815
DANCE SMARTLY (filly) 1988	17	12	2	3	$3,263,835
FAVORITE TRICK (horse) 1995	16	12	0	1	$1,726,793
FLAWLESSLY (filly) 1988	28	16	4	3	$2,572,536
FREE HOUSE (horse) 1994	22	9	5	3	$3,178,971
GENTLEMEN (Arg) (horse) 1992	24	13	4	2	$3,608,558
HOLY BULL (horse) 1991	16	13	0	0	$2,481,760
LEMON DROP KID (horse) 1996	24	10	3	3	$3,245,370
PARADISE CREEK (filly) 1989	25	14	7	1	$3,401,416
PASEANA (Arg) (filly) 1987	36	19	10	2	$3,317,427
REAL QUIET (horse) 1995	20	6	5	6	$3,271,802
RIBOLETTA (Brz) (filly) 1995	28	13	3	3	$1,555,103
SERENA'S SONG (filly) 1992	38	18	11	3	$3,283,388
SHARP CAT (filly) 1994	22	15	3	0	$2,032,575
SILVER CHARM (horse) 1994	24	12	7	2	$6,944,369
SILVERBULLETDAY (filly) 1996	23	15	3	1	$3,093,207
SKIP AWAY (horse) 1993	38	18	10	6	$9,616,360
SKY BEAUTY (filly) 1990	21	15	2	2	$1,336,000
THUNDER GULCH (horse) 1992	16	9	2	2	$2,915,086
TIZNOW (horse) 1997	15	8	4	2	$6,427,830

important races won	special notes
Belmont S., Breeders' Cup Classic, etc.	Racing Hall of Fame, Horse of the Year at three
CCA Oaks, Spinster S., Alabama S., Go For Wand S., etc.	Champion at three
Breeders' Cup Distaff, Beldame S., Matron S., etc.	Champion at four
Santa Anita H., Hollywood Futurity, Hollywood Gold Cup, Oaklawn H., etc.	
Breeders' Cup Classic, Woodward S. (twice), etc.	Horse of the Year at five and six
Breeders' Cup Distaff, Molson Export Million, etc.	Champion at three, won Canadian Triple Crown
Breeders' Cup Juvenile, Hopeful S., Breeders' Futurity, etc.	Horse of the Year at two
Matriarch S. (twice), Ramona H. (three times), etc.	Champion grass mare at four and five
Pacific Classic Stakes, Santa Anita H., Santa Anita Derby, Swaps S., etc.	
Pacific Classic, Hollywood Gold Cup H., Pimlico Special H., etc.	
Travers S., Florida Derby, Metropolitan H., Woodward S., etc.	Horse of the Year at three
Belmont S., Whitney H., Travers S., Woodward S., Futurity S. etc.	Champion at four
Arlington Million, Washington, D.C., International, etc.	Champion grass horse at five
Breeders' Cup Distaff, Apple Blossom H. (twice), etc.	Champion older mare at five and six
Kentucky Derby, Preakness S., Hollywood Gold Cup, Pimlico Special, etc.	Champion at three
Beldame S., Santa Margarita Invitational Handicap, Vanity H., Ruffian H., etc.	Champion at five
Haskell Invitational H., Mother Goose S., Beldame S., etc.	Champion at three
Acorn S., Beldame S., Hollywood Starlet, Ruffian H., Santa Anita Oaks, etc.	
Kentucky Derby, Preakness S., Dubai World Cup, Strub S., etc.	Champion at three
Breeders' Cup Juvenile Fillies, Kentucky Oaks, etc.	Champion filly at two and three
Breeders' Cup Classic, etc.	Horse of the Year at five, champion at three and four
Alabama S., Ruffian H., Shuvee H., etc.	Champion at four, won Filly Triple Crown
Kentucky Derby, Belmont S., Travers S., Florida Derby, etc.	Champion at three
Breeders' Cup Classic (twice), Santa Anita H., etc.	Horse of the Year at three, champion at four

APPENDIX A

Thoroughbred Foundation Sires

All modern Thoroughbreds, regardless of where they are foaled, share a proud ancestral heritage dating back some three hundred years. When long ago students of pedigree began tracing Thoroughbred bloodlines back to their source, they discovered a remarkable fact: three small Middle Eastern stallions imported into England during the late seventeenth and early eighteenth centuries were largely responsible for launching this extraordinary breed of equine athlete. These three progenitors— one a bounty of war, one a royal gift, and one exported or smuggled illegally from the desert of Syria—brought their hot, highly potent blood to the cold shores of England, where they left an indelible genetic imprint on a sport destined to become international in scope and popularity.

The Byerly Turk, the Darley Arabian, and the Godolphin Arabian represent the first great triumvirate of foundation sires. Every modern Thoroughbred without exception can be traced in straight paternal line to one of those three. Later in the 1700s, an equally influential second triumvirate appeared on the scene, comprised of male-line descendants of the famed trio of desert imports. This threesome—Match'em, Herod, and Eclipse—provide the links that carry their famous ancestors forever into the future.

By the mid-eighteenth century, the careful blending of Arabian and native English lines had worked evolutionary magic. Eclipse and company could not rightfully be termed either *eastern* or *native*, for by all appearances an entirely new breed of racehorse had been created—one endowed with greater size, bone, and strength than its imported ancestors had possessed, and with more refinement, speed, and stamina than its English antecedents.

Finally, several American sires have been included herein because of the profound genetic influence they exert from the post-Colonial era through the Civil War. *Diomed, Sir Archy, *Glencoe, Boston, and Lexington have not survived paternally in modern bloodlines, but their names are distantly present in countless nonmale pedigree branches. These stallions provide the cornerstones on which America built its early rough-and-rugged racing industry, a sport that prizes the iron-horse qualities of physical power and durability above all else.

EASTERN FOUNDATION SIRES

c. 1700-1750

The Byerly Turk

Dark brown or black, foaled circa 1679, the earliest days of this original foundation sire are obscure, although he is believed to have been of Turkish origin. His initial appearance on history's stage came in 1688, when English Captain Robert Byerly supposedly captured him from a Turkish officer in the Battle of Buda, in Hungary. For Byerly, this horse became a war charger of rare courage, speed, and stamina, and the captain subsequently rode him alongside William III in the 1690 Battle of the Boyne in Northern Ireland—when William's Protestant forces defeated the Catholic forces of James II. Byerly's Turk—or the Byerly Turk, as he came to be known—was the only one of the three Eastern foundation sires known to have actually raced in Europe; he was recorded as having won a prize of silver in 1690 at an Irish track called Down Royal.

He stood at stud in England for a number of years and died around the turn of the nineteenth century at his owner's Goldsborough Hall, near Yorkshire. The Byerly Turk's son Jigg, a racehorse of unremarkable talent, became the link in an undying chain of influence as the paternal great-grandsire of Herod—one of the three most important Thoroughbred stallions of the late 1700s.

The Darley Arabian

A bay horse, foaled circa 1700, bred in Syria and originally owned by Sheikh Mirzah II, this exquisitely beautiful, mahogany colt caught the attention of British consul Thomas Darley, who—depending upon which story one believes—either purchased him or smuggled him out of the country around 1704. British custom then was to call imported stallions by their owners' names, thus, the magnificent colt was referred to as Darley's Arabian. The possessive was eventually dropped and he became the legend known as the Darley Arabian.

Around 1706, he entered stud at the Darley family estate, near Leedes, where he lived a long life and died in 1730 at approximately 30 years of age. Although the Darley Arabian sired many notable individuals, his place in history was secured by two sons, full brothers named Flying Childers and Bartlett's Childers. The former has been acknowledged as racing's first champion and folklore has bestowed upon him mythical mile-a-minute speed. Bartlett's Childers, also gruesomely known as Bloody Childers because of his tendency to break respiratory blood-vessels

under exertion, could not race but became the Darley Arabian's male-line link to the future through his great-grandson Eclipse. It has been speculated that Flying Childers and Bartlett's Childers were, in fact, one and the same horse, though the truth of this can never be known.

Although the Darley Arabian once shared equal billing with the Byerly Turk and Godolphin Arabian as a forefather of the modern racehorse, over time his male line gained transcendence. Genetic studies have shown that some 95 percent of Thoroughbred paternal lines in existence today trace back to Thomas Darley's eighteenth century Arabian stallion.

The Godolphin Arabian

A bay horse, foaled circa 1724 (although his precise origins remain a mystery), the Godolphin Arabian was probably imported to France from Yemen in the late 1720s, possibly as a gift to King Louis XV from the bey of Tunis.

Highly romanticized legends have evolved regarding this horse, including those penned by author Marguerite Henry in her children's classic *King of the Wind.* In the most popular version, the French royal stud master was so unimpressed with the tiny stallion that he turned him away from the King's stable, after which an Englishman "discovered" him pulling a cart on the streets of Paris. He was purchased and brought to England, where he served as a lowly teaser, used to determine a mare's willingness to receive a stallion for breeding, for a stallion named Hobgoblin at Lord Godolphin's Gogmagog Stud near Cambridgeshire.

One story had it that the Arabian broke loose one day and successfully engaged Hobgoblin in battle for the "attentions" of the mare Roxanna. Another stated that Hobgoblin had simply refused the mare, at which point the teaser was given the job. Whatever the truth, the resulting foal was the remarkable racehorse, Lath.

The Godolphin Arabian thereafter became a marvelous progenitor of early running stock, injecting his hot-blooded energy and refinement into the coarser English mares of the period. His male line once had no superior, although over many generations it bowed to that of the Darley Arabian in terms of sheer numbers and influence. It has, however, survived into modern times through his descendant, 14 generations removed, Man o' War, and through that great stallion's own male descendants. The Godolphin Arabian died at Gogmagog in 1753 at 29 years of age.

THE SECOND TRIUMVIRATE

c. 1750-1800

Match'em

A bay horse by Cade out of a mare by Partner, bred in Northern England by John Holmes, and foaled in 1748, Match'em (also spelled Matchem) was a paternal grandson of the Godolphin Arabian. While a yearling in 1749, he was sold privately to a breeder named William Fenwick, who retained him throughout his long, productive life as a racehorse and sire.

Match'em was small, just a hair above what is regarded as a large pony today, but he was handsome and well made, with a distinct Arabian flair to his physical mold. Racehorses were brought along slowly in the eighteenth century and Match'em was no exception, going unraced until his fifth year. Competing sparingly through the age of ten, he became noted for courage and stamina, if not brilliance, while winning all but 2 of his 12 known races—mostly four-mile events at courses such as Newmarket and York.

Fenwick retired Match'em around 1758 to his Bywell Stud, in Northumberland, where Match'em enjoyed a great deal of success—getting several early classic winners and a notable racehorse and sire in Conductor, who was responsible for carrying Match'em successfully into the modern era through a male-line that would one day include Man o' War.

Matchem lived a long, fruitful life at Bywell, dying there on February 21, 1781, at the age of 33.

Herod

A bay horse by Tartar out of Cypron by Blaze, bred in England by the Duke of Cumberland (William Augustus, son of King George II), Herod was foaled in Yorkshire in 1758. A strong, fine individual, he was a great-great-paternal-grandson of the Byerly Turk and formally named King Herod, although he was generally known simply as Herod.

Herod reached the races as a mature horse of five in 1763 and continued competitively through age nine, distinguishing himself in good company. His true contributions to the sport, however, came later, in the stud at Netherhall, near Suffolk, where he sired around five hundred winners, including some of the finest racehorses of the day. Among those were Woodpecker and undefeated Highflyer, both prominent sires who continued the Herod male line.

The Herod line through yet another son, Florizel, became an important cornerstone in America's Thoroughbred breeding industry of the 1800s. Florizel's son, *Diomed, arrived on U.S. shores in 1798 and launched a male line that, within a century, produced champions and leading sires Lexington and Hanover.

Herod died at Netherhall on May 12, 1780.

Eclipse

A chestnut horse by Marske out of Spiletta by Regulus, bred in England by the Duke of Cumberland (also the breeder of Herod), he was foaled in 1764 during a solar eclipse, thus his name. Eclipse, a great-great-paternal-grandson of the Darley Arabian, was a striking, blaze-faced chestnut, although reportedly coarse in appearance and considered oversized. At a reported height of 16 hands—average for today—he towered above most of his eighteenth century contemporaries.

Upon the Duke's death in 1765, the yearling Eclipse was sold to William Wildman, and for several seasons afterward, it was later whispered, his unearthly speed was put to use by a highwayman in robbing English travelers. This is not likely, as Wildman himself was a respected farmer.

Eclipse began his formal racing career in 1769 and proved spectacularly unbeatable, giving rise to the popular phrase, "Eclipse first, the rest nowhere." Sportsman Dennis O'Kelly eventually bought and retired him with an unblemished 18 for 18 record.

After standing most of his career at O'Kelly's Clay Hill Stud, in Surrey, Eclipse was moved to a farm near Middlesex in 1788 and there died the following year on February 26. The skeleton of Eclipse was later displayed in the Jockey Club Museum at Newmarket, and his hooves—at least *five* of them—were turned into commemorative gold-plated inkstands.

Eclipse was the greatest and most influential of progenitors, not only in his own lifetime, but ever afterward. He is today solely responsible for linking the Darley Arabian's name to twenty-first century American sire lines and is present countless times in the far reaches of every modern Thoroughbred pedigree.

SOME AMERICAN FOUNDATION SIRES

c. 1800-1875

*Diomed

A chestnut horse by Florizel out of a sister to Juno by Spectator, bred in England by Sir Charles Bunbury, and foaled in 1777, *Diomed won the inaugural English Derby in 1780 and was for a time compared favorably to the unbeatable phenomenon, Eclipse. At stud in England, however, he proved disappointing, and his fee dropped to the equivalent of about $8 by the time he was sold for $250 in 1798 to Virginia political figure John Hoomes. *Diomed was 21 years of age when he sailed for America.

Like Eclipse, *Diomed was big and powerful—at 16 hands, he was huge by postcolonial standards. Although he had failed as a sire in his native land, he became one of the most revered of American stallions in the decade following his importation, putting size, speed, and quality into his offspring, and creating what some historians have described as a breed all his own. Among his best were Duroc, Ball's Florizel, leading sire Sir Archy, and the great race mare Haynie's Maria, the latter conceived when *Diomed was 30 years of age. The greatest sporting ambition of future president and noted racing man Andrew Jackson during those years was to beat Maria. He was a man accustomed to winning, but in that, he was thwarted.

Through his son Sir Archy, *Diomed became the male-line ancestor of the great 1850s 4-miler, Boston, and his immortal son, Lexington. He died in 1808 at the age of 31.

Sir Archy

A brown horse by *Diomed out of *Castianira by Rockingham, bred in Virginia by Colonel John Tayloe III and Captain Archibald Randolph, Sir Archy was foaled in 1805. He was initially called Robert Burns, but Tayloe changed his name to Sir Archy to honor cobreeder Randolph. The name *Sir Archy* was frequently spelled *Sir Archie,* both versions acceptable in that era preceding the *American Stud Book.*

Unraced at two, Sir Archy's three-year-old campaign was compromised when he fell ill with distemper—he finished unplaced in both starts that season. In 1809, he was sold for $1,500 to noted turf man W. R. Johnson, for whom he won four of five starts and came to be regarded as one of America's best 4-mile heat specialists.

Sir Archy was sold upon his retirement from racing for a reported $5,000 to Revolutionary War hero and North Carolina political figure William R. Davie. Sometimes referred to as the Godolphin Arabian of America because of his profound influence on the early development of the Thoroughbred in this country, Sir Archy eventually surpassed even his own great sire, *Diomed, in genetic influence. Among his sons were future leading sires Sir Charles and Bertrand, as well as Boston's sire, Timoleon.

At age 28, Sir Archy died on June 7, 1833—the same day on which his best son, Sir Charles, also passed away.

*Glencoe

A chestnut horse by Sultan out of Trampoline by Tramp, bred in England by Lord Jersey, and foaled in 1831, *Glencoe was one of the best racehorses of his era, winning the 1834 Two Thousand Guineas and other important races before being sold for $10,000 to American James Jackson.

A physical beauty except for a noticeable sway to his back, *Glencoe arrived in the United States in 1836 and initially stood at Jackson's famed Alabama breeding farm, The Forks of Cypress. There he remained through 1844, after which he relocated to Tennessee for several seasons, and was then sold in 1849 to A. Keene Richards of Kentucky.

*Glencoe stood his remaining years in the Blue Grass State, although his overall record there was probably diminished by Richards, an ardent secessionist who turned over some of his later offspring, including one ridden by the Thunderbolt of the Confederacy, General John Hunt Morgan, for use as Confederate Civil War mounts. *Glencoe nevertheless led the American sire list on eight occasions and was particularly noted for his outstanding daughters, including Peytona, America's top money winner between 1845 and 1861 ($62,400). Although sons of *Glencoe did not carry on in the male line, daughters of the great stallion were phenomenal producers, especially when crossed with Lexington.

At age 26 on August 25, 1857, *Glencoe died of "lung fever" at Blue Grass Park, near Georgetown, Kentucky.

Boston

A bay horse by Timoleon out of a sister to Tuckahoe by Ball's Florizel, foaled in 1833, and named for a popular card game of the era, Boston was bred in Virginia by John Wickham, best known to history as a defense attorney in Aaron Burr's 1807 treason trial. Wickham was forced to sell Boston as a two-year-old in 1835 to Nathaniel Rives to satisfy an $800 gaming debt. The notoriously vile-tempered colt tempted handlers to castrate or kill him, but fortunately neither course was taken.

Boston went on to become one of America's most notable racehorses and sires. He won 40 of 45 starts, including 30 grueling 4-mile heat races, and earned $51,700—a remarkable sum in an era of small purse money. Nicknamed Old White Nose for his distinctively blazed face, he eventually ranked as America's leading sire of winners three times (1851–1853).

Although blind and in failing health in later life, Boston's fiery spirit remained unconquerable until the night of January 30, 1850. The following morning, the body of the 17-year-old stallion was found in a blood-spattered stall at Colonel E. M. Blackburn's farm, in Woodford County, Kentucky, after an apparently violent battle with death. His two finest offspring, future Racing Hall of Famers Lecomte and Lexington, were foaled weeks later, the latter destined to become the greatest American-born Thoroughbred sire of the nineteenth century.

Lexington

A bay horse by Boston out of Alice Carneal by *Sarpedon, bred in Kentucky by Dr. Elisha Warfield, Lexington was foaled in 1850. Because Dr. Warfield felt he resembled paintings of his ancestor the Darley Arabian, this son of Boston raced initially under the name Darley. When sold in 1853 to sportsman Richard Ten Broeck, Darley's name was changed to Lexington.

A lightly raced winner in six of seven starts, Lexington earned $56,600 and clocked the fastest 4 miles ever run to that time (7:19 ¾) before encroaching blindness forced his retirement. In 1857, he was sold for a believed American record $15,000 to Robert A. Alexander, who vowed to one day sell an offspring of Lexington for more—which he did, with the 1864 sale of Norfolk for $15,001.

Lexington spent most of his stud career at Alexander's Woodburn Stud, near Midway, Kentucky, except for an 1860s wartime interlude when safety concerns sent him to Illinois. As a stallion he had no equal, leading the American sire list 16 times and sending out countless topflight performers. Lexington's record likely would have been even better except that his career coincided with the Civil War, when many of his offspring, prized for speed and stamina, were utilized as cavalry mounts or were stolen by guerrilla soldiers, as in the case of unbeaten Asteroid.

Lexington's best racing progeny included champions Kentucky, Asteroid, Norfolk, Duke of Magenta, Harry Bassett, Sultana, and Tom Bowling. His post–Civil War stud fee of $500 was almost unheard of in America at that time. He died at Woodburn on July 1, 1875. Since 1877 his skeleton has been in the possession of the Smithsonian Institution in Washington, D. C.

APPENDIX B

American Yearling Sales Averages 1908–2001

The American Thoroughbred industry of the twentieth century often marched to its own drummer, its yearling auction prices rising and falling with little obvious connection to what was happening in the world around it. These internal fluctuations were determined by such factors as the passage of legislation unfavorable to racing, overproduction of foals (supply exceeding demand), or the appearance of a superstar such as Man o' War or Secretariat to inflame the public's imagination.

There were times, however, when equine sales were clearly and profoundly affected by the grander scheme of things. The Great Depression and U.S. involvement in World War II brought yearling prices tumbling down, as did widespread fear leading up to the Korean conflict. The 1988 yearling market dropped sharply in response to the record stock market decline of October 1987. Conversely, when the Dow began scaling the heights in the late 1990s, so too did Thoroughbred auction prices. Both reached all-time highs in the year 2000—the Dow at 11,723 (January 14), yearling averages at $54,384.

*1923 Kentucky Derby winner Zev easily defeated English Derby winner *Papyrus in the International Match at Belmont Park*

French champion*Epinard finished second in all three International Specials of 1924. American fans loved him.

Year	Yearlings Sold	Average Price	National Events
1908	745	$344	Antiwagering laws passed in New York; Dow is at 86 pts.; the nation is suffering from a major monetary crisis
1909	691	$412	Antiwagering laws passed in California
1910	550	$325	Major racetracks close in New York and California
1911	390	$230	
1912	243	$517	High point of Progressive Reform Movement
1913	316	$472	Racing resumes in New York. An economic recession lasts for two years, until the outbreak of war in Europe.
1914	398	$654	WWI begins; New York Stock Exchange closes July—December
1915	375	$695	U.S. grants credits to Britain as U.S. goods flow to Allied nations. The *Lusitania* sinks.
1916	426	$932	
1917	643	$1,030	U.S. enters WWI; stock market drops 35% April—December
1918	509	$827	One million U.S. troops are in Europe; inflation rate is 18%
1919	335	$2,140	End of the war; crisis over League of Nations
1920	400	$1,727	Man o' War's classic season; "Normalcy" arrives with election of Warren Harding as U.S. President
1921	395	$2,274	Postwar recession is short-lived except in agriculture, lasting through the Great Depression
1922	534	$2,200	Consumer goods economy rises with the spread of credit
1923	640	$2,016	Period of New Era Capitalism and speculative boom lasting to the end of the decade
1924	600	$2,230	Harding dies, succeeded by Coolidge. End of free immigration to the U.S.
1925	582	$3,208	
1926	751	$2,640	
1927	703	$2,759	Beginning of a runaway bull stock market
1928	852	$2,269	Hoover is elected President
1929	855	$2,539	Stock market crashes in October
1930	1,030	$1,966	Great Depression begins

Year	Yearlings Sold	Average Price	National Events
1931	1,070	$980	Economy worsens
1932	952	$570	Roosevelt elected President with the promise of a New Deal to end Great Depression
1933	813	$696	All-time high unemployment rate at 25%. Agricultural subsidies instituted through the AAA.
1934	746	$825	Economic recovery begins—unemployment at 22%. Discontent rises with major strikes.
1935	831	$1,192	Social Security Act, Wagner Labor Relations Act, work relief passed
1936	892	$1,576	Unemployment declines to 17%. Industrial unions are formed; triumph of labor unions in the steel and auto industries, and the CIO was founded.
1937	877	$1,676	
1938	985	$1,564	Revival of American military production
1939	1,150	$1,459	World War II begins; American neutrality proclaimed
1940	1,259	$1,186	France falls and U.S. supports survival of Britain. Roosevelt elected to an unprecedented third term
1941	1,072	$1,215	Pearl Harbor is attacked; U.S. enters WWII
1942	1,061	$638	U.S. economy is booming, becoming the arsenal of the free world
1943	873	$1,866	Start of victory in Europe and Asia
1944	818	$3,917	GI Bill of Rights passed; wage/price controls work; Roosevelt is elected a fourth time; inflation is held in check
1945	986	$5,146	WWII ends; postwar economic boom begins
1946	1,287	$5,909	Housing boom and suburbanization of the nation
1947	1,465	$4,184	Television becomes a mass medium
1948	1,629	$3,625	Truman defeats Dewey in upset. Military is desegregated
1949	1,818	$2,835	Agricultural subsidies are increased
1950	1,739	$2,921	Korean War; start of the Red Scare and McCarthyism
1951	1,695	$4,039	
1952	1,640	$4,321	Eisenhower is elected President
1953	1,637	$4,470	End of Korean War; death of Stalin

Year	Yearlings Sold	Average Price	National Events
1954	1,625	$4,973	Peak of Red Scare
1955	1,583	$5,452	McCarthy repudiated
1956	1,672	$5,299	End of Red Scare; Montgomery Bus Boycott; Brown vs. Board of Education
1957	1,638	$5,427	
1958	1,783	$5,022	
1959	1,716	$5,747	Castro revolution in Cuba
1960	1,911	$5,263	Kennedy beats Nixon
1961	2,021	$5,529	Bay of Pigs
1962	2,279	$5,528	
1963	2,436	$5,543	Kennedy is assassinated; Lyndon Johnson is sworn in
1964	2,648	$6,041	Civil Rights Act passed; Johnson is reelected
1965	2,849	$6,247	Great Society and War on Poverty are instituted
1966	3,282	$6,066	Increased involvement in Vietnam
1967	3,375	$6,374	Escalation of number of U.S. military in Nam; Great Society programs cut back; Antiwar Movement escalates
1968	3,480	$7,567	Robert Kennedy and Martin Luther King Jr. assassinated; Nixon elected, ends Johnson reforms; moves to deregulate economy
1969	3,325	$7,424	
1970	3,420	$7,386	Environmental movement emerges
1971	3,541	$8,735	Antiwar activities lead to governmental repression
1972	4,145	$9,159	Secretariat races; Watergate break-in; Nixon reelected
1973	4,256	$12,231	U.S. pulls troops out of Vietnam; oil embargo after U.S. aids Israel in Yom Kippur War
1974	4,584	$10,729	Nixon resigns
1975	4,918	$10,917	Energy crisis deepens
1976	5,178	$13,037	Ford loses election to Jimmy Carter
1977	5,267	$16,252	
1978	6,029	$19,659	Iran hostage crisis

Year	Yearlings Sold	Average Price	National Events
1979	6,326	$24,768	
1980	7,079	$29,683	Inflation rate is 13.48—highest since 1947; Reagan is elected Pres.
1981	7,963	$35,359	
1982	8,174	$32,991	Deep national recession
1983	8,705	$41,258	Economy rebounds, inflation rate declines to 3.21
1984	9,268	$41,396	Reagan reelected; Soviet-U.S. arms accord negotiated; Iran-Contra crisis
1985	8,420	$41,311	
1986	8,206	$34,285	
1987	8,845	$35,441	Stock market plunges, largest percent drop in history
1988	9,083	$31,250	Bush is elected President
1989	8,317	$33,899	Berlin Wall falls
1990	8,471	$30,320	National debt triples in 10 years; Persian Gulf War
1991	7,888	$27,201	Collapse of the Soviet Union; Cold War ends
1992	7,992	$22,651	Clinton is elected President
1993	7,459	$25,143	Beginning of the longest economic growth spurt in U.S. history
1994	7,751	$27,183	
1995	7,830	$31,075	
1996	8,036	$34,518	Clinton is reelected
1997	8,067	$38,145	Dow tops 7,000; 8,000
1998	8,248	$42,942	Dow tops 9,000
1999	8,757	$50,263	Dow tops 10,000; 11,000; low inflation and unemployment
2000	9,553	$54,384	Dow is at an all-time high of 11,723 on January 14; George W. Bush elected President
2001	9,032	$52,402	Market declines; World Trade Center is destroyed in terrorist attacks on September 11; Operation Enduring Freedom, major U.S.-led war on terrorism begins

Statistical information from 1908-1988 from the *Daily Racing Form's American Racing Manual*

Data from 1989-2001 from *Thoroughbred Times*

Appendix C

Leading American Money Winners

The listing at right includes top earnings records for both male and female Thoroughbreds who raced in America during the past 180 years. Current American leading earner Cigar is not number one internationally—that honor goes to T. M. Opera O, whose Japanese earnings totaled $14,811,347 through 2001. Earnings opportunities for fillies and mares have historically been unequal to those available to male runners, so a separate listing is included below. Note that Peytona and Miss Woodford held the money title regardless of gender, and that the latter in 1885 became the first American Thoroughbred to top $100,000. While most of the earnings for Trinycarol (Ven) and Dahlia were banked abroad, both were eligible for inclusion here by virtue of having also raced in North America.

LEADING AMERICAN DISTAFF MONEY WINNERS			
Years Title Held	Mare	Record	Earnings
1845–1885	Peytona	Unknown	$66,000
1885–1925	Miss Woodford	48-37-7-2	$118,270
1925–1931	Princess Doreen	94-34-15-17	$174,745
1931–1945	Top Flight	16-12-0-0	$275,900
1945–1947	Busher	21-15-3-1	$334,035
1947–1951	Gallorette	72-21-20-13	$445,535
1951–1962	Bewitch	55-20-10-11	$462,605
1962–1971	Cicada	42-23-8-6	$783,674
1971–1974	Shuvee	44-16-10-6	$890,445
1974–1982	Dahlia *	48-15-3-7	$1,545,139
1982–1983	Trinycarol (Ven)	29-18-3-1	$2,647,171
1983–1986	All Along (Fr) **	21-9-4-2	$3,015,764
1986–1991	Lady's Secret	45-25-8-3	$3,021,425
1991–1996	Dance Smartly	17-12-2-3	$3,263,835
1996–present	Serena's Song ***	38-18-11-3	$3,283,388

* Allez France briefly passed Dahlia in mid-1975. **Earnings include a $1 million bonus for winning Rothmans, Turf Classic, and Washington, D. C., International in 1983. The above list includes runners who started at least once in North America. ***In 2002, Spain surpassed Serena's Song as the all-time leading distaff money winner with $3,540,542.

294

LEADING AMERICAN MONEY WINNERS

Years Title Held	Horse	Record	Earnings
1823–1845	American Eclipse	8-8-0-0	$56,700
1845–1861	Peytona (f.)	8-6-2-0	$66,000
1861–1881	Planet *	31-27-4-0	$69,700
1881–1881	Hindoo	35-30-3-2	$71,875
1881–1885	Parole	138-59-28-17	$82,816
1885–1889	Miss Woodford (f.)	48-37-7-2	$118,270
1889–1892	Hanover	50-32-14-2	$118,887
1892–1893	Kingston	138-89-33-12	$138,917
1893–1920	Domino	25-19-2-1	$193,550
1920–1923	Man o' War	21-20-1-0	$249,465
1923–1930	Zev	43-23-8-5	$313,639
1930–1931	Gallant Fox	17-11-3-2	$328,165
1931–1940	Sun Beau	74-33-12-10	$376,744
1940–1942	Seabiscuit	89-33-15-13	$437,730
1942–1947	Whirlaway	60-32-15-9	$561,161
1947–1950	Stymie **	131-35-33-28	$918,485
1950–1956	Citation	45-32-10-2	$1,085,760
1956–1958	Nashua	30-22-4-1	$1,288,565
1958–1964	Round Table	66-43-8-5	$1,749,869
1964–1979	Kelso	63-39-12-2	$1,977,896
1979–1980	Affirmed	29-22-5-1	$2,393,818
1980–1981	Spectacular Bid	30-26-2-1	$2,781,607
1981–1988	John Henry	83-39-15-9	$6,597,947
1988–1996	Alysheba	26-11-8-2	$6,679,242
1996–present	Cigar	33-19-4-5	$9,999,815

* Planet last raced five days before the Civil War was ignited by the attack of Fort Sumter.
**Assault held the title for two weeks during the summer of 1947.

Appendix D

Selected Bibliography

Much of the information on the history of horse racing comes from a variety of sources that can be difficult to find. Many of the sources were published from the late 1800s to the early 1900s and are now out of print. All efforts were made to provide complete information for every entry. The following is a list of books, magazines, journals, and newspapers that were used to research this book. This bibliography is by no means a complete record of all the works and sources the author has consulted.

Ainslie, Tom. *Ainslie's Complete Guide to Thoroughbred Racing.* New York: Simon and Schuster, 1979.

Alexander, David. *The Sound of Horses.* New York: Bobbs-Merrill, 1966.

American Thoroughbred Breeders Association. *American Race Horses.* Lexington: Thoroughbred Owners and Breeders Association 1936–1963.

The Blood-Horse (1930–present).

Bruce, B.G. *The Livestock Record* 1–42 (1875–1895).

Daily Racing Form. *American Racing Manual.* Daily Racing Form Publishing Co, 1909–1995.

Sanders, Bruce D. *American Stud Book.* 30 vols. New York: The Jockey Club, 1873–present.

Arcaro, Eddie. *I Ride to Win.* New York: Greenberg Publishing, 1951.

Beckwith, B. K. *The Longden Legend.* New York: A. S. Barnes and Company, 1973.

Blanchard, Elizabeth, and Manley Wellman. *The Life and Times of Sir Archie.* Chapel Hill: Chapel Hill University of North Carolina Press, 1958.

British Bloodstock Agency, Ltd. *Bloodstock Breeders' Annual Review.* London: British Bloodstock Agency, 1912–1981.

The British Racehorse (1949–1981).

Chew, Peter. *The Kentucky Derby—The First 100 Years.* Boston: Houghton Mifflin Co., 1974.

Clark, John H. *Trader Clark—Six Decades of Racing Lore.* Lexington: Thoroughbred Publications, Inc., 1991.

Compiled by The Blood-Horse staff. *The Great Ones.* Lexington: The Blood-Horse, 1970.

Crickmore, H. G. *Krik's Guide to the Turf, 1877–1884.* New York.

The European Racehorse (1981–1988).

General Stud Book Containing Pedigrees of Race Horses. 43 vols. London: Weatherbys and Sons, 1827–present.

Glasscock, C. B. *Lucky Baldwin: The Story of an Unconventional Success.* New York: A. L. Burt, 1935.

Goodwin's Annual Official Turf Guide. New York: Goodwin Brothers, 1882–1908.

Harrison, Fairfax. *Early American Turf Stock.* 2 vols. Virginia: The Old Dominion Press 1730–1830, 1935.

Hervey, John, Walter Vosburgh, Robert F. Kelley, and William H. Rudy. *Racing in America—1665–1979.* 6 vols. New York: The Jockey Club.

Hewitt, Abram S. *Sire Lines.* Lexington: Thoroughbred Owners and Breeders Association, 1977.

———. *The Great Breeders and Their Methods.* Lexington: Thoroughbred Publishers, Inc., 1982.

Hildreth, Samuel C., and James R. Crowell. *The Spell of the Turf.* Philadelphia: J. B. Lippincott Company, 1926.

Hollingsworth, Kent. *The Wizard of the Turf—John E. Madden of Hamburg Place.* Lexington: The Blood-Horse, 1965.

Hoofprints of the Century. Lexington: Record Publishing Co, 1975.

Jennings, Frank. *From Here to the Bugle.* Lexington: The Thoroughbred Press, 1949.

Johnson, Charlene R. *Florida Thoroughbred.* Gainesville: University Press of Florida, 1993.

Keene, Foxhall. *Full Tilt—The Sporting Memoirs of Foxhall Keene.* New York: Derrydale Press, 1938.

Leach, Brownie. *The Kentucky Derby Diamond Jubilee (1875–1949).* New York: Dial Press, 1949.

Mackay-Smith, Alexander. *The Race Horses of America.* Saratoga Springs: The National Museum of Racing, 1981.

Macy, Alan. *The Romance of the Derby Stakes.* London: Hutchinson, 1930.

Menke, Frank. *Down the Stretch: The Story of Colonel Matt J. Winn.* New York: Smith and Durrell, 1944.

Merry, Thomas G. *The American Thoroughbred.* Los Angeles: Commercial Printing House, 1905.

Nack, William. *Big Red of Meadow Stable: Secretariat, the Making of a Champion.* New York: Arthur Fields Books, 1975.

New York Spirit of the Times—The American Gentleman's Newspaper 1–124 (1861–1892).

O'Connor, Winnie. *Jockeys, Crooks, and Kings.* New York: Jonathan Cape and Harrison Smith, 1930.

Palmer, Joe H. *Names in Pedigrees.* Lexington: Thoroughbred Owners and Breeders Association, 1939.

———. *This Was Racing.* New York: A. S. Barnes and Company, 1953.

Privman, Jay. *Breeders' Cup—Thoroughbred Racing's Championship Day.* Louisville: Moonlight Press, 2000.

Racing Form Charts of American Racing, Daily Racing Form Publishing Co., Triangle Publications, Inc., Daily Racing Form, Inc. 1909–1980

Robertson, William H. P. *The History of Thoroughbred Racing in America.* New Jersey: Prentice-Hall, Inc., 1964.

Rosenfeld, Richard. *American Aurora—The Suppressed History of our Nation's Beginnings and the Heroic Newspaper that Tried to Report It.* New York: Saint Martin's Press, 1997.

Sanders, Bruce. *Turf, Field and Farm* 1–55 (1865–1892).

Schwartz, Jane. *Ruffian: Burning from the Start.* New York: Ballantine Books, 1991.

The Thoroughbred of California—The California Thoroughbred (Arcadia, Calif.) (1937–present).

The Thoroughbred Record (Lexington) 43–224 (1896–1990).

The Thoroughbred Times (Lexington) (1985–2000).

Turf, Field and Farm (New York) (1860–1890).

Vosburgh, Walter, Charles Lanier, Frank Bryan, and James Cooley. *Thoroughbred Types—1900–1926.* New York.

(From left) *Bob and Beverly Lewis, Gary Stevens, W. T. Young, and D. Wayne Lukas earned their share of the sport's most coveted prizes.*

Wall, John F. *Thoroughbred Bloodlines—An Elementary Study.* Baltimore: Monumental Printing Company, 1936.

Waller, George. *Saratoga—Saga of an Impious Era.* New Jersey: Prentice-Hall, Inc., 1966.

Wettereau, Bruce. *The New York Public Library Book of Chronologies.* New York: Prentice-Hall Press, 1990.

Whitney, Cornelius Vanderbilt. *High Peaks.* Lexington: University Press of Kentucky, 1977.

Glossary

* (asterisk): when placed in front of a horse's name, denotes a horse who was imported to the United States from a foreign country other than Canada. The asterisk was replaced in 1976 by abbreviated country codes appearing after a horse's name and in parentheses.

American standard (American record): the fastest time for a specific distance ever recorded in America regardless of track

American Stud Book: published by the Jockey Club for more than a century, these volumes record officially recognized American and imported Thoroughbred bloodlines

automatic hotwalker: a stationary, motor-driven machine equipped with several long rotating "arms" to which horses are tied and walked in a circle until they are cooled out after a race or workout

backstretch: the part of a track's racing surface that lies across the infield from the grandstands. This term is also used in reference to the stable area of a racetrack.

bay: a coat color that can range from light brown to nearly black and is always accompanied by a black mane and tail

bloodstock: horses bred for racing

bowed tendon: a severe strain or rupture of the tendon that runs below the knee at the back of the foreleg, giving the leg a bowed appearance. This injury can vary in seriousness, although most horses with residual breeding value are retired from racing upon bowing a tendon.

break a maiden: to win for the first time; a horse who wins for the first time has broken his maiden

broodmare sire: maternal grandsire

campaign: a one-year racing season

cannon bone: the long bone extending from the knee to the fetlock, or ankle

card: the daily program of races offered at a given track

chestnut: a coat color that is reddish or golden in hue, with a mane and tale of similar or lighter coloring

claimer: a horse running in a claiming race. Usually, claimers are not top-class runners and their owners are willing to risk losing them in claiming company.

claiming race: a race in which the horses may be claimed, or purchased, by another owner for a prespecified price determined in the conditions of the race.

classics: important and often historically traditional races held specifically for three-year-olds. Most racing countries conduct classic events. North American classics include the Kentucky Derby, Preakness Stakes, and Belmont Stakes.

colt: an intact male horse under the age of five

covering: a discreet term used to describe the act of a stallion breeding a mare

daily double: a wager in which the bettor must correctly pick the winners of two specific races

dispersal: an auction wherein the equine holdings of a particular owner are sold

distaffer: a female racehorse of any age

exacta (also perfecta): a wager in which the bettor attempts to pick the first two finishers of a race in a specific order

filly: a female horse under the age of five

full-card simulcasting: the live televised transmission of a full day's racing card from a specific racetrack to off-track sites for wagering purposes

furlong: a unit of distance that equals one-eighth of a mile

gelding: a castrated male horse

General Stud Book: England's official record of pedigrees. It has been published in numerous volumes for more than two hundred years and includes the names and lineages of all recognized English Thoroughbreds.

graded stakes (Grade 1, 2, 3): the highest classes of races recognized in the United States, with Grade 1's being the most important. The Kentucky Derby is a Grade 1 race.

group stakes (Group 1, 2, 3): same as above, except this term is used in Europe and other foreign countries to rate important racing events

hand: a unit of measure equal to four inches, used to determine the height of horses at the top of the shoulder

handicap: a race in which an artificial disadvantage, or advantage, is imposed on a horse to equalize his or her chances of winning. The horse carries weight, the amount of which is assigned by a track's racing secretary based on that horse's past performances.

handle: the total amount of money wagered in pari-mutuel races

hock: the joint in a horse's hind leg between the thigh and the cannon bone that resembles the human ankle but is elevated and bends backward

intertrack simulcasting: televised transmission of live racing from one racetrack to another

juvenile: a two-year-old colt or filly

length: a distance that roughly approximates that of a horse's length from head to tail

maiden: a horse of either sex who has not yet won a race

maiden race: a race for non-winners

mare: a female horse five years of age or older. If she is younger than five but has had a foal, she is also referred to as a mare.

parade to post: the procession of horses onto the racetrack prior to a race as they make their way to the starting gate

pari-mutuel wagering: a type of betting, which originated in France during the 1800s, that employs ticket machines instead of human bookmakers. Money wagered on the competitors finishing in the first three places is pooled and later divided, minus taxes and operating revenue, among all who hold winning tickets.

perfecta (also exacta): a wager in which the bettor attempts to pick the first two finishers of a race in a specific order

photo-finish camera: a camera positioned to photograph the finish of a race. Resulting photos can verify the winner of a finish otherwise too close to call.

place: to finish second in a race

post: the starting gate

purse: the total money awarded in a race

quinella: a wager in which the bettor tries to pick the top two finishers in either order

race times: during much of the twentieth century, North American races were timed to the fifth of a second. In the mid-1990s, the sport gradually changed over to timing to the hundredths of a second, and thus changed from fractions to decimals.

racing secretary: the racetrack official who determines what types of races will be run, assigns weights to be carried in handicaps, and other such policies

ringing: illegally substituting one horse for another in a race. With modern blood-typing identification methods, ringing became virtually impossible by the late twentieth century.

sesamoid: two small bones with attached ligaments at the back of the fetlock joint, which is located at the base of the cannon bone. Sesamoid injuries can be catastrophic to a racehorse.

shadow roll: a strap, usually wool, that is attached to the noseband of a horse's bridle theoretically to prevent him from looking down and spooking at shadows

show: to finish third in a race

simulcasting: the live television transmission of races to other tracks and wagering facilities, enabling more people to wager on the races

stakes: prestigious races that generally offer more money than nonstakes events. Some stakes are invitational; others require paid nomination for eligibility.

start: a race. A horse with 10 starts has raced 10 times.

stayer: racing slang for a horse noted for his or her ability to successfully race over a long distance of ground, generally beyond a mile and a quarter by modern American standards

syndication: the sale of a racehorse or breeding prospect into multiple ownership portions. Stallions may have 40 or more individual owners.

takeout: money deducted from the track's pari-mutuel wagering pool to be used for operating revenue and taxes

totalizator board: a large electronic board, usually located in the infield directly in front of the grandstands, that displays information such as current odds on each horse and the amount of money wagered

totalizator: A machine that sells and records wagers, and calculates odds and payoffs

track standard (track record): the fastest time for a specific distance run at a specific racetrack

trifecta (triple wager): a wager in which a bettor attempts to pick the top three finishers of a race in the exact order

Triple Crown winner: the title achieved by a horse in the United States who has won the three classic races: the Kentucky Derby, Preakness Stakes, and Belmont Stakes. Other countries have Triple Crowns as well, and New York offers a filly triple called the Triple Tiara.

turf: a grass track used for racing; also a general term used to describe the sport or business of horse racing

twin double: a wager in which the bettor tries to pick the winners of four designated races

walkover: a race in which only one horse is entered

winningest: an editorial term used to describe a trainer (or jockey) who saddled (or rode) more winners than any other, either during a specific time frame or for all-time. *Five-time winningest* means he trained (or rode) more winners than any other American trainer in each of five years.

world standard (world record): the fastest time for a specific distance recorded anywhere in the world

INDEX